WELCOME

— FIRST —
"SEGAR'S WIMPY"
AN INTRODUCTION
BY KEVIN HUIZENGA →

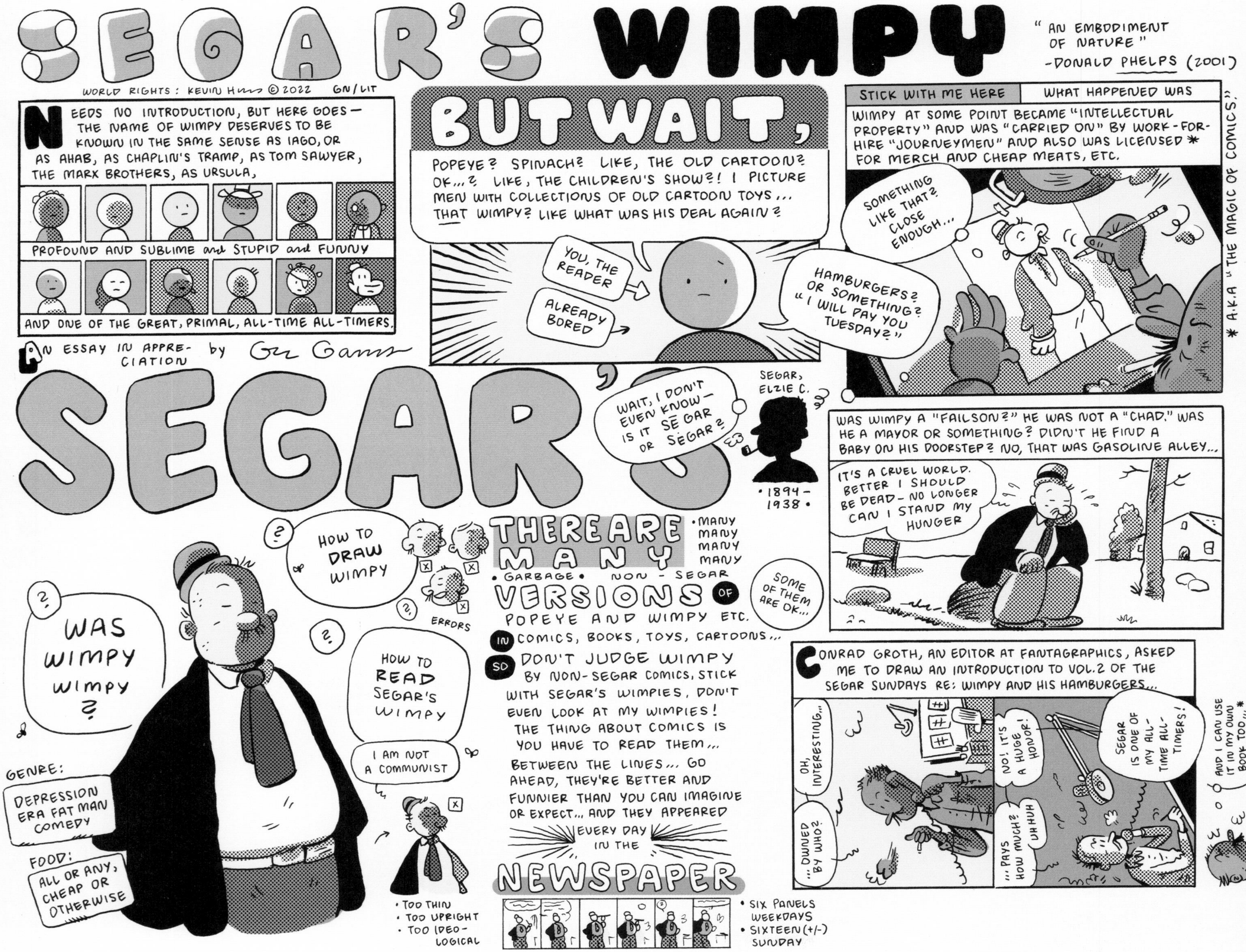

SEGAR'S WIMPY
"AN EMBODIMENT OF NATURE" -DONALD PHELPS (2001)
WORLD RIGHTS: KEVIN H[illegible] © 2022 GN/LIT
NEEDS NO INTRODUCTION, BUT HERE GOES— THE NAME OF WIMPY DESERVES TO BE KNOWN IN THE SAME SENSE AS IAGO, OR AS AHAB, AS CHAPLIN'S TRAMP, AS TOM SAWYER, THE MARX BROTHERS, AS URSULA,
PROFOUND AND SUBLIME and STUPID and FUNNY
AND ONE OF THE GREAT, PRIMAL, ALL-TIME ALL-TIMERS.
BUT WAIT,
POPEYE? SPINACH? LIKE, THE OLD CARTOON? OK...? LIKE, THE CHILDREN'S SHOW?! I PICTURE MEN WITH COLLECTIONS OF OLD CARTOON TOYS... THAT WIMPY? LIKE WHAT WAS HIS DEAL AGAIN?
YOU, THE READER
ALREADY BORED
HAMBURGERS? OR SOMETHING? "I WILL PAY YOU TUESDAY?"
STICK WITH ME HERE
WHAT HAPPENED WAS
WIMPY AT SOME POINT BECAME "INTELLECTUAL PROPERTY" AND WAS "CARRIED ON" BY WORK-FOR-HIRE "JOURNEYMEN" AND ALSO WAS LICENSED * FOR MERCH AND CHEAP MEATS, ETC.
SOMETHING LIKE THAT? CLOSE ENOUGH...
* A.K.A "THE MAGIC OF COMICS."
AN ESSAY IN APPRECIATION by [signature]
SEGAR'S
WAIT, I DON'T EVEN KNOW— IS IT SE GAR OR SEGAR?
SEGAR, ELZIE C.
• 1894 - 1938 •
WAS WIMPY A "FAILSON?" HE WAS NOT A "CHAD." WAS HE A MAYOR OR SOMETHING? DIDN'T HE FIND A BABY ON HIS DOORSTEP? NO, THAT WAS GASOLINE ALLEY...
IT'S A CRUEL WORLD. BETTER I SHOULD BE DEAD– NO LONGER CAN I STAND MY HUNGER
HOW TO DRAW WIMPY
ERRORS
THERE ARE MANY •MANY MANY MANY MANY
• GARBAGE • NON-SEGAR VERSIONS OF POPEYE AND WIMPY ETC.
IN COMICS, BOOKS, TOYS, CARTOONS...
SOME OF THEM ARE OK...
SO DON'T JUDGE WIMPY BY NON-SEGAR COMICS, STICK WITH SEGAR'S WIMPIES, DON'T EVEN LOOK AT MY WIMPIES! THE THING ABOUT COMICS IS YOU HAVE TO READ THEM... BETWEEN THE LINES... GO AHEAD, THEY'RE BETTER AND FUNNIER THAN YOU CAN IMAGINE OR EXPECT... AND THEY APPEARED EVERY DAY IN THE NEWSPAPER
• SIX PANELS WEEKDAYS
• SIXTEEN (+/-) SUNDAY
WAS WIMPY WIMPY?
HOW TO READ SEGAR'S WIMPY
I AM NOT A COMMUNIST
• TOO THIN
• TOO UPRIGHT
• TOO IDEOLOGICAL
GENRE:
DEPRESSION ERA FAT MAN COMEDY
FOOD:
ALL OR ANY, CHEAP OR OTHERWISE
CONRAD GROTH, AN EDITOR AT FANTAGRAPHICS, ASKED ME TO DRAW AN INTRODUCTION TO VOL. 2 OF THE SEGAR SUNDAYS RE: WIMPY AND HIS HAMBURGERS...
OH, INTERESTING...
...OWNED BY WHO?
NO! IT'S A HUGE HONOR!
...PAYS HOW MUCH?
UHHUH
SEGAR IS ONE OF MY ALL-TIME ALL-TIMERS!
AND I CAN USE IT IN MY OWN BOOK TOO...*

LETS GO BACK TO 1932
"ALL OVER AMERICA, MEN WERE DRIFTING LIKE SARGASSO WEED IN A VAST DEAD SEA OF RUINED INDUSTRY." THIS WAS THE DEPRESSION!
– LOREN EISELEY
TRUE POVERTY IS TERRIBLE,,, NO JOKE! MANY WOMEN AND MEN WERE WIPED OUT!!! THIS IS THE CONTEXT... WORKING CLASS SCENARIOS,,, GRAPES OF WRATH, UPTON SINCLAIR, LET US NOW PRAISE FAMOUS MEN,,,
THE COMEDY TYPE THAT WIMPY WAS, WAS VERY COMMON: THE PRETENDER, THE PATHETIC NON-EARNER, THE TRICKSTER MOOCH,,, TO IMAGINE WIMPY DOING ANYTHING IS TO IMAGINE A SCHEME UNDERWAY,,,
Z-Z Z-Z-Z- Z-Z
HARD, COLD STEELY LIFE-
NOBODY'S PAL-
'TIS THE WAY OF THINGS- SORROW IS MY HERITAGE- ALAS-
HUNGER MY FOE- MY NATURAL ENEMY
HE WILL TAKE FOOD FROM A POOR HUNGRY CHILD,,, (SEE 5/29/32)
OH, THAT'S HOW YOU DRAW HIM,,,
THIS LOOKS TERRI BLE!
I GUESS I COULD TRACE SOME JPGS,,, CRANK THIS OUT,,,
THIS WHOLE THING IS A TERRIBLE IDEA.
OR DANGLE A BURGER BEFORE A HUNGRY DOWN-AND-OUT-ER AND THEN SLOWLY EAT IT IN FRONT OF HIM!
(SEE 7/16/1933)
CHOKE OUT HIS OWN GRANDMOTHER FOR FOOD! * (SEE 11/26/1933)
ETC.
[BORED]
SCROLL SCROLL
WIMPY
AN ESSAY IN APPRE-CIATION
SEGAR'S
• WAS BORN IN CHESTER, ILLINOIS
• WAS BASED ON: "WINDY" BILL SCHUCHERT, WELL-INGTON J. REYNOLDS, H. HILLARD WIMPEE.
TO SCALE
= 70 MILES
= 8 YRS
I'LL BE THE WARE OF SEGAR!
I COULD DO THE BOOK DESIGN...
WELL, I BETTER DO SOME RESEARCH.
ACH! THESE POP. UP WINDOWS
SOURCES:
○ POPEYE THE SAILORPEDIA
○ KING FEATURES SYNDICATE
○ HBO MAX
BURGER TRIVIA
SOURCES
○ STEVE BLATCHFORD
○ HERITAGE AUCTIONS
○ BRIAN BAYNES
SOURCES
○ WIKIWAND
○ BOOMERMAGAZINE .COM
○ WIMPYPEDIA
○ FANTAGRAPHICS
○ RICK MAR SCH ALL
... LIKE WRITE SOMETHING?
DRAW IT?
OK HMM
OH, COVEY IS?
WHO AM I FOOLING? I DON'T HAVE TIME FOR THIS!
Google
TIMELINE
NOW
1958
2022 YOU ARE HERE
2014
1993
1977
1941 WWII
DEPRESSION
1938 DEATH OF SEGAR
1931 WIMPY FIRST APPEA RANCE
1929 POPEYE FIRST APPEA RANCE
1919 THIMBLE THEATRE BEGINS
1894 SEGAR BORN, ILLI NOIS
ADS FIELDER, MICHIANA ×
GLENN GANGES IN: ×
TRAILER #2 SHOW MORE
* ACTUALLY POPEYE IN DISGUISE, BUT STILL!

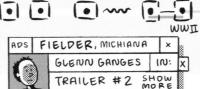

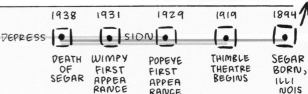

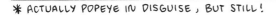

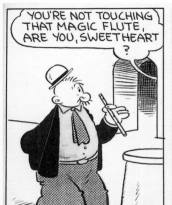

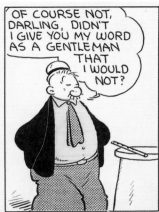

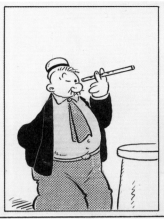

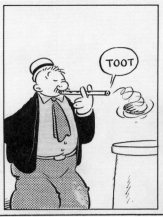

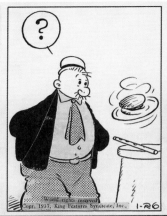

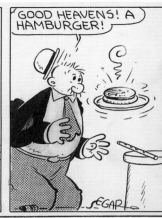

YOU'RE NOT TOUCHING THAT MAGIC FLUTE, ARE YOU, SWEETHEART ?
OF COURSE NOT, DARLING, DIDN'T I GIVE YOU MY WORD AS A GENTLEMAN THAT I WOULD NOT?
TOOT
?
GOOD HEAVENS! A HAMBURGER!
World rights reserved. Copr. 1937, King Features Syndicate, Inc.
1-26
SEGAR
SEGAR'S
THE STRIP ABOVE APPEARED LESS THAN A YEAR BEFORE SEGAR'S DEATH AT AGE 43.
EFFORTLESSLY LEGIBLE ... HEADS ON A HORIZONTAL, SMALL CHANGES, BIG EFFECTS, A PERFECTLY TIMED SEQUENCE,
AND SEE! HOW, IN THE LAST PANEL, THE DOTS ENLARGE THE SMALLEST LEGIBLE AMOUNT.
AN ESSAY IN APPRECIATION:
WIMPY'S EYES
ARE THE PEACEABLY HALF-CLOSED TYPE, NINETY-NINE PERCENT OF THE TIME, BUT OCCASIONALLY WILL POP OPEN. IT'S A GOOD BIT, FUNNY, SUBTLE.
• ORIG. 4.5 × 20.5 INCHES
WHEN THEY POP
OPEN, AMAZING!
THE MAGIC OF COMICS / EYES WIDEN
HEAD SIZE CONSISTENT
HYPHEN - BECOMES • DOT
NOT TO MENTION— NOTICE HOW WIMPY'S MID-SECTION COMPRESSES THE SMALLEST LEGIBLE AMOUNT!
IN PANELS 3 → 4
AND HERE ARE SOME MORE
COMMON ERRORS IN NON-SEGAR WIMPYS:
☒ HEADS TOO BIG
☒ LEGS TOO THIN
☒ EXTRANEOUS LINES
☒ TOO SOLID
☒ GRID:
☒ ONE-POINT PERSPECTIVE
☒ ISOMETRIC
☒ SEGAR'S GRID: IS NEITHER
☒ NOR:
$450?
$300...
OK
TUESDAY?!
• PRINTED AT "ACTUAL SIZE" OF SEGAR'S ORIGINAL DRAWING

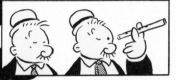

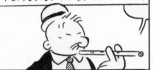

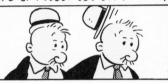

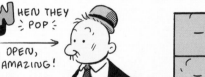

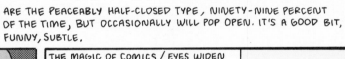

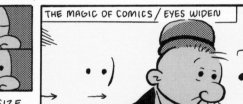

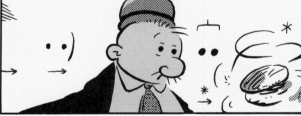

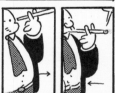

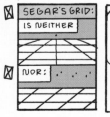

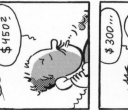

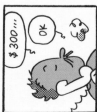

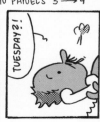

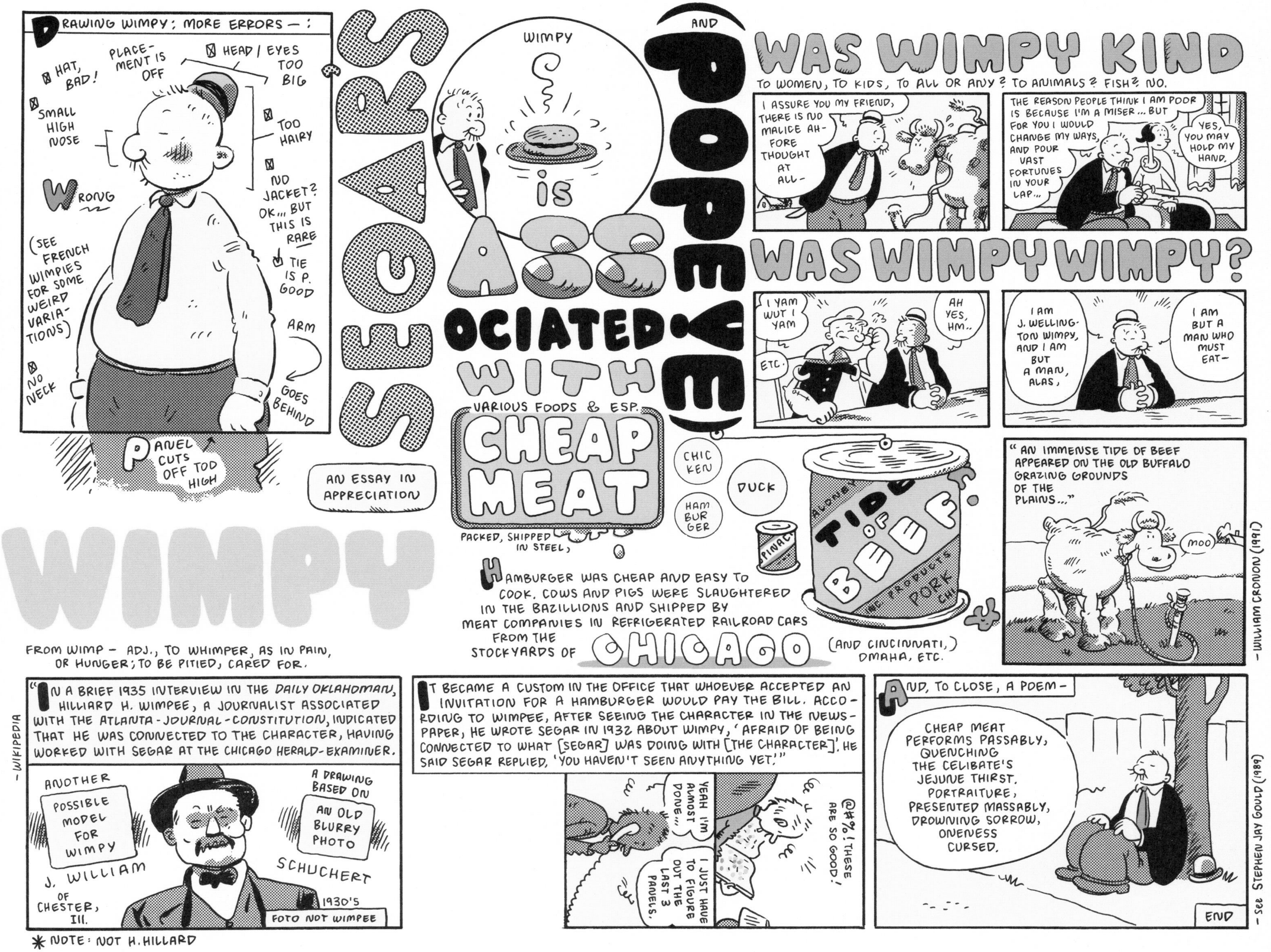

DRAWING WIMPY: MORE ERRORS — :
☒ HAT, BAD!
PLACEMENT IS OFF
☒ HEAD / EYES TOO BIG
☒ SMALL HIGH NOSE
☒ TOO HAIRY
WRONG
☒ NO JACKET? OK... BUT THIS IS RARE
(SEE FRENCH WIMPIES FOR SOME WEIRD VARIATIONS)
☑ TIE IS P. GOOD
ARM GOES BEHIND
☒ NO NECK
PANEL CUTS OFF TOO HIGH
SEGAR'S
AND
(POPEYE)
WIMPY
IS ASSOCIATED WITH
VARIOUS FOODS & ESP.
CHEAP MEAT
PACKED, SHIPPED IN STEEL,
AN ESSAY IN APPRECIATION
CHICKEN
DUCK
HAMBURGER
SPINACH
ALDNEY
TIDE OF BEEF
PRODUCTS
PORK
CHI
WIMPY
FROM WIMP – ADJ., TO WHIMPER, AS IN PAIN, OR HUNGER; TO BE PITIED, CARED FOR.
HAMBURGER WAS CHEAP AND EASY TO COOK. COWS AND PIGS WERE SLAUGHTERED IN THE BAZILLIONS AND SHIPPED BY MEAT COMPANIES IN REFRIGERATED RAILROAD CARS FROM THE STOCKYARDS OF
CHICAGO
(AND CINCINNATI,) OMAHA, ETC.
WAS WIMPY KIND
TO WOMEN, TO KIDS, TO ALL OR ANY? TO ANIMALS? FISH? NO.
I ASSURE YOU MY FRIEND, THERE IS NO MALICE AHFORE THOUGHT AT ALL—
THE REASON PEOPLE THINK I AM POOR IS BECAUSE I'M A MISER... BUT FOR YOU I WOULD CHANGE MY WAYS, AND POUR VAST FORTUNES IN YOUR LAP...
YES, YOU MAY HOLD MY HAND.
WAS WIMPY WIMPY?
I YAM WUT I YAM
ETC.
AH YES, HM..
I AM J. WELLINGTON WIMPY, AND I AM BUT A MAN, ALAS,
I AM BUT A MAN WHO MUST EAT—
"AN IMMENSE TIDE OF BEEF APPEARED ON THE OLD BUFFALO GRAZING GROUNDS OF THE PLAINS..."
MOO
— WILLIAM CRONON (1991)
"IN A BRIEF 1935 INTERVIEW IN THE DAILY OKLAHOMAN, HILLIARD H. WIMPEE, A JOURNALIST ASSOCIATED WITH THE ATLANTA-JOURNAL-CONSTITUTION, INDICATED THAT HE WAS CONNECTED TO THE CHARACTER, HAVING WORKED WITH SEGAR AT THE CHICAGO HERALD-EXAMINER.
— WIKIPEDIA
IT BECAME A CUSTOM IN THE OFFICE THAT WHOEVER ACCEPTED AN INVITATION FOR A HAMBURGER WOULD PAY THE BILL. ACCORDING TO WIMPEE, AFTER SEEING THE CHARACTER IN THE NEWSPAPER, HE WROTE SEGAR IN 1932 ABOUT WIMPY, 'AFRAID OF BEING CONNECTED TO WHAT [SEGAR] WAS DOING WITH [THE CHARACTER]'. HE SAID SEGAR REPLIED, 'YOU HAVEN'T SEEN ANYTHING YET.'"
ANOTHER
POSSIBLE MODEL FOR WIMPY
A DRAWING BASED ON
AN OLD BLURRY PHOTO
J. WILLIAM SCHUCHERT
OF CHESTER, ILL.
1930'S
FOTO NOT WIMPEE
* NOTE: NOT H. HILLARD
YEAH I'M ALMOST DONE...
I JUST HAVE TO FIGURE OUT THE LAST 3 PANELS.
@#%! THESE ARE SO GOOD!
AND, TO CLOSE, A POEM—
CHEAP MEAT
PERFORMS PASSABLY,
QUENCHING
THE CELIBATE'S
JEJUNE THIRST.
PORTRAITURE,
PRESENTED MASSABLY,
DROWNING SORROW,
ONENESS
CURSED.
END
— see STEPHEN JAY GOULD (1989)

DESIGN: Jacob Covey
EDITORIAL: Conrad Groth & Gary Groth
PRODUCTION: Paul Baresh
PUBLICITY: Jacquelene Cohen
VP / ASSOCIATE PUBLISHER: Eric Reynolds
PRESIDENT / PUBLISHER: Gary Groth

FANTAGRAPHICS BOOKS, INC.
7563 Lake City Way NE
Seattle, WA 98115

www.fantagraphics.com
facebook.com/fantagraphics
@fantagraphics

ISBN: 978-1-68396-668-5
LOC: 2022936613
First Fantagraphics Books edition:
Fall 2022
Printed in China

OUR FEATURE:

POPEYE

THE E.C. SEGAR POPEYE SUNDAYS

STARRING IN:

"Wimpy & His Hamburgers"

VOLUME TWO OF A SERIES

March 1932 – November 1933

GROTH & SON, IN ASSOCIATION WITH KING FEATURES SYNDICATE

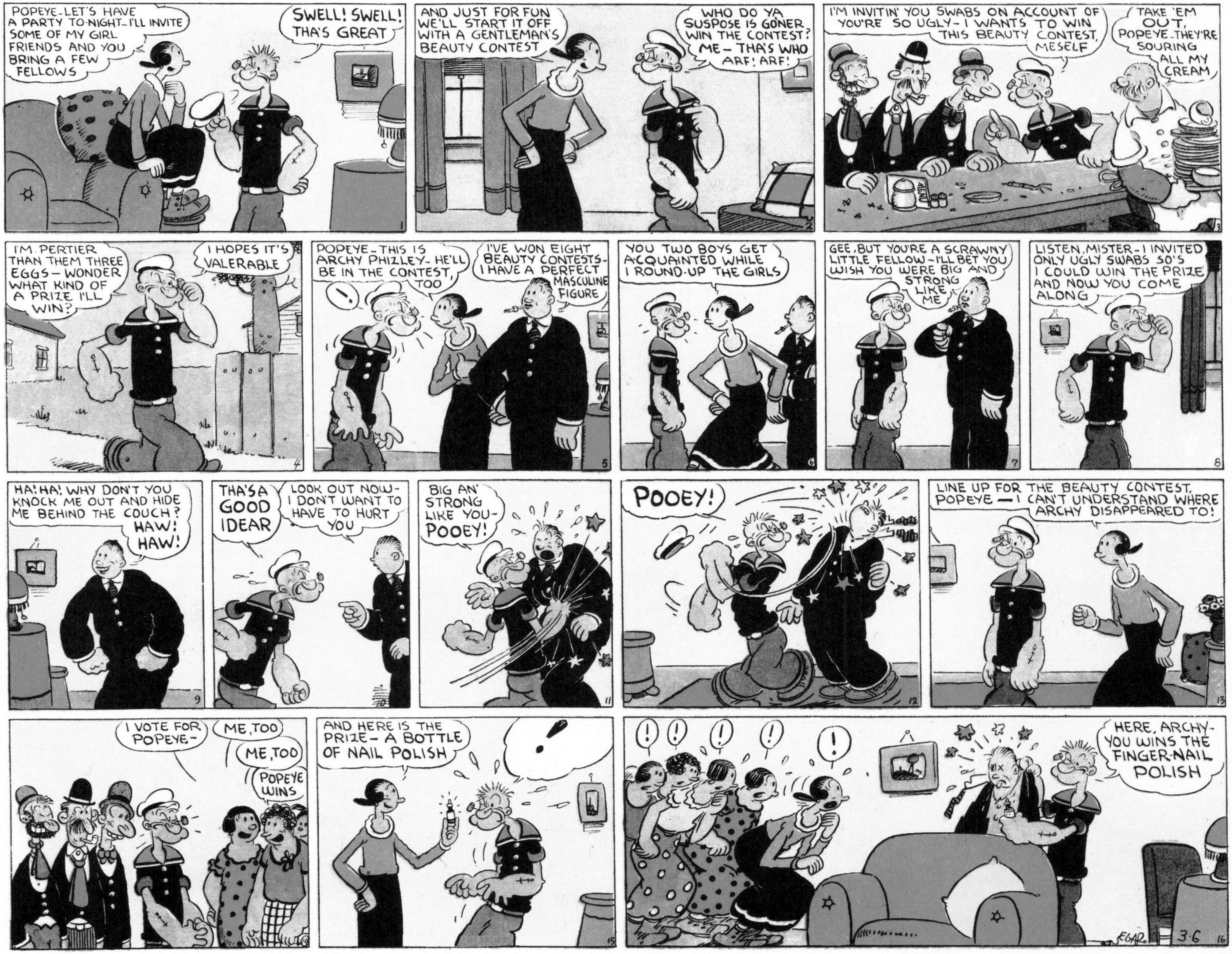
POPEYE-LET'S HAVE A PARTY TO-NIGHT-I'LL INVITE SOME OF MY GIRL FRIENDS AND YOU BRING A FEW FELLOWS
SWELL! SWELL! THA'S GREAT
AND JUST FOR FUN WE'LL START IT OFF WITH A GENTLEMAN'S BEAUTY CONTEST
WHO DO YA SUSPOSE IS GONER WIN THE CONTEST? ME- THA'S WHO ARF! ARF!
I'M INVITIN' YOU SWABS ON ACCOUNT OF YOU'RE SO UGLY- I WANTS TO WIN THIS BEAUTY CONTEST, MESELF
TAKE 'EM OUT, POPEYE-THEY'RE SOURING ALL MY CREAM
I'M PERTIER THAN THEM THREE EGGS- WONDER WHAT KIND OF A PRIZE I'LL WIN?
I HOPES IT'S VALERABLE
POPEYE-THIS IS ARCHY PHIZLEY- HE'LL BE IN THE CONTEST, TOO
I'VE WON EIGHT BEAUTY CONTESTS- I HAVE A PERFECT MASCULINE FIGURE
!
YOU TWO BOYS GET ACQUAINTED WHILE I ROUND-UP THE GIRLS
GEE, BUT YOU'RE A SCRAWNY LITTLE FELLOW-I'LL BET YOU WISH YOU WERE BIG AND STRONG LIKE ME
LISTEN, MISTER-I INVITED ONLY UGLY SWABS SO'S I COULD WIN THE PRIZE AND NOW YOU COME ALONG
HA! HA! WHY DON'T YOU KNOCK ME OUT AND HIDE ME BEHIND THE COUCH? HAW! HAW!
THA'S A GOOD IDEAR
LOOK OUT NOW- I DON'T WANT TO HAVE TO HURT YOU
BIG AN' STRONG LIKE YOU- POOEY!
POOEY!
LINE UP FOR THE BEAUTY CONTEST, POPEYE — I CAN'T UNDERSTAND WHERE ARCHY DISAPPEARED TO!
I VOTE FOR POPEYE-
ME, TOO
ME, TOO
POPEYE WINS
AND HERE IS THE PRIZE- A BOTTLE OF NAIL POLISH
!
! ! ! ! !
HERE, ARCHY- YOU WINS THE FINGER-NAIL POLISH
SEGAR 3-6

9. March 6, 1932

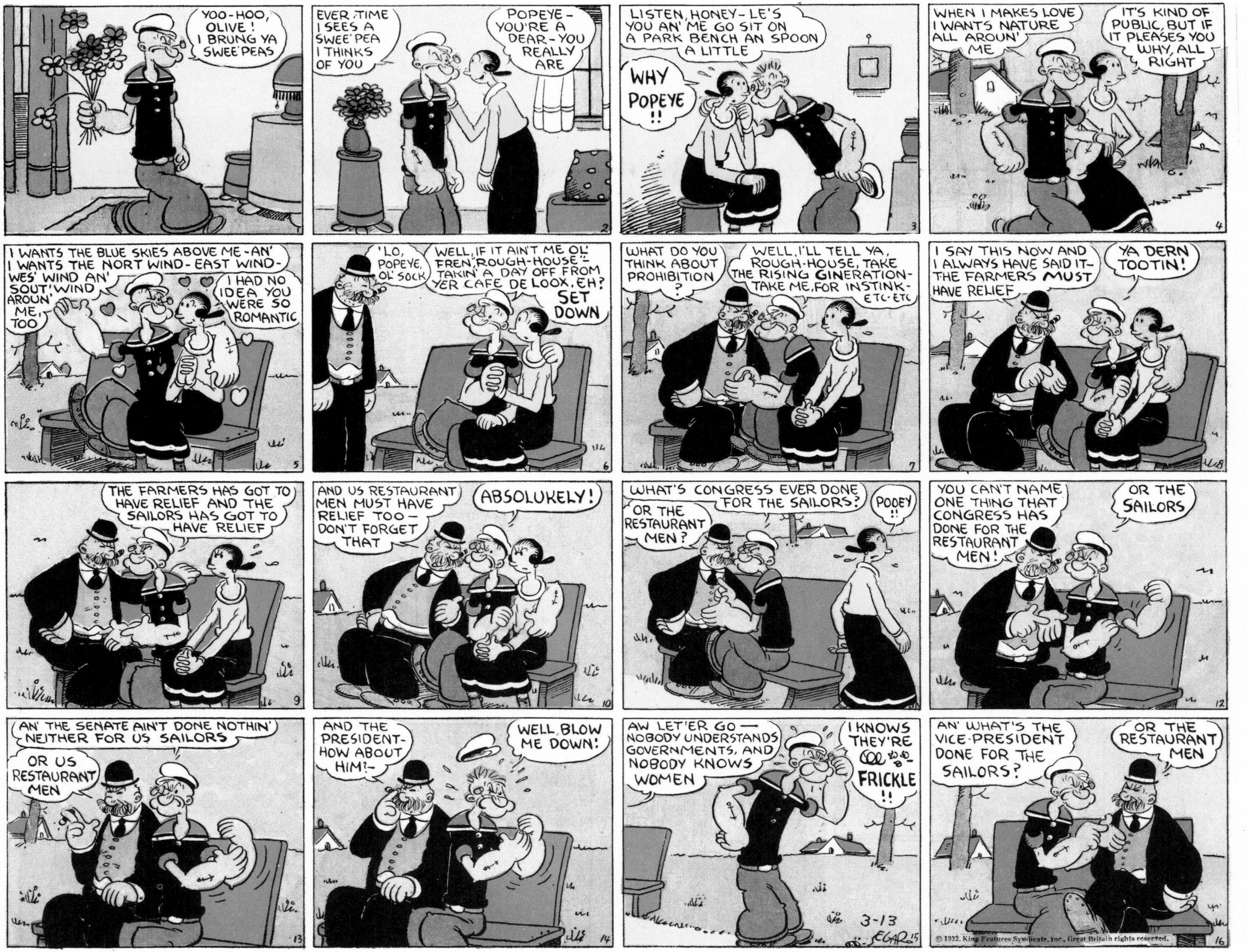
YOO-HOO, OLIVE! I BRUNG YA SWEE'PEAS
EVER TIME I SEES A SWEE'PEA I THINKS OF YOU
POPEYE - YOU'RE A DEAR - YOU REALLY ARE
LISTEN, HONEY - LE'S YOU AN' ME GO SIT ON A PARK BENCH AN SPOON A LITTLE
WHY POPEYE !!
WHEN I MAKES LOVE I WANT'S NATURE ALL AROUN' ME
IT'S KIND OF PUBLIC, BUT IF IT PLEASES YOU WHY, ALL RIGHT
I WANTS THE BLUE SKIES ABOVE ME - AN' I WANTS THE NORT WIND - EAST WIND - WES' WIND AN' SOUT' WIND AROUN' ME, TOO
I HAD NO IDEA YOU WERE SO ROMANTIC
'LO, POPEYE, OL' SOCK
WELL, IF IT AIN'T ME OL' FREN' "ROUGH-HOUSE" - TAKIN' A DAY OFF FROM YER CAFE DE LOOX, EH?
SET DOWN
WHAT DO YOU THINK ABOUT PROHIBITION ?
WELL, I'LL TELL YA, ROUGH-HOUSE, TAKE THE RISING GINERATION - TAKE ME, FOR INSTINK - ETC - ETC
I SAY THIS NOW AND I ALWAYS HAVE SAID IT - THE FARMERS MUST HAVE RELIEF
YA DERN TOOTIN!
THE FARMERS HAS GOT TO HAVE RELIEF AND THE SAILORS HAS GOT TO HAVE RELIEF
AND US RESTAURANT MEN MUST HAVE RELIEF TOO - DON'T FORGET THAT
ABSOLUKELY!
WHAT'S CONGRESS EVER DONE FOR THE SAILORS?
OR THE RESTAURANT MEN?
PODEY !!
YOU CAN'T NAME ONE THING THAT CONGRESS HAS DONE FOR THE RESTAURANT MEN!
OR THE SAILORS
AN' THE SENATE AIN'T DONE NOTHIN' NEITHER FOR US SAILORS
OR US RESTAURANT MEN
AND THE PRESIDENT - HOW ABOUT HIM? -
WELL BLOW ME DOWN!
AW LET'ER GO — NOBODY UNDERSTANDS GOVERNMENTS, AND NOBODY KNOWS WOMEN
I KNOWS THEY'RE FRICKLE !!
3-13
SEGAR
AN' WHAT'S THE VICE-PRESIDENT DONE FOR THE SAILORS?
OR THE RESTAURANT MEN
© 1932, King Features Syndicate, Inc., Great Britain rights reserved.

10. March 13, 1932

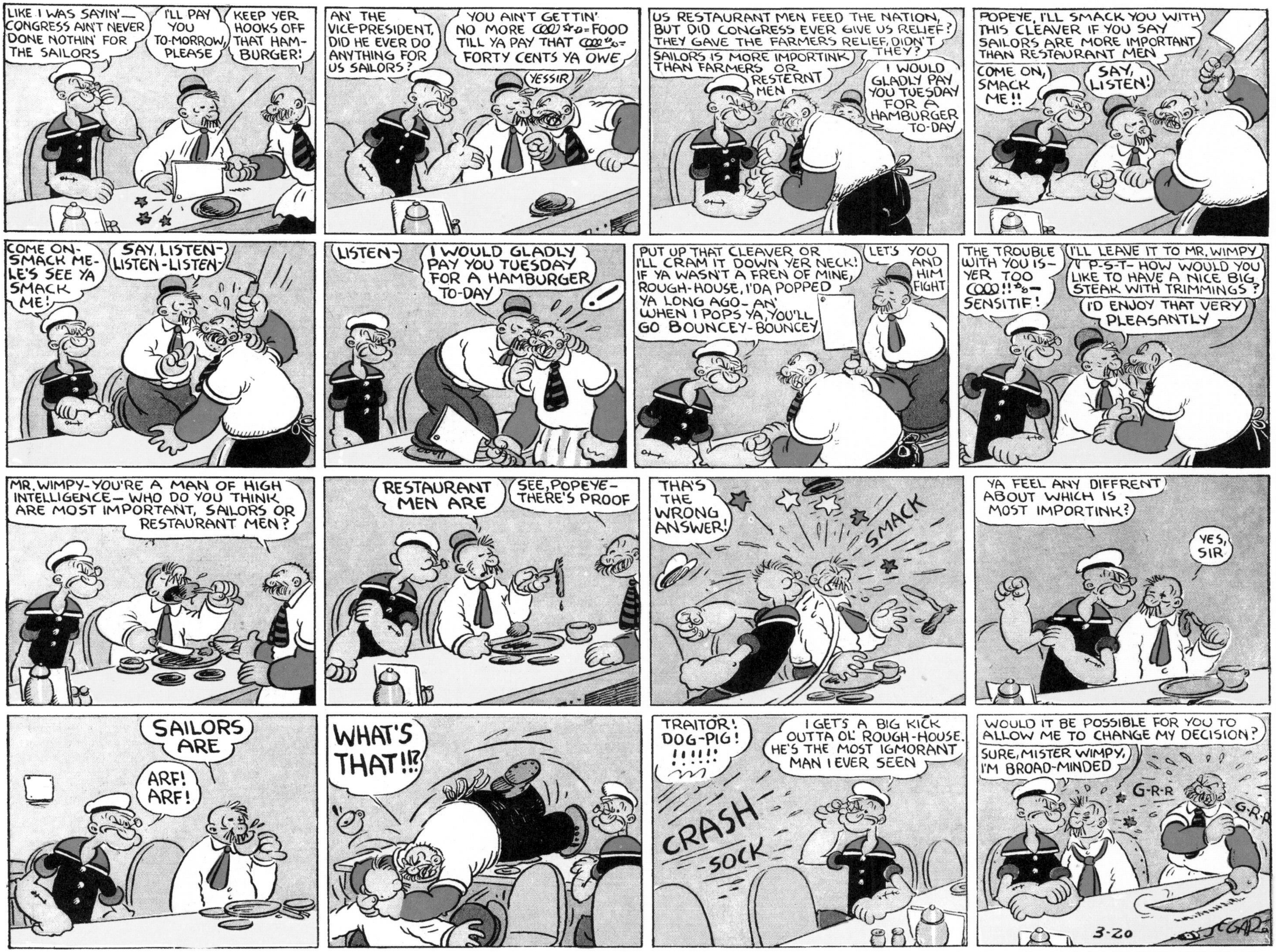
LIKE I WAS SAYIN'— CONGRESS AIN'T NEVER DONE NOTHIN' FOR THE SAILORS
I'LL PAY YOU TO-MORROW, PLEASE
KEEP YER HOOKS OFF THAT HAM-BURGER!
AN' THE VICE-PRESIDENT, DID HE EVER DO ANYTHING FOR US SAILORS?
YOU AIN'T GETTIN' NO MORE FOOD TILL YA PAY THAT FORTY CENTS YA OWE
YESSIR
US RESTAURANT MEN FEED THE NATION, BUT DID CONGRESS EVER GIVE US RELIEF? THEY GAVE THE FARMERS RELIEF, DIDN'T THEY?
SAILORS IS MORE IMPORTINK THAN FARMERS OR RESTERNT MEN
I WOULD GLADLY PAY YOU TUESDAY FOR A HAMBURGER TO-DAY
POPEYE, I'LL SMACK YOU WITH THIS CLEAVER IF YOU SAY SAILORS ARE MORE IMPORTANT THAN RESTAURANT MEN
COME ON, SMACK ME!!
SAY, LISTEN!
COME ON- SMACK ME- LE'S SEE YA SMACK ME!
SAY, LISTEN- LISTEN- LISTEN-
LISTEN-
I WOULD GLADLY PAY YOU TUESDAY FOR A HAMBURGER TO-DAY
!
PUT UP THAT CLEAVER OR I'LL CRAM IT DOWN YER NECK! IF YA WASN'T A FREN OF MINE, ROUGH-HOUSE, I'DA POPPED YA LONG AGO- AN' WHEN I POPS YA, YOU'LL GO BOUNCEY-BOUNCEY
LET'S YOU AND HIM FIGHT
THE TROUBLE WITH YOU IS- YER TOO SENSITIF!
I'LL LEAVE IT TO MR. WIMPY
P-S-T- HOW WOULD YOU LIKE TO HAVE A NICE BIG STEAK WITH TRIMMINGS?
I'D ENJOY THAT VERY PLEASANTLY
MR. WIMPY- YOU'RE A MAN OF HIGH INTELLIGENCE- WHO DO YOU THINK ARE MOST IMPORTANT, SAILORS OR RESTAURANT MEN?
RESTAURANT MEN ARE
SEE, POPEYE- THERE'S PROOF
THA'S THE WRONG ANSWER!
SMACK
YA FEEL ANY DIFFRENT ABOUT WHICH IS MOST IMPORTINK?
YES, SIR
SAILORS ARE
ARF! ARF!
WHAT'S THAT!!?
TRAITOR! DOG-PIG! !!!!!
I GETS A BIG KICK OUTTA OL' ROUGH-HOUSE. HE'S THE MOST IGMORANT MAN I EVER SEEN
CRASH
SOCK
WOULD IT BE POSSIBLE FOR YOU TO ALLOW ME TO CHANGE MY DECISION?
SURE, MISTER WIMPY, I'M BROAD-MINDED
G-R-R
G-R-R
3-20
SEGAR

11. March 20, 1932

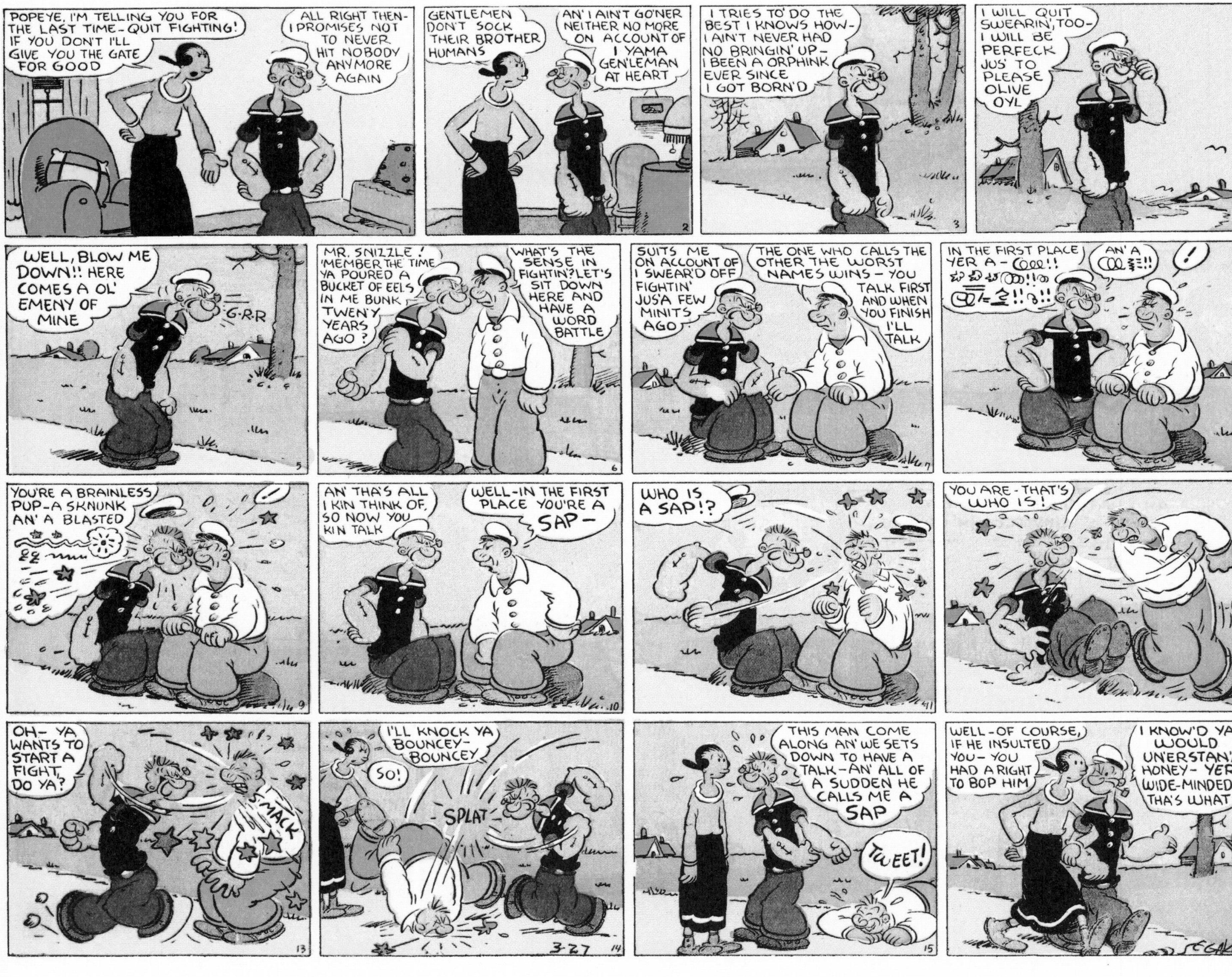
POPEYE, I'M TELLING YOU FOR THE LAST TIME - QUIT FIGHTING! IF YOU DON'T I'LL GIVE YOU THE GATE FOR GOOD
ALL RIGHT THEN - I PROMISES NOT TO NEVER HIT NOBODY ANYMORE AGAIN
GENTLEMEN DON'T SOCK THEIR BROTHER HUMANS
AN' I AIN'T GO'NER NEITHER NO MORE ON ACCOUNT OF I YAMA GEN'LEMAN AT HEART
I TRIES TO' DO THE BEST I KNOWS HOW - I AIN'T NEVER HAD NO BRINGIN' UP - I BEEN A ORPHINK EVER SINCE I GOT BORN'D
I WILL QUIT SWEARIN', TOO - I WILL BE PERFECK JUS' TO PLEASE OLIVE OYL
WELL, BLOW ME DOWN!! HERE COMES A OL' EMENY OF MINE
G-R-R
MR. SNIZZLE! 'MEMBER THE TIME YA POURED A BUCKET OF EELS IN ME BUNK TWEN'Y YEARS AGO?
WHAT'S THE SENSE IN FIGHTIN? LET'S SIT DOWN HERE AND HAVE A WORD BATTLE
SUITS ME ON ACCOUNT OF I SWEAR'D OFF FIGHTIN' JUS'A FEW MINITS AGO
THE ONE WHO CALLS THE OTHER THE WORST NAMES WINS - YOU TALK FIRST AND WHEN YOU FINISH I'LL TALK
IN THE FIRST PLACE YER A -
AN' A
!
YOU'RE A BRAINLESS PUP - A SKNUNK AN' A BLASTED
!
AN' THA'S ALL I KIN THINK OF, SO NOW YOU KIN TALK
WELL - IN THE FIRST PLACE YOU'RE A SAP -
WHO IS A SAP!?
YOU ARE - THAT'S WHO IS!
OH - YA WANTS TO START A FIGHT, DO YA?
SMACK
I'LL KNOCK YA BOUNCEY-BOUNCEY
SO!
SPLAT
3-27
THIS MAN COME ALONG AN' WE SETS DOWN TO HAVE A TALK - AN' ALL OF A SUDDEN HE CALLS ME A SAP
TWEET!
WELL - OF COURSE, IF HE INSULTED YOU - YOU HAD A RIGHT TO BOP HIM
I KNOW'D YA WOULD UN'ERSTAN', HONEY - YER WIDE-MINDED - THA'S WHAT

12. March 27, 1932

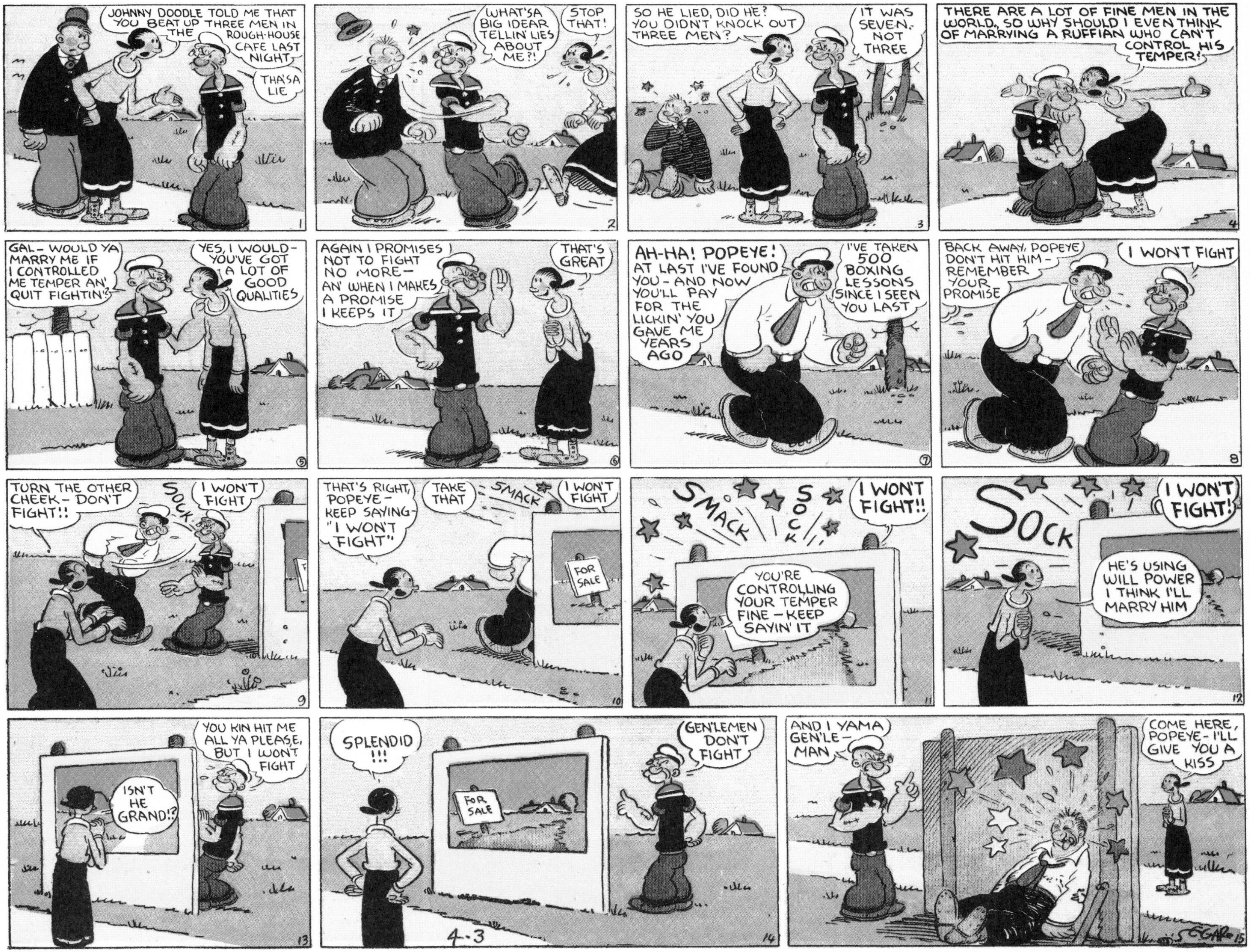
JOHNNY DOODLE TOLD ME THAT YOU BEAT UP THREE MEN IN THE ROUGH-HOUSE CAFE LAST NIGHT
THA'SA LIE
WHAT'SA BIG IDEAR TELLIN' LIES ABOUT ME?!
STOP THAT!
SO HE LIED, DID HE? YOU DIDN'T KNOCK OUT THREE MEN?
IT WAS SEVEN - NOT THREE
THERE ARE A LOT OF FINE MEN IN THE WORLD, SO WHY SHOULD I EVEN THINK OF MARRYING A RUFFIAN WHO CAN'T CONTROL HIS TEMPER!
GAL- WOULD YA MARRY ME IF I CONTROLLED ME TEMPER AN' QUIT FIGHTIN'?
YES, I WOULD- YOU'VE GOT A LOT OF GOOD QUALITIES
AGAIN I PROMISES NOT TO FIGHT NO MORE— AN' WHEN I MAKES A PROMISE I KEEPS IT
THAT'S GREAT
AH-HA! POPEYE! AT LAST I'VE FOUND YOU - AND NOW YOU'LL PAY FOR THE LICKIN' YOU GAVE ME YEARS AGO
I'VE TAKEN 500 BOXING LESSONS SINCE I SEEN YOU LAST
BACK AWAY, POPEYE DON'T HIT HIM- REMEMBER YOUR PROMISE
I WON'T FIGHT
TURN THE OTHER CHEEK- DON'T FIGHT!!
SOCK
I WON'T FIGHT
THAT'S RIGHT, POPEYE- KEEP SAYING- "I WON'T FIGHT"
TAKE THAT
SMACK
I WON'T FIGHT
FOR SALE
SMACK
SOCK
I WON'T FIGHT!!
YOU'RE CONTROLLING YOUR TEMPER FINE - KEEP SAYIN' IT
SOCK
I WON'T FIGHT!
HE'S USING WILL POWER I THINK I'LL MARRY HIM
YOU KIN HIT ME ALL YA PLEASE, BUT I WON'T FIGHT
ISN'T HE GRAND!?
SPLENDID !!!
FOR SALE
GEN'LEMEN DON'T FIGHT
4-3
AND I YAMA GEN'LE-MAN
COME HERE, POPEYE- I'LL GIVE YOU A KISS
SEGAR

13. April 3, 1932

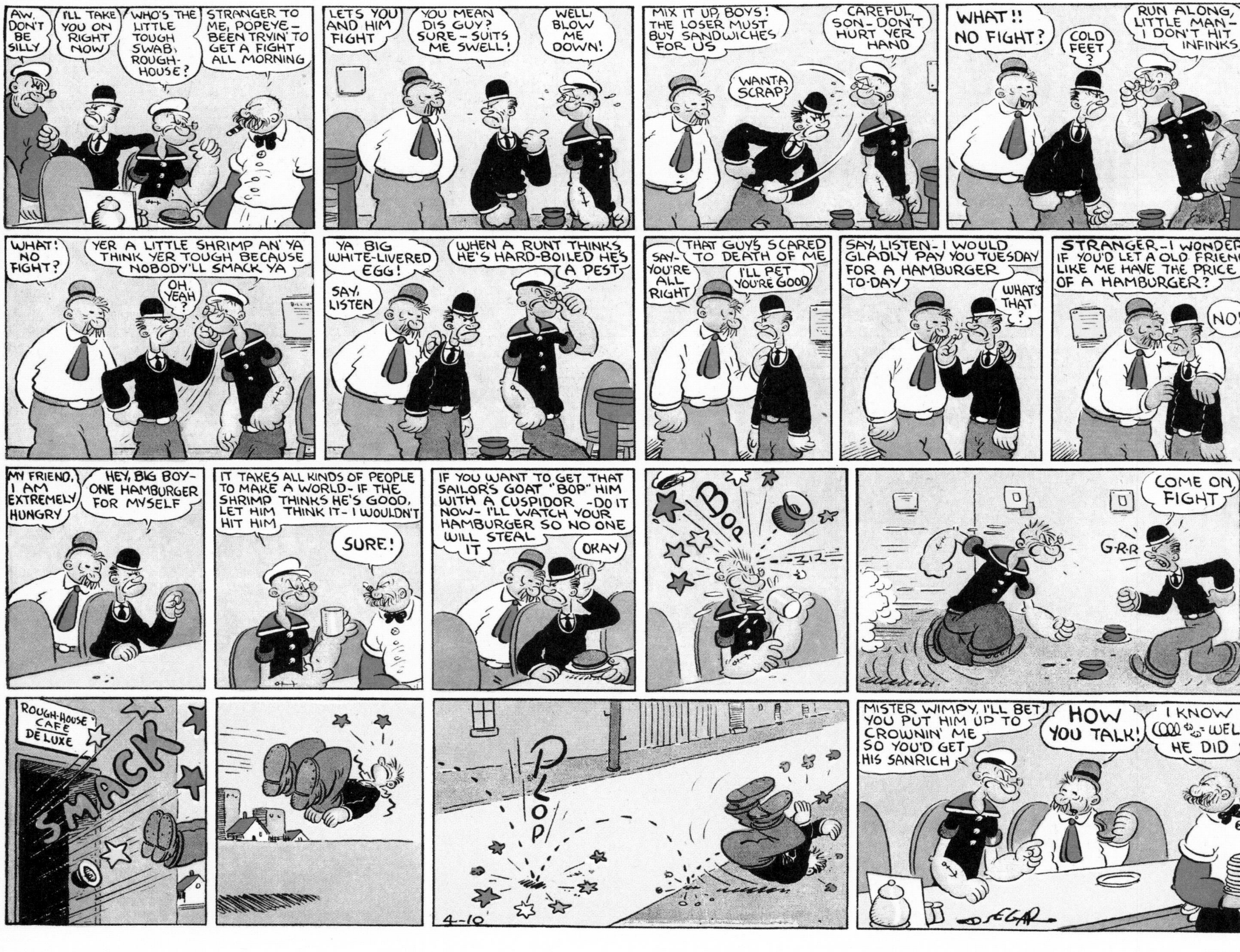

AW, DON'T BE SILLY
I'LL TAKE YOU ON RIGHT NOW
WHO'S THE LITTLE TOUGH SWAB, ROUGH-HOUSE?
STRANGER TO ME, POPEYE— BEEN TRYIN' TO GET A FIGHT ALL MORNING
LETS YOU AND HIM FIGHT
YOU MEAN DIS GUY? SURE—SUITS ME SWELL!
WELL, BLOW ME DOWN!
MIX IT UP, BOYS! THE LOSER MUST BUY SANDWICHES FOR US
CAREFUL, SON—DON'T HURT YER HAND
WANTA SCRAP?
WHAT!! NO FIGHT?
COLD FEET ?
RUN ALONG, LITTLE MAN— I DON'T HIT INFINKS
WHAT! NO FIGHT?
YER A LITTLE SHRIMP AN' YA THINK YER TOUGH BECAUSE NOBODY'LL SMACK YA
OH, YEAH ?
YA BIG WHITE-LIVERED EGG!
WHEN A RUNT THINKS HE'S HARD-BOILED HE'S A PEST
SAY, LISTEN
THAT GUY'S SCARED TO DEATH OF ME
SAY— YOU'RE ALL RIGHT
I'LL BET YOU'RE GOOD
SAY, LISTEN— I WOULD GLADLY PAY YOU TUESDAY FOR A HAMBURGER TO-DAY
WHAT'S THAT ?
STRANGER— I WONDER IF YOU'D LET A OLD FRIEND LIKE ME HAVE THE PRICE OF A HAMBURGER?
NO!
MY FRIEND, I AM EXTREMELY HUNGRY
HEY, BIG BOY— ONE HAMBURGER FOR MYSELF
IT TAKES ALL KINDS OF PEOPLE TO MAKE A WORLD— IF THE SHRIMP THINKS HE'S GOOD, LET HIM THINK IT— I WOULDN'T HIT HIM
SURE!
IF YOU WANT TO GET THAT SAILOR'S GOAT "BOP" HIM WITH A CUSPIDOR —DO IT NOW— I'LL WATCH YOUR HAMBURGER SO NO ONE WILL STEAL IT
OKAY
BOP
COME ON, FIGHT
G-R-R
ROUGH-HOUSE CAFE DE LUXE
SMACK
PLOP
4-10
MISTER WIMPY, I'LL BET YOU PUT HIM UP TO CROWNIN' ME SO YOU'D GET HIS SANRICH
HOW YOU TALK!
I KNOW —WELL HE DID
SEGAR

14. April 10, 1932

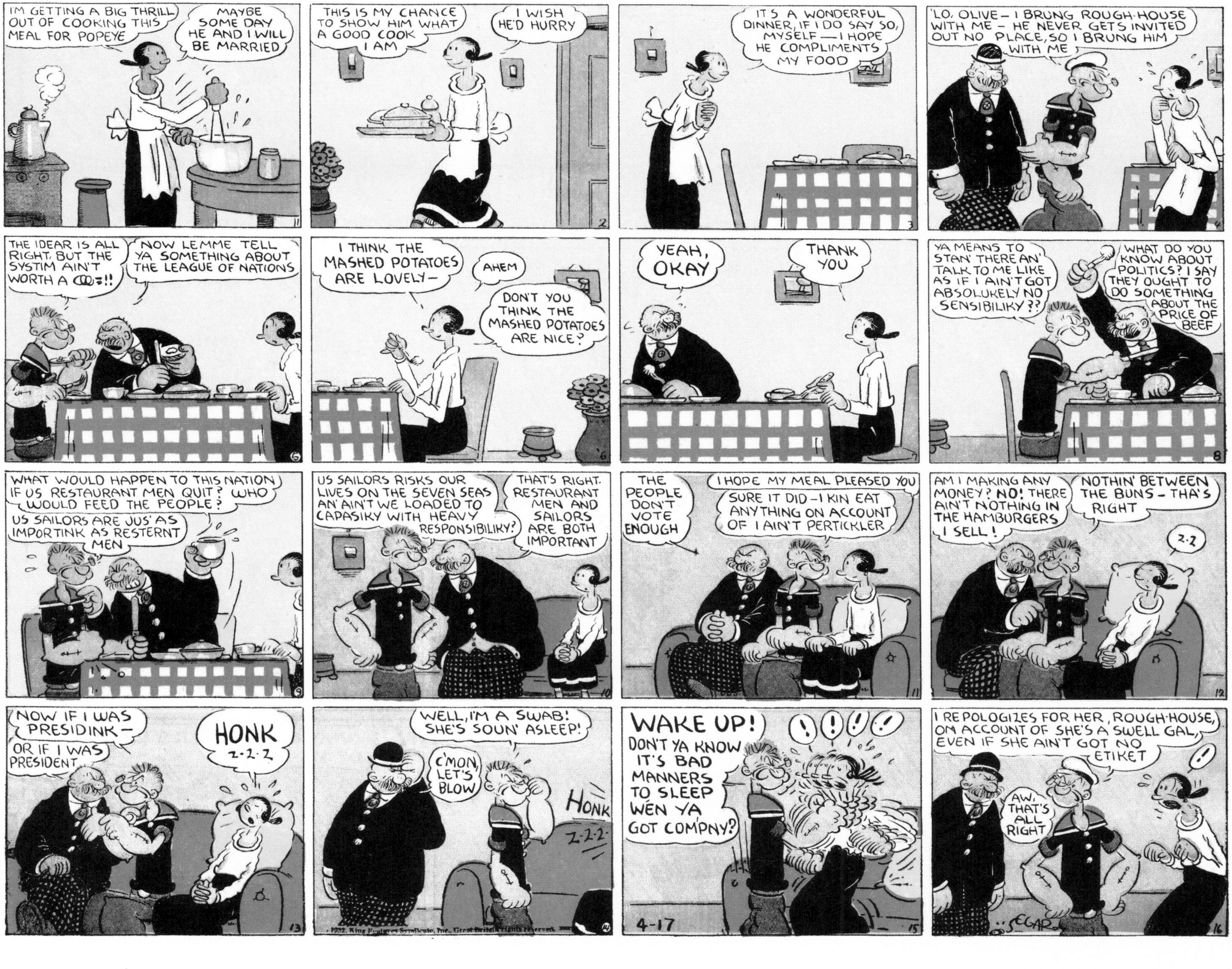
I'M GETTING A BIG THRILL OUT OF COOKING THIS MEAL FOR POPEYE
MAYBE SOME DAY HE AND I WILL BE MARRIED
THIS IS MY CHANCE TO SHOW HIM WHAT A GOOD COOK I AM
I WISH HE'D HURRY
IT'S A WONDERFUL DINNER, IF I DO SAY SO, MYSELF — I HOPE HE COMPLIMENTS MY FOOD
'LO, OLIVE — I BRUNG ROUGH-HOUSE WITH ME — HE NEVER GETS INVITED OUT NO PLACE, SO I BRUNG HIM WITH ME
THE IDEAR IS ALL RIGHT, BUT THE SYSTIM AIN'T WORTH A !!
NOW LEMME TELL YA SOMETHING ABOUT THE LEAGUE OF NATIONS
I THINK THE MASHED POTATOES ARE LOVELY —
AHEM
DON'T YOU THINK THE MASHED POTATOES ARE NICE?
YEAH, OKAY
THANK YOU
YA MEANS TO STAN' THERE AN' TALK TO ME LIKE AS IF I AIN'T GOT ABSOLUKELY NO SENSIBILIKY??
WHAT DO YOU KNOW ABOUT POLITICS? I SAY THEY OUGHT TO DO SOMETHING ABOUT THE PRICE OF BEEF
WHAT WOULD HAPPEN TO THIS NATION IF US RESTAURANT MEN QUIT? WHO WOULD FEED THE PEOPLE?
US SAILORS ARE JUS' AS IMPORTINK AS RESTERNT MEN
US SAILORS RISKS OUR LIVES ON THE SEVEN SEAS AN' AIN'T WE LOADED TO CAPASIKY WITH HEAVY RESPONSIBILIKY?
THAT'S RIGHT. RESTAURANT MEN AND SAILORS ARE BOTH IMPORTANT
THE PEOPLE DON'T VOTE ENOUGH
I HOPE MY MEAL PLEASED YOU
SURE IT DID — I KIN EAT ANYTHING ON ACCOUNT OF I AIN'T PERTICKLER
AM I MAKING ANY MONEY? NO! THERE AIN'T NOTHING IN THE HAMBURGERS I SELL!
NOTHIN' BETWEEN THE BUNS — THA'S RIGHT
Z-Z
NOW IF I WAS PRESIDINK —
OR IF I WAS PRESIDENT
HONK Z-Z-Z
WELL, I'M A SWAB! SHE'S SOUN' ASLEEP!
C'MON LET'S BLOW
HONK Z-Z-Z
WAKE UP!
DON'T YA KNOW IT'S BAD MANNERS TO SLEEP WEN YA GOT COMP'NY?
!!!!
I REPOLOGIZES FOR HER, ROUGH-HOUSE, ON ACCOUNT OF SHE'S A SWELL GAL, EVEN IF SHE AIN'T GOT NO ETIKET
!
AW, THAT'S ALL RIGHT
4-17
SEGAR

15. April 17, 1932

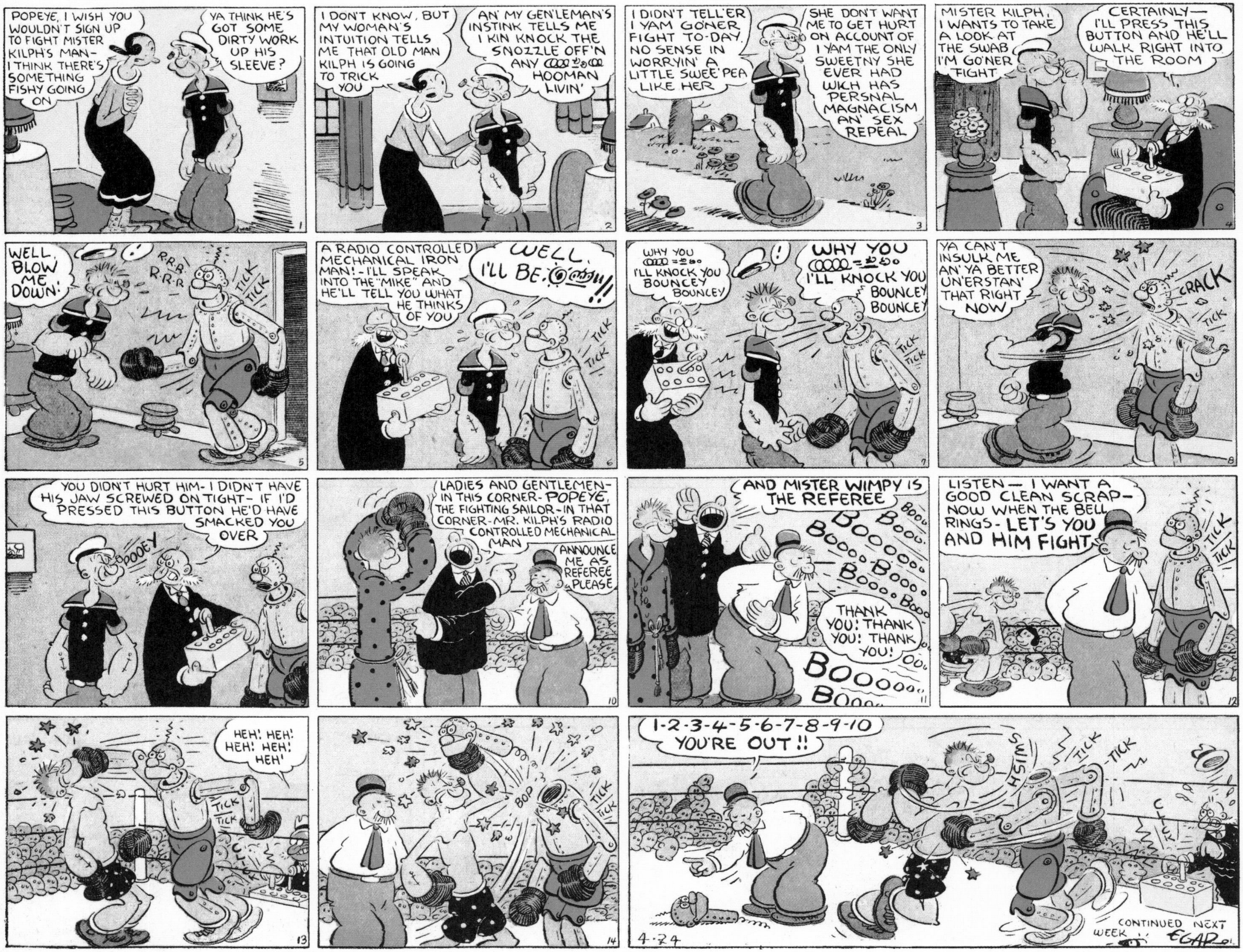
POPEYE, I WISH YOU WOULDN'T SIGN UP TO FIGHT MISTER KILPH'S MAN- I THINK THERE'S SOMETHING FISHY GOING ON
YA THINK HE'S GOT SOME DIRTY WORK UP HIS SLEEVE?
I DON'T KNOW, BUT MY WOMAN'S INTUITION TELLS ME THAT OLD MAN KILPH IS GOING TO TRICK YOU
AN' MY GEN'LEMAN'S INSTINK TELLS ME I KIN KNOCK THE SNOZZLE OFF'N ANY HOOMAN LIVIN'
I DIDN'T TELL'ER I YAM GO'NER FIGHT TO-DAY. NO SENSE IN WORRYIN' A LITTLE SWEE'PEA LIKE HER
SHE DON'T WANT ME TO GET HURT ON ACCOUNT OF I YAM THE ONLY SWEETNY SHE EVER HAD WICH HAS PERSNAL MAGNACISM AN' SEX REPEAL
MISTER KILPH, I WANTS TO TAKE A LOOK AT THE SWAB I'M GO'NER FIGHT
CERTAINLY— I'LL PRESS THIS BUTTON AND HE'LL WALK RIGHT INTO THE ROOM
WELL, BLOW ME DOWN!
R-R-R R-R-R
TICK TICK
A RADIO CONTROLLED MECHANICAL IRON MAN! - I'LL SPEAK INTO THE "MIKE" AND HE'LL TELL YOU WHAT HE THINKS OF YOU
WELL, I'LL BE. !!
TICK TICK
WHY YOU I'LL KNOCK YOU BOUNCEY BOUNCEY
WHY YOU I'LL KNOCK YOU BOUNCEY BOUNCEY
TICK TICK
YA CAN'T INSULK ME AN' YA BETTER UN'ERSTAN' THAT RIGHT NOW
CRACK
TICK
YOU DIDN'T HURT HIM- I DIDN'T HAVE HIS JAW SCREWED ON TIGHT- IF I'D PRESSED THIS BUTTON HE'D HAVE SMACKED YOU OVER
POOEY
LADIES AND GENTLEMEN- IN THIS CORNER- POPEYE, THE FIGHTING SAILOR- IN THAT CORNER- MR. KILPH'S RADIO CONTROLLED MECHANICAL MAN
ANNOUNCE ME AS REFEREE PLEASE
AND MISTER WIMPY IS THE REFEREE
BOOOO BOOOO BOOOOOOO BOOOO BOOOO BOOOO
THANK YOU! THANK YOU! THANK YOU!
BOOOOOO
LISTEN— I WANT A GOOD CLEAN SCRAP- NOW WHEN THE BELL RINGS- LET'S YOU AND HIM FIGHT
TICK TICK
HEH! HEH! HEH! HEH! HEH!
TICK TICK
CLICK
BOP
TICK TICK
1-2-3-4-5-6-7-8-9-10 YOU'RE OUT!!
SWISH
TICK
TICK
CLICK
4·24
CONTINUED NEXT WEEK

16. April 24, 1932

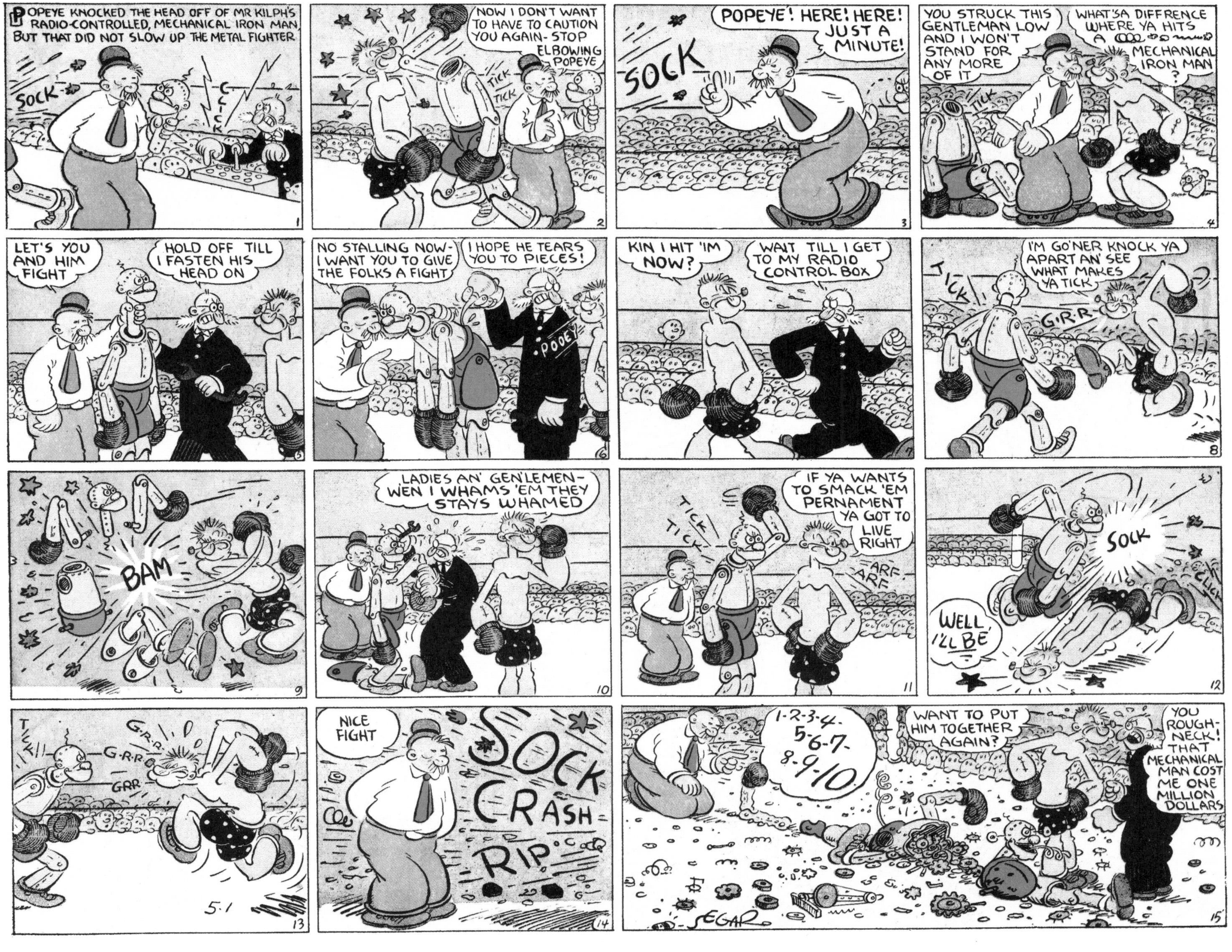
POPEYE KNOCKED THE HEAD OFF OF MR KILPH'S RADIO-CONTROLLED, MECHANICAL IRON MAN, BUT THAT DID NOT SLOW UP THE METAL FIGHTER
SOCK
CLICK
NOW I DON'T WANT TO HAVE TO CAUTION YOU AGAIN - STOP ELBOWING POPEYE
TICK TICK
SOCK
POPEYE! HERE! HERE! JUST A MINUTE!
YOU STRUCK THIS GENTLEMAN LOW AND I WON'T STAND FOR ANY MORE OF IT
WHAT'SA DIFFRENCE WHERE YA HITS A MECHANICAL IRON MAN?
TICK
LET'S YOU AND HIM FIGHT
HOLD OFF TILL I FASTEN HIS HEAD ON
NO STALLING NOW - I WANT YOU TO GIVE THE FOLKS A FIGHT
I HOPE HE TEARS YOU TO PIECES!
POOEY
KIN I HIT 'IM NOW?
WAIT TILL I GET TO MY RADIO CONTROL BOX
TICK
I'M GO'NER KNOCK YA APART AN' SEE WHAT MAKES YA TICK
G-R-R
BAM
LADIES AN' GEN'LEMEN - WEN I WHAMS 'EM THEY STAYS WHAMED
TICK TICK
IF YA WANTS TO SMACK 'EM PERNAMENT YA GOT TO LIVE RIGHT
ARF ARF
SOCK
CLICK
WELL I'LL BE
TICK
G-R-R
G-R-R
GRR
5-1
NICE FIGHT
SOCK
CRASH
RIP
1-2-3-4-5-6-7-8-9-10
WANT TO PUT HIM TOGETHER AGAIN?
YOU ROUGH-NECK! THAT MECHANICAL MAN COST ME ONE MILLION DOLLARS
SEGAR

17. May 1, 1932

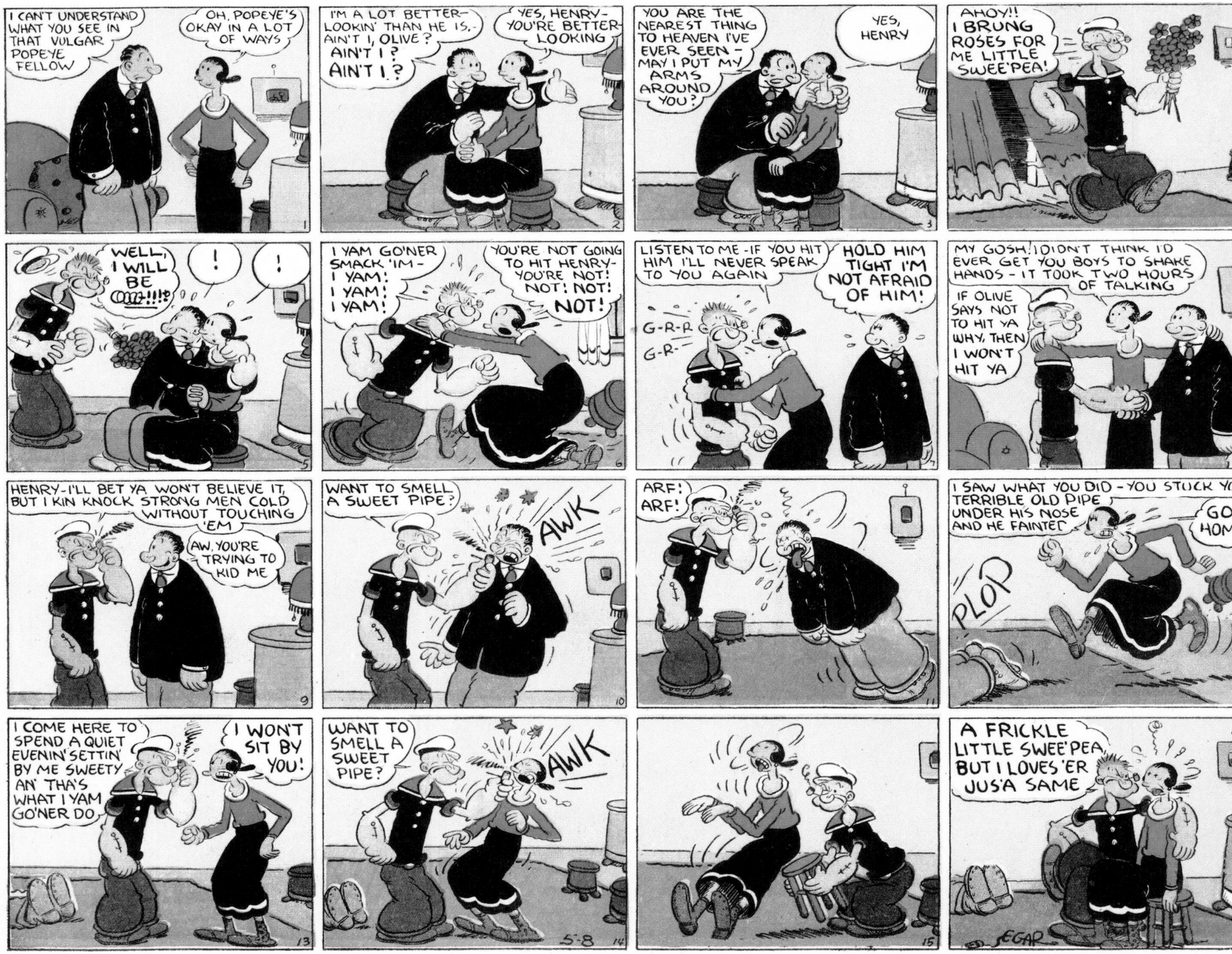
I CAN'T UNDERSTAND WHAT YOU SEE IN THAT VULGAR POPEYE FELLOW
OH, POPEYE'S OKAY IN A LOT OF WAYS
I'M A LOT BETTER-LOOKIN' THAN HE IS. AIN'T I, OLIVE? AIN'T I? AIN'T I?
YES, HENRY-YOU'RE BETTER LOOKING
YOU ARE THE NEAREST THING TO HEAVEN I'VE EVER SEEN - MAY I PUT MY ARMS AROUND YOU?
YES, HENRY
AHOY!! I BRUNG ROSES FOR ME LITTLE SWEE'PEA!
WELL, I WILL BE
!
!
I YAM GO'NER SMACK 'IM - I YAM! I YAM! I YAM!
YOU'RE NOT GOING TO HIT HENRY - YOU'RE NOT! NOT! NOT! NOT!
LISTEN TO ME - IF YOU HIT HIM I'LL NEVER SPEAK TO YOU AGAIN
HOLD HIM TIGHT I'M NOT AFRAID OF HIM!
G-R-R
G-R-
MY GOSH! I DIDN'T THINK I'D EVER GET YOU BOYS TO SHAKE HANDS - IT TOOK TWO HOURS OF TALKING
IF OLIVE SAYS NOT TO HIT YA WHY, THEN I WON'T HIT YA
HENRY - I'LL BET YA WON'T BELIEVE IT, BUT I KIN KNOCK STRONG MEN COLD WITHOUT TOUCHING 'EM
AW, YOU'RE TRYING TO KID ME
WANT TO SMELL A SWEET PIPE?
AWK
ARF! ARF!
I SAW WHAT YOU DID - YOU STUCK YOUR TERRIBLE OLD PIPE UNDER HIS NOSE AND HE FAINTED
GO HOME!
PLOP
I COME HERE TO SPEND A QUIET EVENIN' SETTIN' BY ME SWEETY AN' THA'S WHAT I YAM GO'NER DO
I WON'T SIT BY YOU!
WANT TO SMELL A SWEET PIPE?
AWK
5-8
A FRICKLE LITTLE SWEE'PEA, BUT I LOVES 'ER JUS'A SAME

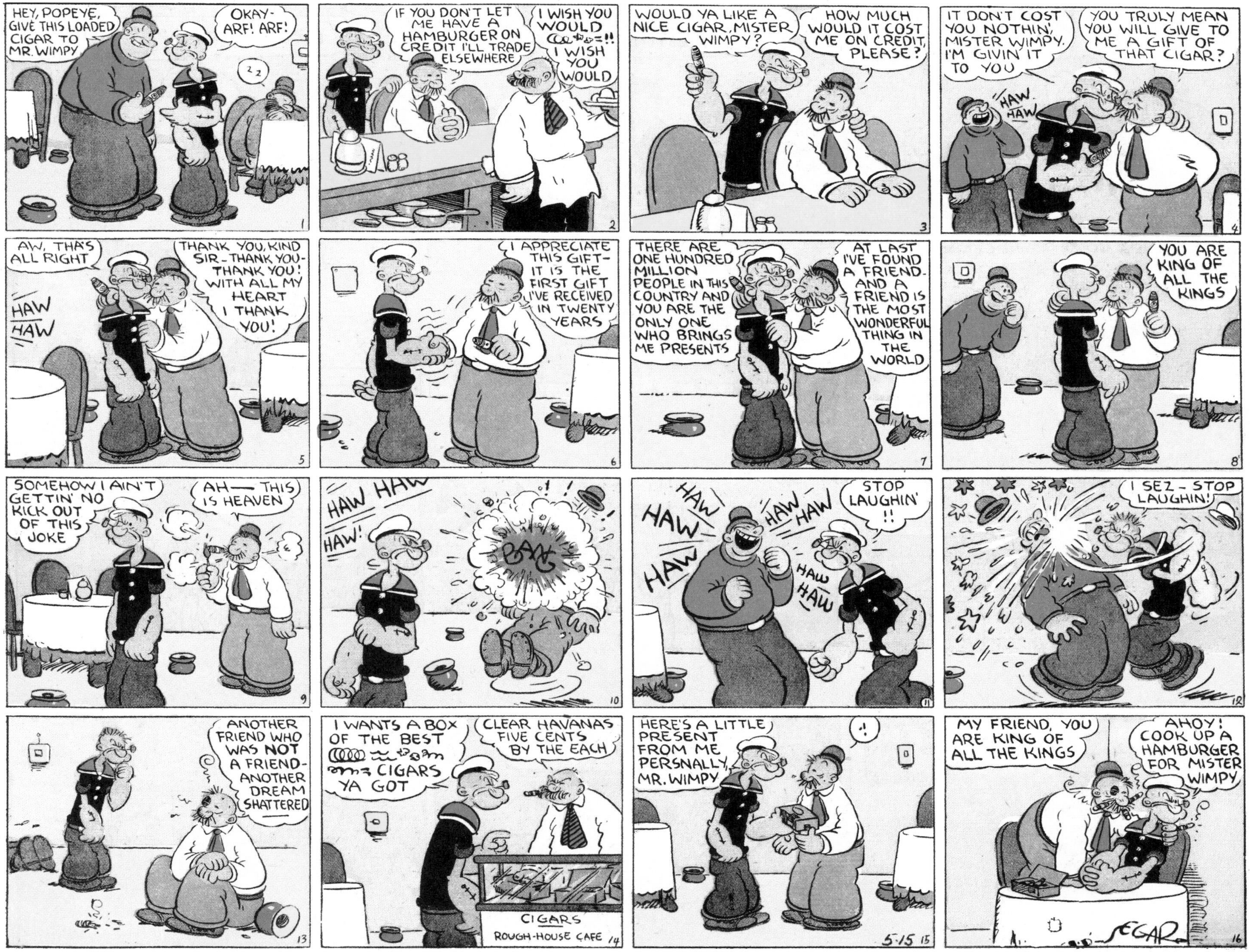
HEY, POPEYE, GIVE THIS LOADED CIGAR TO MR. WIMPY
OKAY- ARF! ARF!
IF YOU DON'T LET ME HAVE A HAMBURGER ON CREDIT I'LL TRADE ELSEWHERE
I WISH YOU WOULD
!!
I WISH YOU WOULD
WOULD YA LIKE A NICE CIGAR, MISTER WIMPY?
HOW MUCH WOULD IT COST ME ON CREDIT, PLEASE?
IT DON'T COST YOU NOTHIN', MISTER WIMPY. I'M GIVIN' IT TO YOU
YOU TRULY MEAN YOU WILL GIVE TO ME A GIFT OF THAT CIGAR?
HAW. HAW
AW, THA'S ALL RIGHT
THANK YOU, KIND SIR - THANK YOU - THANK YOU! WITH ALL MY HEART I THANK YOU!
HAW HAW
I APPRECIATE THIS GIFT- IT IS THE FIRST GIFT I'VE RECEIVED IN TWENTY YEARS
THERE ARE ONE HUNDRED MILLION PEOPLE IN THIS COUNTRY AND YOU ARE THE ONLY ONE WHO BRINGS ME PRESENTS
AT LAST I'VE FOUND A FRIEND- AND A FRIEND IS THE MOST WONDERFUL THING IN THE WORLD
YOU ARE KING OF ALL THE KINGS
SOMEHOW I AIN'T GETTIN' NO KICK OUT OF THIS JOKE
AH — THIS IS HEAVEN
HAW HAW
HAW!
BANG
HAW HAW HAW
HAW HAW
STOP LAUGHIN' !!
HAW HAW
I SEZ - STOP LAUGHIN'!
ANOTHER FRIEND WHO WAS NOT A FRIEND- ANOTHER DREAM SHATTERED
I WANTS A BOX OF THE BEST CIGARS YA GOT
CLEAR HAVANAS FIVE CENTS BY THE EACH
CIGARS
ROUGH-HOUSE CAFE
HERE'S A LITTLE PRESENT FROM ME PERSNALLY, MR. WIMPY
!
5-15
MY FRIEND, YOU ARE KING OF ALL THE KINGS
AHOY! COOK UP A HAMBURGER FOR MISTER WIMPY
SEGAR

19. May 15, 1932

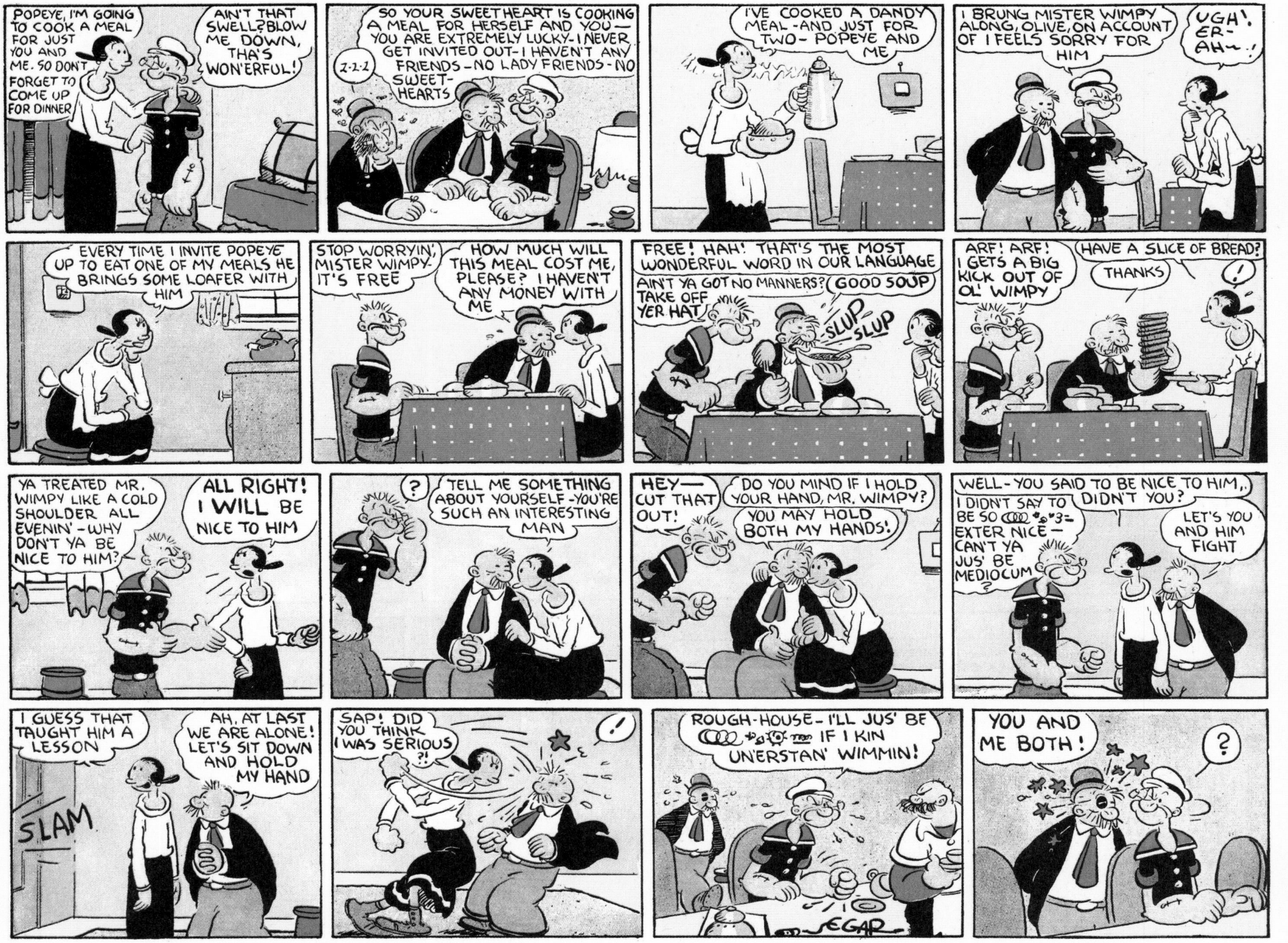
POPEYE, I'M GOING TO COOK A MEAL FOR JUST YOU AND ME. SO DON'T FORGET TO COME UP FOR DINNER
AIN'T THAT SWELL? BLOW ME DOWN, THA'S WON'ERFUL!
SO YOUR SWEETHEART IS COOKING A MEAL FOR HERSELF AND YOU — YOU ARE EXTREMELY LUCKY - I NEVER GET INVITED OUT - I HAVEN'T ANY FRIENDS - NO LADY FRIENDS - NO SWEET-HEARTS
Z-Z-Z
I'VE COOKED A DANDY MEAL - AND JUST FOR TWO - POPEYE AND ME
I BRUNG MISTER WIMPY ALONG, OLIVE, ON ACCOUNT OF I FEELS SORRY FOR HIM
UGH! ER-AH~!
EVERY TIME I INVITE POPEYE UP TO EAT ONE OF MY MEALS HE BRINGS SOME LOAFER WITH HIM
STOP WORRYIN', MISTER WIMPY - IT'S FREE
HOW MUCH WILL THIS MEAL COST ME, PLEASE? I HAVEN'T ANY MONEY WITH ME
FREE! HAH! THAT'S THE MOST WONDERFUL WORD IN OUR LANGUAGE
AIN'T YA GOT NO MANNERS? TAKE OFF YER HAT
GOOD SOUP
SLUP - SLUP
ARF! ARF! I GETS A BIG KICK OUT OF OL' WIMPY
HAVE A SLICE OF BREAD?
THANKS
!
YA TREATED MR. WIMPY LIKE A COLD SHOULDER ALL EVENIN' - WHY DON'T YA BE NICE TO HIM?
ALL RIGHT! I WILL BE NICE TO HIM
?
TELL ME SOMETHING ABOUT YOURSELF - YOU'RE SUCH AN INTERESTING MAN
HEY— CUT THAT OUT!
DO YOU MIND IF I HOLD YOUR HAND, MR. WIMPY?
YOU MAY HOLD BOTH MY HANDS!
WELL - YOU SAID TO BE NICE TO HIM,, DIDN'T YOU?
I DIDN'T SAY TO BE SO EXTER NICE — CAN'T YA JUS' BE MEDIOCUM?
LET'S YOU AND HIM FIGHT
I GUESS THAT TAUGHT HIM A LESSON
AH, AT LAST WE ARE ALONE! LET'S SIT DOWN AND HOLD MY HAND
SLAM
SAP! DID YOU THINK I WAS SERIOUS ?!
!
ROUGH-HOUSE - I'LL JUS' BE IF I KIN UN'ERSTAN' WIMMIN!
SEGAR
YOU AND ME BOTH!
?

20. May 22, 1932

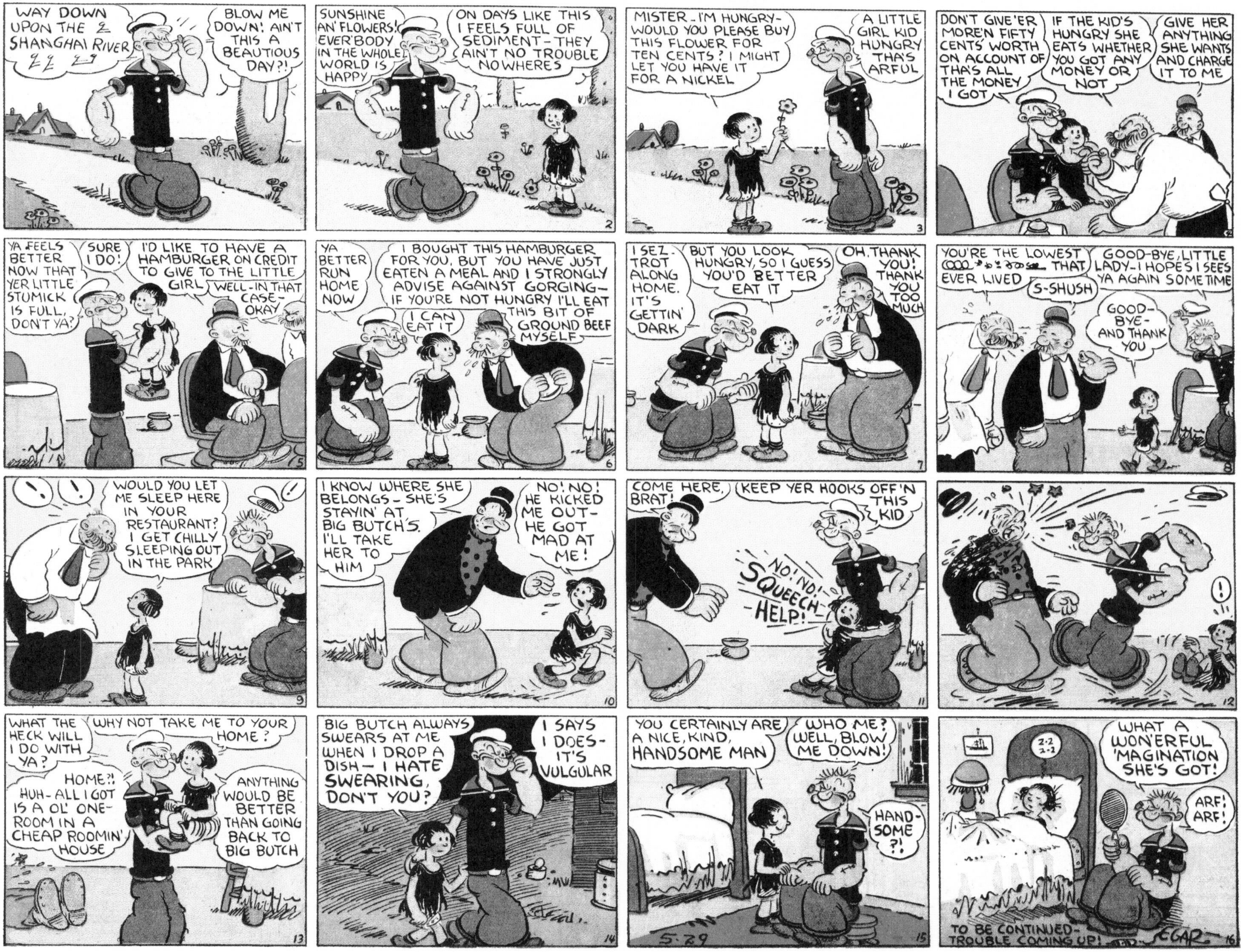
WAY DOWN UPON THE SHANGHAI RIVER
BLOW ME DOWN! AIN'T THIS A BEAUTIOUS DAY?!
SUNSHINE AN' FLOWERS! EVER'BODY IN THE WHOLE WORLD IS HAPPY
ON DAYS LIKE THIS I FEELS FULL OF SEDIMENT - THEY AIN'T NO TROUBLE NOWHERES
MISTER - I'M HUNGRY - WOULD YOU PLEASE BUY THIS FLOWER FOR TEN CENTS? I MIGHT LET YOU HAVE IT FOR A NICKEL
A LITTLE GIRL KID HUNGRY THA'S ARFUL
DON'T GIVE 'ER MORE'N FIFTY CENTS' WORTH ON ACCOUNT OF THA'S ALL THE MONEY I GOT
IF THE KID'S HUNGRY SHE EATS WHETHER YOU GOT ANY MONEY OR NOT
GIVE HER ANYTHING SHE WANTS AND CHARGE IT TO ME
YA FEELS BETTER NOW THAT YER LITTLE STUMICK IS FULL, DON'T YA?
SURE I DO!
I'D LIKE TO HAVE A HAMBURGER ON CREDIT TO GIVE TO THE LITTLE GIRL
WELL - IN THAT CASE - OKAY
YA BETTER RUN HOME NOW
I BOUGHT THIS HAMBURGER FOR YOU, BUT YOU HAVE JUST EATEN A MEAL AND I STRONGLY ADVISE AGAINST GORGING - IF YOU'RE NOT HUNGRY I'LL EAT THIS BIT OF GROUND BEEF MYSELF
I CAN EAT IT
I SEZ TROT ALONG HOME. IT'S GETTIN' DARK
BUT YOU LOOK HUNGRY, SO I GUESS YOU'D BETTER EAT IT
OH, THANK YOU! THANK YOU TOO MUCH
YOU'RE THE LOWEST THAT EVER LIVED
S-SHUSH
GOOD-BYE, LITTLE LADY - I HOPES I SEES YA AGAIN SOME TIME
GOOD-BYE - AND THANK YOU
! !
WOULD YOU LET ME SLEEP HERE IN YOUR RESTAURANT? I GET CHILLY SLEEPING OUT IN THE PARK
!
I KNOW WHERE SHE BELONGS - SHE'S STAYIN' AT BIG BUTCH'S. I'LL TAKE HER TO HIM
NO! NO! HE KICKED ME OUT - HE GOT MAD AT ME!
COME HERE, BRAT!
KEEP YER HOOKS OFF'N THIS KID
NO! NO!
SQUEECH
HELP!
!
WHAT THE HECK WILL I DO WITH YA?
WHY NOT TAKE ME TO YOUR HOME?
HOME?! HUH - ALL I GOT IS A OL' ONE-ROOM IN A CHEAP ROOMIN' HOUSE
ANYTHING WOULD BE BETTER THAN GOING BACK TO BIG BUTCH
BIG BUTCH ALWAYS SWEARS AT ME WHEN I DROP A DISH - I HATE SWEARING, DON'T YOU?
I SAYS I DOES - IT'S VULGULAR
YOU CERTAINLY ARE A NICE, KIND, HANDSOME MAN
WHO ME? WELL, BLOW ME DOWN!
HANDSOME?!
5-29
WHAT A WON'ERFUL 'MAGINATION SHE'S GOT!
ARF! ARF!
TO BE CONTINUED - TROUBLE COMING UP!
SEGAR

21. May 29, 1932

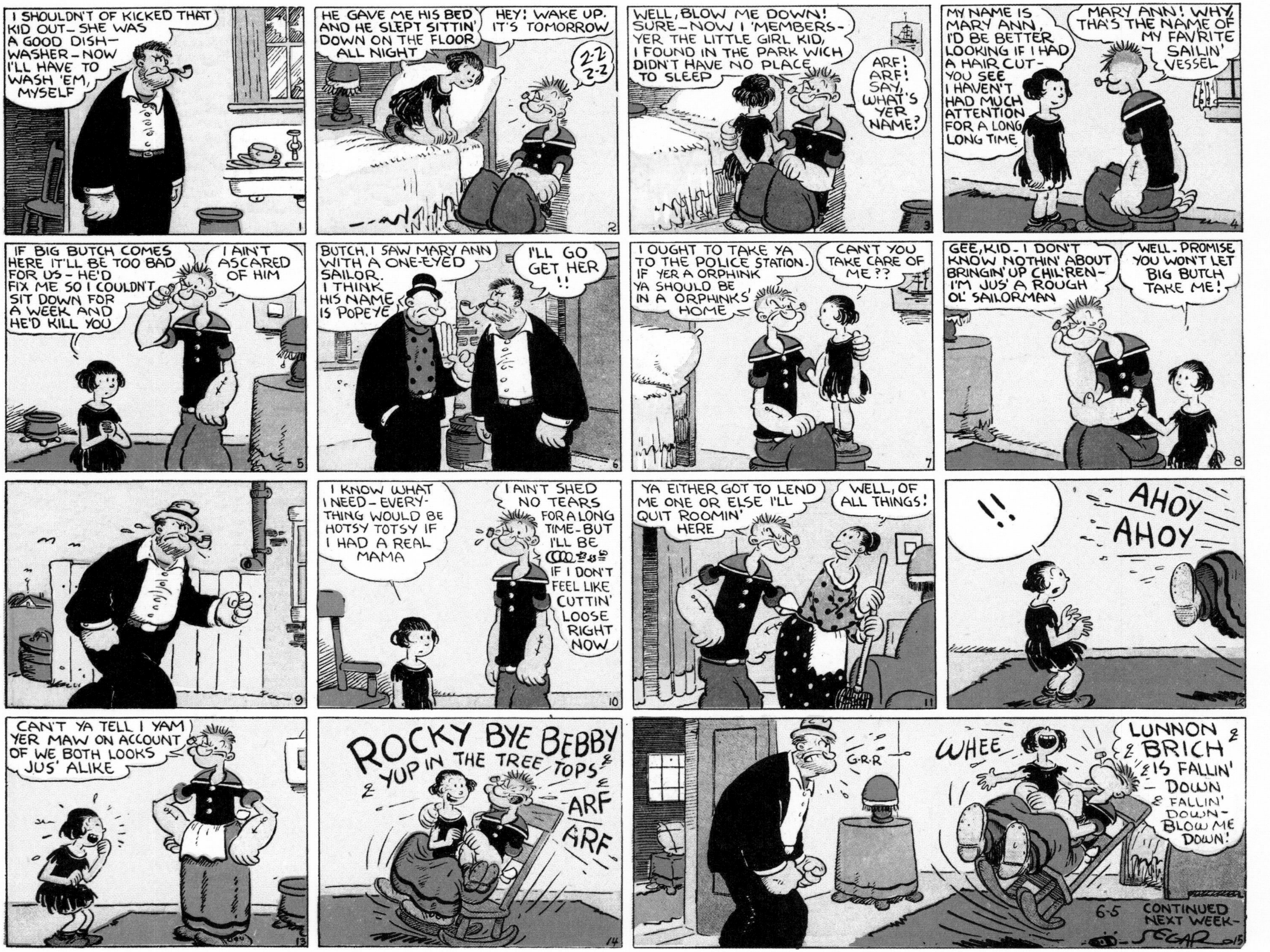

I SHOULDN'T OF KICKED THAT KID OUT—SHE WAS A GOOD DISH-WASHER—NOW I'LL HAVE TO WASH 'EM, MYSELF
1
HE GAVE ME HIS BED AND HE SLEPT SITTIN' DOWN ON THE FLOOR ALL NIGHT
HEY! WAKE UP. IT'S TOMORROW
Z-Z Z-Z
2
WELL, BLOW ME DOWN! SURE—NOW I 'MEMBERS—YER THE LITTLE GIRL KID, I FOUND IN THE PARK WICH DIDN'T HAVE NO PLACE TO SLEEP
ARF! ARF! SAY, WHAT'S YER NAME?
3
MY NAME IS MARY ANN, I'D BE BETTER LOOKING IF I HAD A HAIR CUT—YOU SEE I HAVEN'T HAD MUCH ATTENTION FOR A LONG LONG TIME
MARY ANN! WHY, THA'S THE NAME OF MY FAV'RITE SAILIN' VESSEL
4
IF BIG BUTCH COMES HERE IT'LL BE TOO BAD FOR US—HE'D FIX ME SO I COULDN'T SIT DOWN FOR A WEEK AND HE'D KILL YOU
I AIN'T ASCARED OF HIM
5
BUTCH, I SAW MARY ANN WITH A ONE-EYED SAILOR. I THINK HIS NAME IS POPEYE
I'LL GO GET HER !!
6
I OUGHT TO TAKE YA TO THE POLICE STATION. IF YER A ORPHINK YA SHOULD BE IN A ORPHINKS' HOME
CAN'T YOU TAKE CARE OF ME??
7
GEE, KID—I DON'T KNOW NOTHIN' ABOUT BRINGIN' UP CHIL'REN—I'M JUS' A ROUGH OL' SAILORMAN
WELL—PROMISE YOU WON'T LET BIG BUTCH TAKE ME!
8
9
I KNOW WHAT I NEED—EVERYTHING WOULD BE HOTSY TOTSY IF I HAD A REAL MAMA
I AIN'T SHED NO TEARS FOR A LONG TIME—BUT I'LL BE IF I DON'T FEEL LIKE CUTTIN' LOOSE RIGHT NOW
10
YA EITHER GOT TO LEND ME ONE OR ELSE I'LL QUIT ROOMIN' HERE
WELL, OF ALL THINGS!
11
!!
AHOY AHOY
12
CAN'T YA TELL I YAM YER MAW ON ACCOUNT OF WE BOTH LOOKS JUS' ALIKE
13
ROCKY BYE BEBBY YUP IN THE TREE TOPS
ARF ARF
14
G-R-R
WHEE
LUNNON BRICH IS FALLIN' DOWN FALLIN' DOWN—BLOW ME DOWN!
6-5
CONTINUED NEXT WEEK—
SEGAR
15

22. June 5, 1932

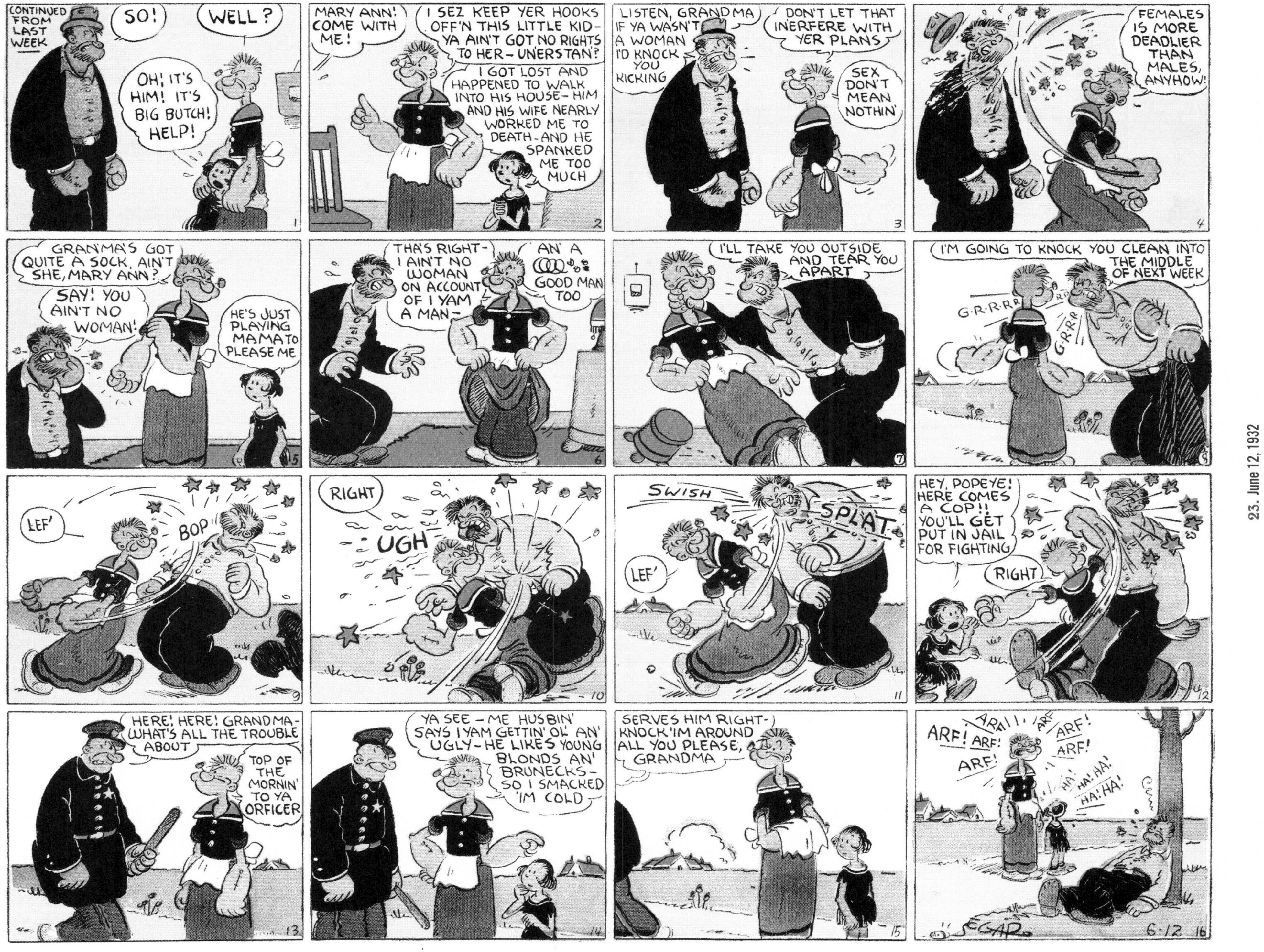
CONTINUED FROM LAST WEEK
SO!
WELL?
OH! IT'S HIM! IT'S BIG BUTCH! HELP!
MARY ANN! COME WITH ME!
I SEZ KEEP YER HOOKS OFF'N THIS LITTLE KID- YA AIN'T GOT NO RIGHTS TO HER-UNERSTAN'?
I GOT LOST AND HAPPENED TO WALK INTO HIS HOUSE-HIM AND HIS WIFE NEARLY WORKED ME TO DEATH-AND HE SPANKED ME TOO MUCH
LISTEN, GRANDMA IF YA WASN'T A WOMAN I'D KNOCK YOU KICKING
DON'T LET THAT INERFERE WITH YER PLANS
SEX DON'T MEAN NOTHIN'
FEMALES IS MORE DEADLIER THAN MALES, ANYHOW!
GRAN'MA'S GOT QUITE A SOCK, AIN'T SHE, MARY ANN?
SAY! YOU AIN'T NO WOMAN!
HE'S JUST PLAYING MAMA TO PLEASE ME
THA'S RIGHT- I AIN'T NO WOMAN ON ACCOUNT OF I YAM A MAN-
AN' A
GOOD MAN TOO
I'LL TAKE YOU OUTSIDE AND TEAR YOU APART
I'M GOING TO KNOCK YOU CLEAN INTO THE MIDDLE OF NEXT WEEK
G-R-R-RR
G-R-R-R
LEF'
BOP
RIGHT
UGH
SWISH
SPLAT
LEF'
HEY, POPEYE! HERE COMES A COP!! YOU'LL GET PUT IN JAIL FOR FIGHTING
RIGHT
HERE! HERE! GRANDMA- WHAT'S ALL THE TROUBLE ABOUT
TOP OF THE MORNIN' TO YA ORFICER
YA SEE-ME HUSBIN' SAYS I YAM GETTIN' OL' AN' UGLY-HE LIKES YOUNG BLONDS AN' BRUNECKS- SO I SMACKED 'IM COLD
SERVES HIM RIGHT- KNOCK 'IM AROUND ALL YOU PLEASE, GRANDMA
ARF! ARF! ARF! ARF! ARF! ARF! ARF!
HA! HA! HA! HA! HA!
SEGAR
6-12

23. June 12, 1932

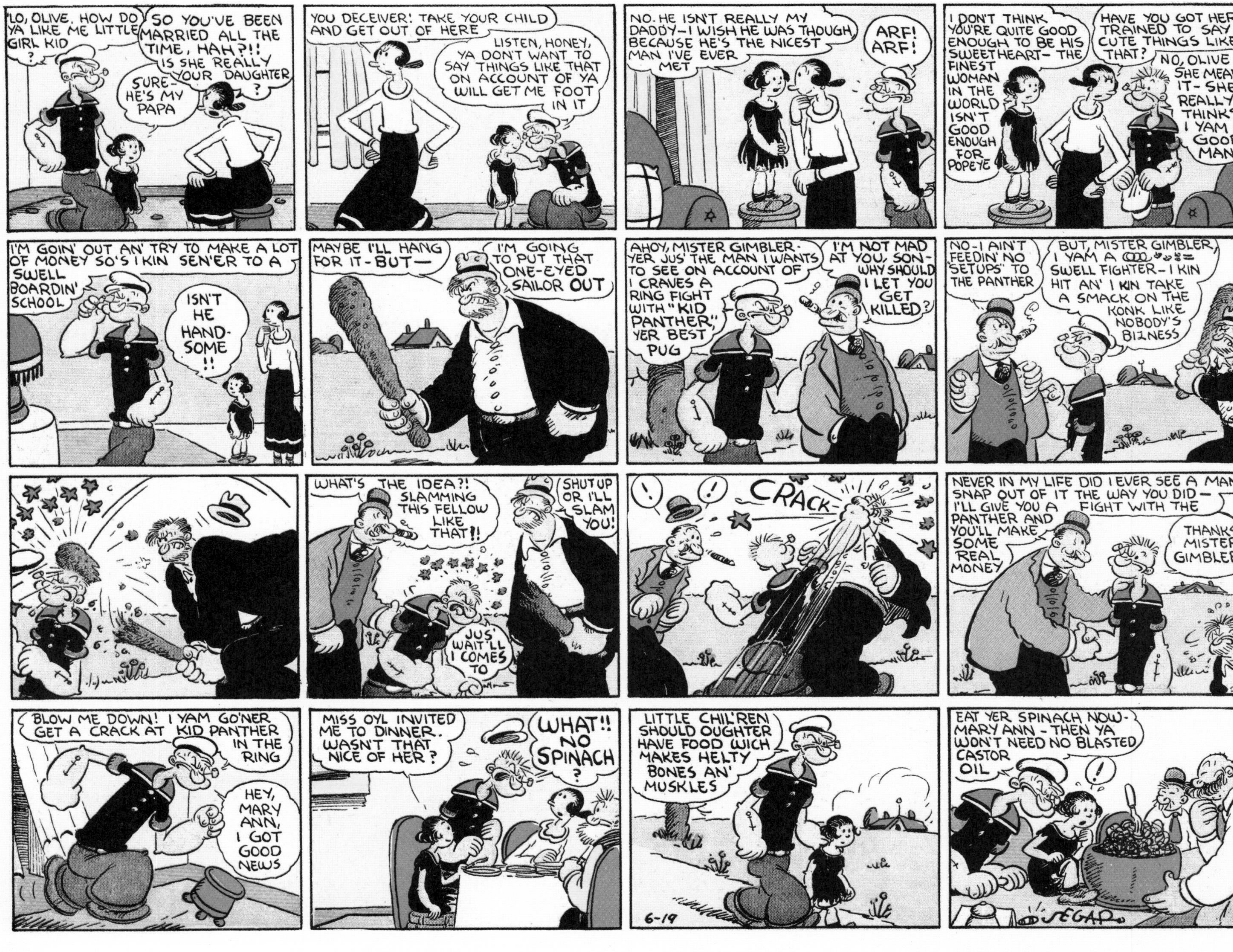
'LO, OLIVE. HOW DO YA LIKE ME LITTLE GIRL KID?
SO YOU'VE BEEN MARRIED ALL THE TIME, HAH?!! IS SHE REALLY YOUR DAUGHTER?
SURE— HE'S MY PAPA
YOU DECEIVER! TAKE YOUR CHILD AND GET OUT OF HERE
LISTEN, HONEY, YA DON'T WANT TO SAY THINGS LIKE THAT ON ACCOUNT OF YA WILL GET ME FOOT IN IT
NO. HE ISN'T REALLY MY DADDY—I WISH HE WAS THOUGH, BECAUSE HE'S THE NICEST MAN I'VE EVER MET
ARF! ARF!
I DON'T THINK YOU'RE QUITE GOOD ENOUGH TO BE HIS SWEETHEART— THE FINEST WOMAN IN THE WORLD ISN'T GOOD ENOUGH FOR POPEYE
HAVE YOU GOT HER TRAINED TO SAY CUTE THINGS LIKE THAT?
NO, OLIVE— SHE MEANS IT— SHE REALLY THINKS I YAM A GOOD MAN
I'M GOIN' OUT AN' TRY TO MAKE A LOT OF MONEY SO'S I KIN SEN'ER TO A SWELL BOARDIN' SCHOOL
ISN'T HE HANDSOME!!
MAYBE I'LL HANG FOR IT-BUT—
I'M GOING TO PUT THAT ONE-EYED SAILOR OUT
AHOY, MISTER GIMBLER- YER JUS' THE MAN I WANTS TO SEE ON ACCOUNT OF I CRAVES A RING FIGHT WITH "KID PANTHER," YER BEST PUG
I'M NOT MAD AT YOU, SON- WHY SHOULD I LET YOU GET KILLED?
NO-I AIN'T FEEDIN' NO "SETUPS" TO THE PANTHER
BUT, MISTER GIMBLER, I YAM A SWELL FIGHTER- I KIN HIT AN' I KIN TAKE A SMACK ON THE KONK LIKE NOBODY'S BIZNESS
WHAT'S THE IDEA?! SLAMMING THIS FELLOW LIKE THAT!!
SHUT UP OR I'LL SLAM YOU!
JUS' WAIT'LL I COMES TO
!
!
CRACK
NEVER IN MY LIFE DID I EVER SEE A MAN SNAP OUT OF IT THE WAY YOU DID— I'LL GIVE YOU A FIGHT WITH THE PANTHER AND YOU'LL MAKE SOME REAL MONEY
THANKS, MISTER GIMBLER
BLOW ME DOWN! I YAM GO'NER GET A CRACK AT KID PANTHER IN THE RING
HEY, MARY ANN, I GOT GOOD NEWS
MISS OYL INVITED ME TO DINNER. WASN'T THAT NICE OF HER?
WHAT!! NO SPINACH?
LITTLE CHIL'REN SHOULD OUGHTER HAVE FOOD WICH MAKES HELTY BONES AN' MUSKLES
6-19
EAT YER SPINACH NOW- MARY ANN - THEN YA WON'T NEED NO BLASTED CASTOR OIL
!
SEGAR

24. June 19, 1932

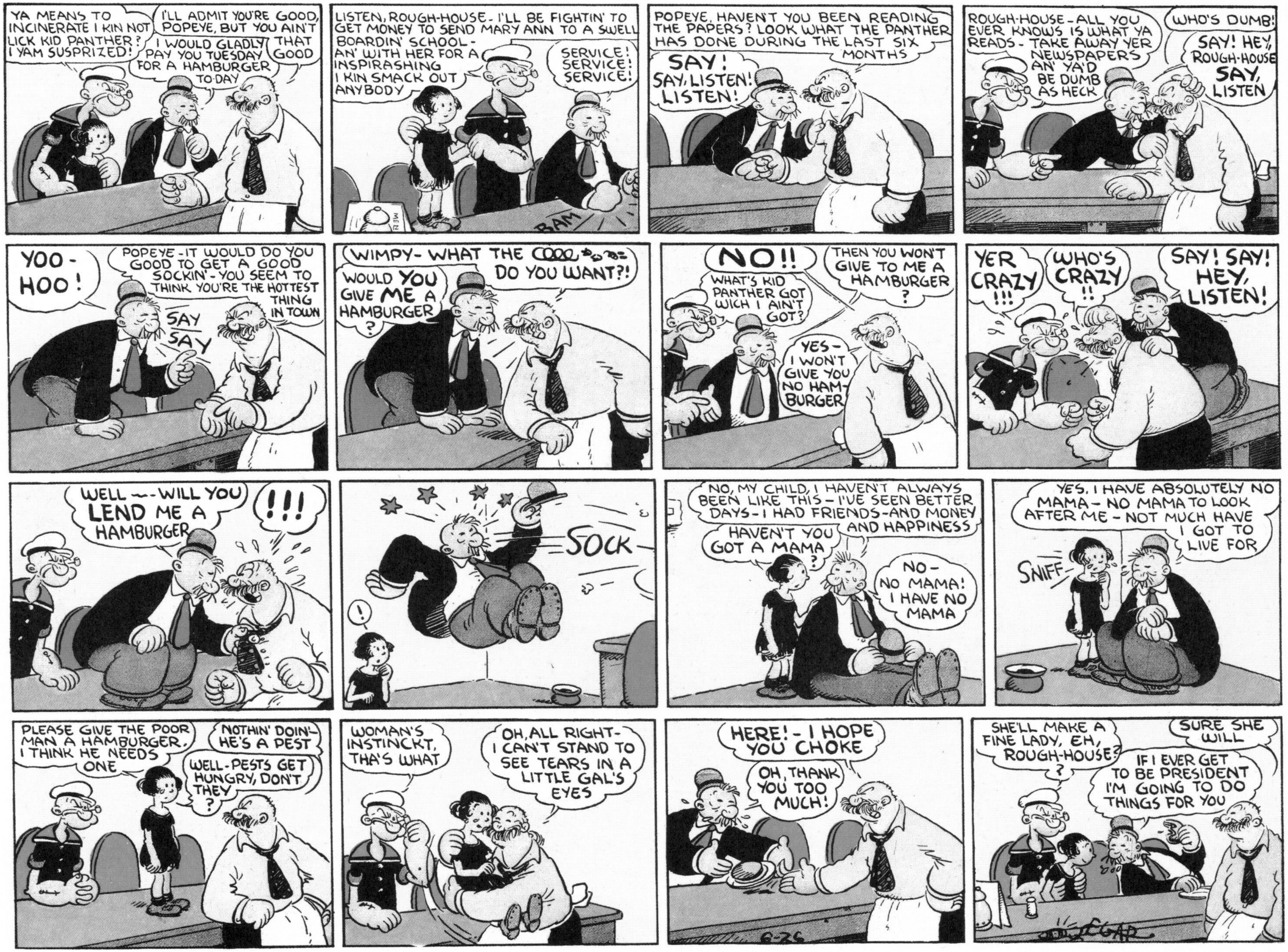
YA MEANS TO INCINERATE I KIN NOT LICK KID PANTHER? I YAM SUSPRIZED!
I'LL ADMIT YOU'RE GOOD, POPEYE, BUT YOU AIN'T THAT GOOD
I WOULD GLADLY PAY YOU TUESDAY FOR A HAMBURGER TO-DAY
LISTEN, ROUGH-HOUSE - I'LL BE FIGHTIN' TO GET MONEY TO SEND MARY ANN TO A SWELL BOARDIN' SCHOOL - AN' WITH HER FOR A INSPIRASHING I KIN SMACK OUT ANYBODY
SERVICE! SERVICE! SERVICE!
BAM
POPEYE, HAVEN'T YOU BEEN READING THE PAPERS? LOOK WHAT THE PANTHER HAS DONE DURING THE LAST SIX MONTHS
SAY! SAY, LISTEN! LISTEN!
ROUGH-HOUSE - ALL YOU EVER KNOWS IS WHAT YA READS - TAKE AWAY YER NEWSPAPERS AN' YA'D BE DUMB AS HECK
WHO'S DUMB!
SAY! HEY, ROUGH-HOUSE SAY, LISTEN
YOO-HOO!
POPEYE - IT WOULD DO YOU GOOD TO GET A GOOD SOCKIN' - YOU SEEM TO THINK YOU'RE THE HOTTEST THING IN TOWN
SAY SAY
WIMPY - WHAT THE DO YOU WANT?!
WOULD YOU GIVE ME A HAMBURGER?
NO!!
WHAT'S KID PANTHER GOT WICH I AIN'T GOT?
THEN YOU WON'T GIVE TO ME A HAMBURGER?
YES - I WON'T GIVE YOU NO HAMBURGER
YER CRAZY !!!
WHO'S CRAZY !!
SAY! SAY! HEY, LISTEN!
WELL -- WILL YOU LEND ME A HAMBURGER
!!!
SOCK
!
NO, MY CHILD, I HAVEN'T ALWAYS BEEN LIKE THIS - I'VE SEEN BETTER DAYS - I HAD FRIENDS - AND MONEY AND HAPPINESS
HAVEN'T YOU GOT A MAMA?
NO - NO MAMA! I HAVE NO MAMA
YES, I HAVE ABSOLUTLY NO MAMA - NO MAMA TO LOOK AFTER ME - NOT MUCH HAVE I GOT TO LIVE FOR
SNIFF
PLEASE GIVE THE POOR MAN A HAMBURGER. I THINK HE NEEDS ONE
NOTHIN' DOIN' - HE'S A PEST
WELL - PESTS GET HUNGRY, DON'T THEY?
WOMAN'S INSTINCKT, THA'S WHAT
OH, ALL RIGHT - I CAN'T STAND TO SEE TEARS IN A LITTLE GAL'S EYES
HERE! - I HOPE YOU CHOKE
OH, THANK YOU TOO MUCH!
6-26
SHE'LL MAKE A FINE LADY, EH, ROUGH-HOUSE?
SURE SHE WILL
IF I EVER GET TO BE PRESIDENT I'M GOING TO DO THINGS FOR YOU
SEGAR

25. June 26, 1932

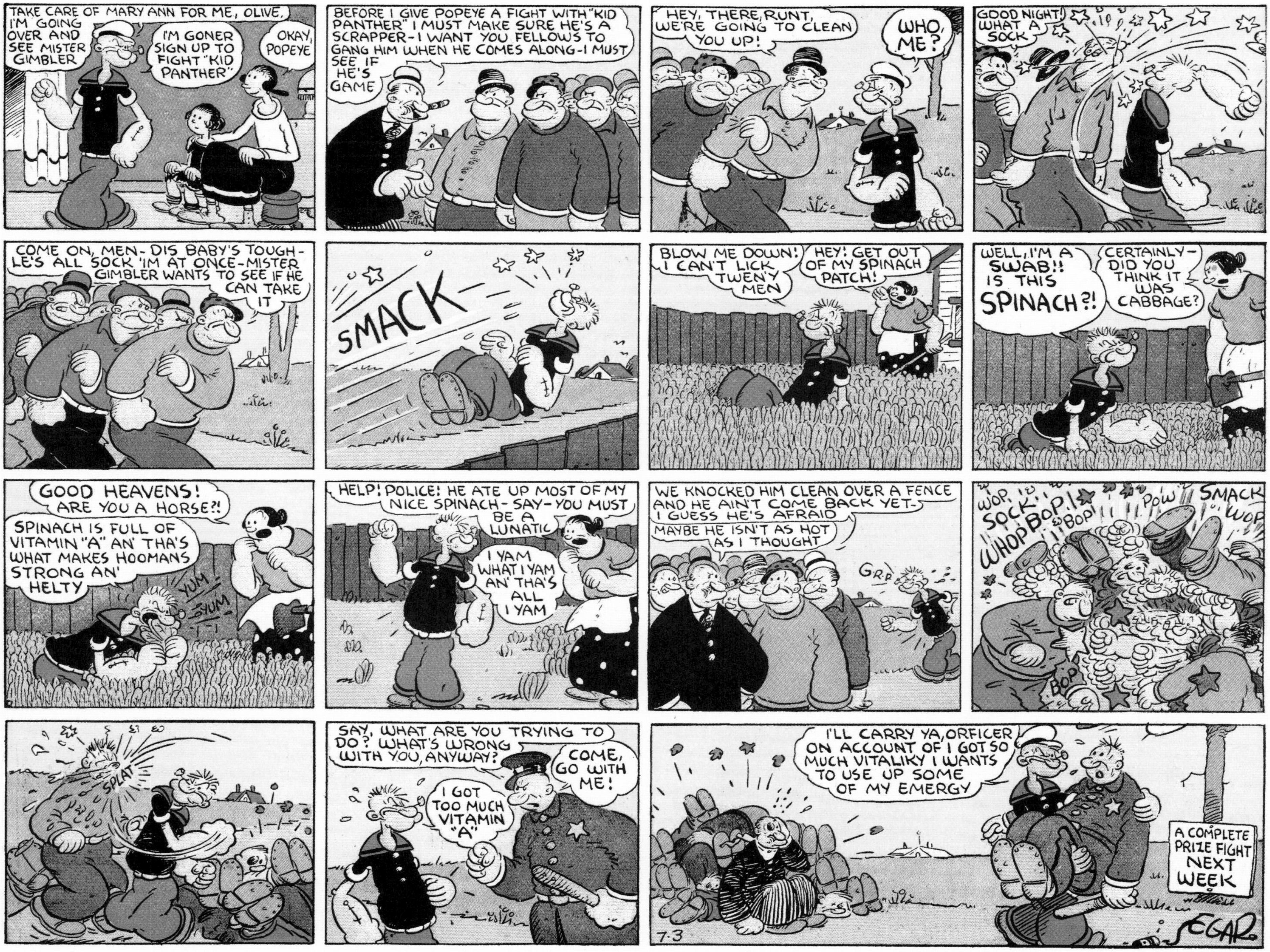
TAKE CARE OF MARY ANN FOR ME, OLIVE, I'M GOING OVER AND SEE MISTER GIMBLER
I'M GONER SIGN UP TO FIGHT "KID PANTHER"
OKAY, POPEYE
BEFORE I GIVE POPEYE A FIGHT WITH "KID PANTHER" I MUST MAKE SURE HE'S A SCRAPPER - I WANT YOU FELLOWS TO GANG HIM WHEN HE COMES ALONG - I MUST SEE IF HE'S GAME
HEY, THERE, RUNT, WE'RE GOING TO CLEAN YOU UP!
WHO, ME?
GOOD NIGHT! WHAT A SOCK
COME ON, MEN - DIS BABY'S TOUGH - LE'S ALL SOCK 'IM AT ONCE - MISTER GIMBLER WANTS TO SEE IF HE CAN TAKE IT
SMACK
BLOW ME DOWN! I CAN'T LICK TWEN'Y MEN
HEY! GET OUT OF MY SPINACH PATCH!
WELL, I'M A SWAB!! IS THIS SPINACH?!
CERTAINLY - DID YOU THINK IT WAS CABBAGE?
GOOD HEAVENS! ARE YOU A HORSE?!
SPINACH IS FULL OF VITAMIN "A" AN' THA'S WHAT MAKES HOOMANS STRONG AN' HELTY
YUM
YUM
HELP! POLICE! HE ATE UP MOST OF MY NICE SPINACH - SAY - YOU MUST BE A LUNATIC
I YAM WHAT I YAM AN' THA'S ALL I YAM
WE KNOCKED HIM CLEAN OVER A FENCE AND HE AIN'T COME BACK YET - I GUESS HE'S AFRAID
MAYBE HE ISN'T AS HOT AS I THOUGHT
GRR
WOP SOCK WHOP BOP! BOP! POW SMACK WOP
BOP
SPLAT
SAY, WHAT ARE YOU TRYING TO DO? WHAT'S WRONG WITH YOU, ANYWAY?
COME, GO WITH ME!
I GOT TOO MUCH VITAMIN "A"
I'LL CARRY YA, ORFICER ON ACCOUNT OF I GOT SO MUCH VITALIKY I WANTS TO USE UP SOME OF MY EMERGY
A COMPLETE PRIZE FIGHT NEXT WEEK
7-3
SEGAR

26. July 3, 1932

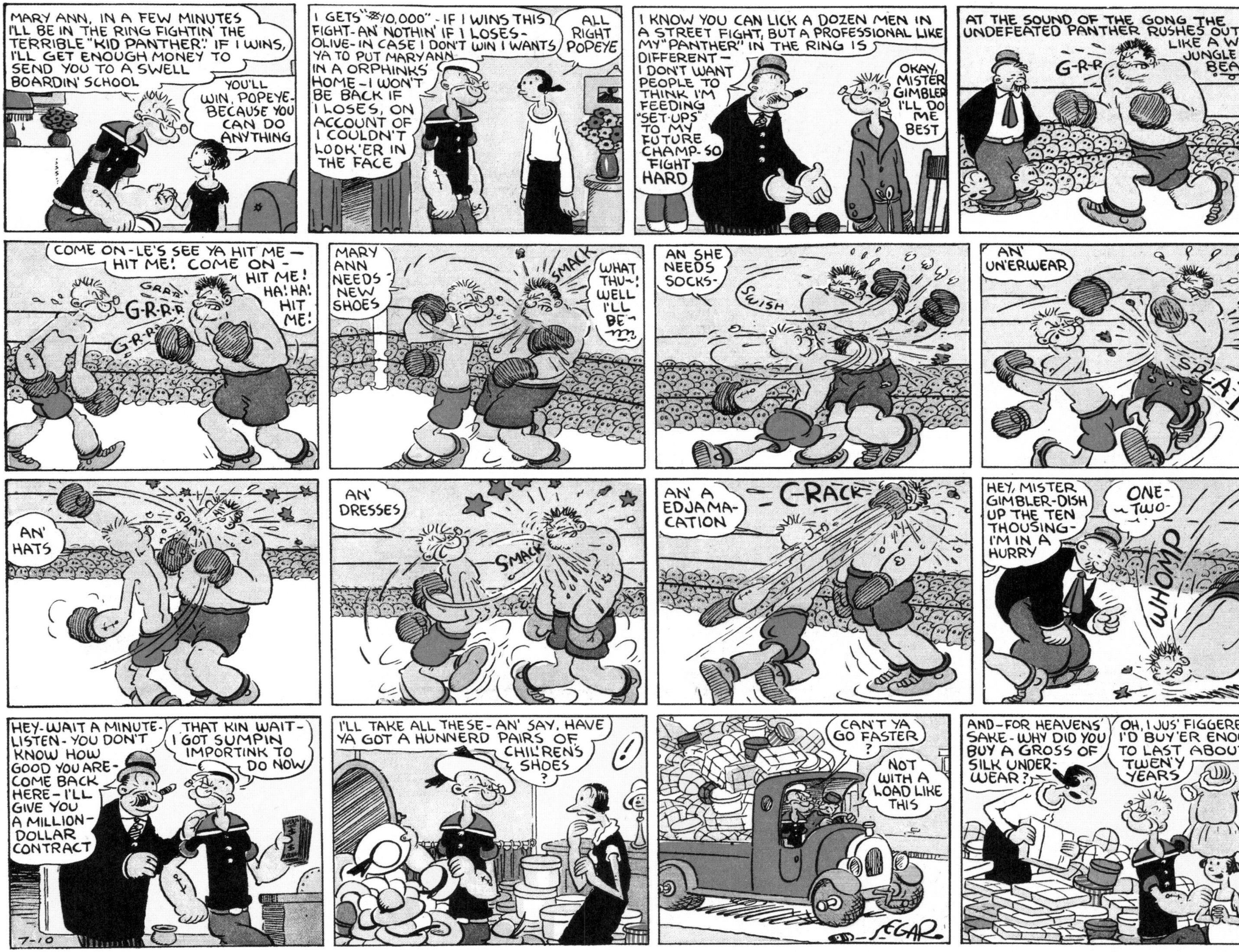

MARY ANN, IN A FEW MINUTES I'LL BE IN THE RING FIGHTIN' THE TERRIBLE "KID PANTHER." IF I WINS, I'LL GET ENOUGH MONEY TO SEND YOU TO A SWELL BOARDIN' SCHOOL
YOU'LL WIN, POPEYE- BECAUSE YOU CAN DO ANYTHING
I GETS "$10,000" - IF I WINS THIS FIGHT - AN' NOTHIN' IF I LOSES - OLIVE - IN CASE I DON'T WIN I WANTS YA TO PUT MARY ANN IN A ORPHINKS' HOME - I WON'T BE BACK IF I LOSES, ON ACCOUNT OF I COULDN'T LOOK 'ER IN THE FACE
ALL RIGHT POPEYE
I KNOW YOU CAN LICK A DOZEN MEN IN A STREET FIGHT, BUT A PROFESSIONAL LIKE MY "PANTHER" IN THE RING IS DIFFERENT - I DON'T WANT PEOPLE TO THINK I'M FEEDING "SET-UPS" TO MY FUTURE CHAMP - SO FIGHT HARD
OKAY, MISTER GIMBLER I'LL DO ME BEST
AT THE SOUND OF THE GONG THE UNDEFEATED PANTHER RUSHES OUT LIKE A WILD JUNGLE BEAST
G-R-R
COME ON - LE'S SEE YA HIT ME - HIT ME! COME ON - HIT ME! HA! HA! HIT ME!
GRRR
G-R-R-R
G-R-R
MARY ANN NEEDS NEW SHOES
SMACK
WHAT THU -! WELL I'LL BE -
AN SHE NEEDS SOCKS -
SWISH
AN' UN'ERWEAR
SPLAT
AN' HATS
SPLAT
AN' DRESSES
SMACK
AN' A EDJAMACATION
CRACK
HEY, MISTER GIMBLER - DISH UP THE TEN THOUSING - I'M IN A HURRY
ONE - TWO -
WHOMP
HEY - WAIT A MINUTE - LISTEN - YOU DON'T KNOW HOW GOOD YOU ARE - COME BACK HERE - I'LL GIVE YOU A MILLION-DOLLAR CONTRACT
THAT KIN WAIT - I GOT SUMPIN IMPORTINK TO DO NOW
7-10
I'LL TAKE ALL THESE - AN' SAY, HAVE YA GOT A HUNNERD PAIRS OF CHIL'REN'S SHOES ?
!
CAN'T YA GO FASTER ?
NOT WITH A LOAD LIKE THIS
SEGAR
AND - FOR HEAVENS' SAKE - WHY DID YOU BUY A GROSS OF SILK UNDER-WEAR ?
OH, I JUS' FIGGERED I'D BUY 'ER ENOUGH TO LAST ABOUT TWEN'Y YEARS

27. July 10, 1932

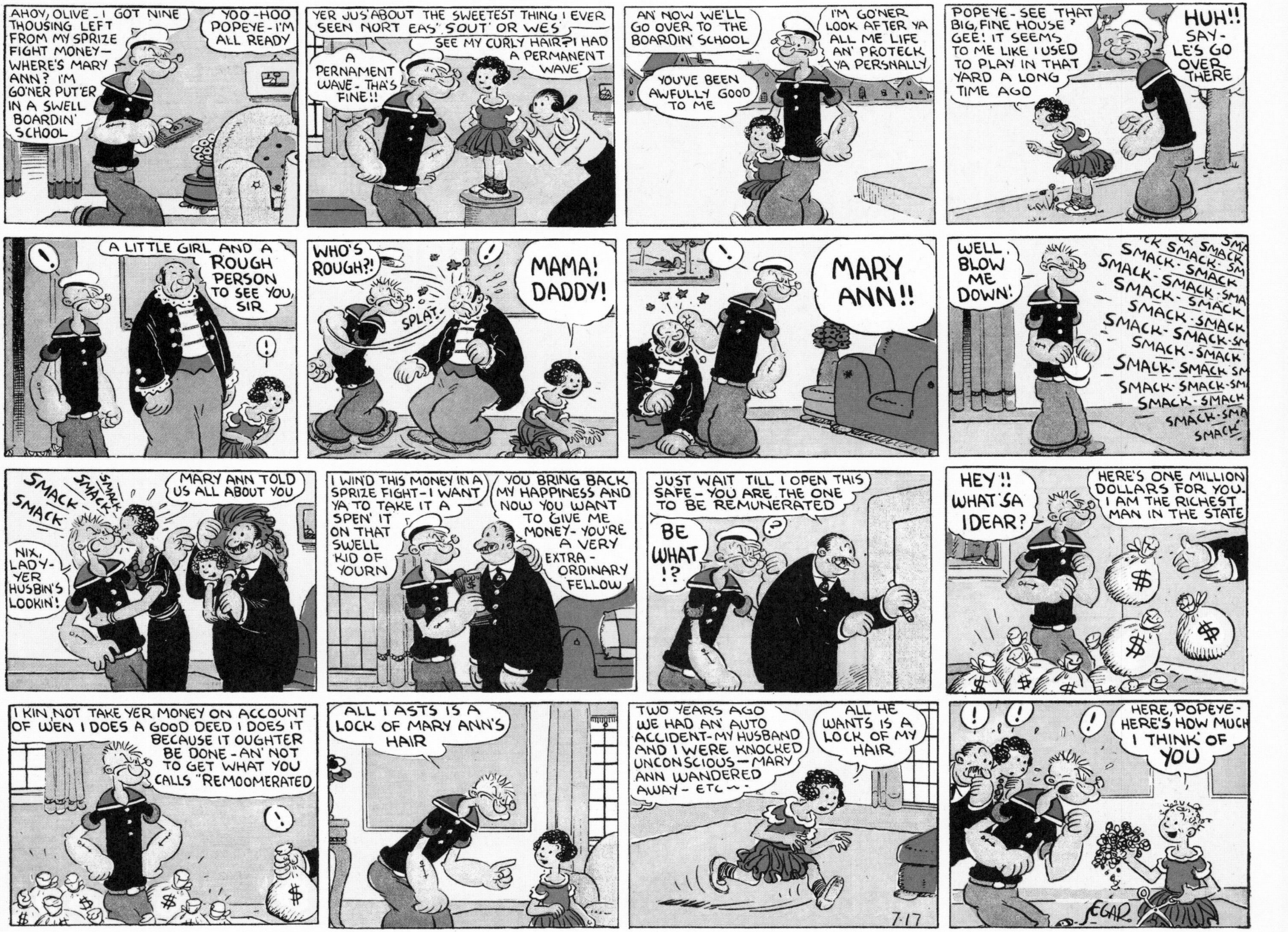

AHOY, OLIVE - I GOT NINE THOUSING LEFT FROM MY SPRIZE FIGHT MONEY— WHERE'S MARY ANN? I'M GO'NER PUT'ER IN A SWELL BOARDIN' SCHOOL
YOO-HOO POPEYE - I'M ALL READY
YER JUS' ABOUT THE SWEETEST THING I EVER SEEN NORT EAS' SOUT' OR WES'
SEE MY CURLY HAIR? I HAD A PERMANENT WAVE
A PERNAMENT WAVE - THA'S FINE!!
AN' NOW WE'LL GO OVER TO THE BOARDIN' SCHOOL
I'M GO'NER LOOK AFTER YA ALL ME LIFE AN' PROTECK YA PERSNALLY
YOU'VE BEEN AWFULLY GOOD TO ME
POPEYE - SEE THAT BIG, FINE HOUSE? GEE! IT SEEMS TO ME LIKE I USED TO PLAY IN THAT YARD A LONG TIME AGO
HUH!! SAY - LE'S GO OVER THERE
!
A LITTLE GIRL AND A ROUGH PERSON TO SEE YOU, SIR
!
WHO'S ROUGH?!
!
SPLAT
MAMA! DADDY!
!
MARY ANN!!
WELL, BLOW ME DOWN!
SMACK-SMACK
SMACK-SMACK
SMACK-SMACK
SMACK-SMACK
SMACK-SMACK
SMACK-SMACK
SMACK-SMACK
SMACK-SMACK
SMACK-SMACK
SMACK
SMACK SMACK SMACK SMACK
MARY ANN TOLD US ALL ABOUT YOU
NIX, LADY - YER HUSBIN'S LOOKIN'!
I WIN'D THIS MONEY IN A SPRIZE FIGHT - I WANT YA TO TAKE IT A SPEN' IT ON THAT SWELL KID OF YOURN
YOU BRING BACK MY HAPPINESS AND NOW YOU WANT TO GIVE ME MONEY - YOU'RE A VERY EXTRA-ORDINARY FELLOW
JUST WAIT TILL I OPEN THIS SAFE - YOU ARE THE ONE TO BE REMUNERATED
BE WHAT!?
?
HEY!! WHAT'SA IDEAR?
HERE'S ONE MILLION DOLLARS FOR YOU. I AM THE RICHEST MAN IN THE STATE
I KIN NOT TAKE YER MONEY ON ACCOUNT OF WEN I DOES A GOOD DEED I DOES IT BECAUSE IT OUGHTER BE DONE - AN' NOT TO GET WHAT YOU CALLS "REMOOMERATED
!
ALL I ASTS IS A LOCK OF MARY ANN'S HAIR
TWO YEARS AGO WE HAD AN' AUTO ACCIDENT - MY HUSBAND AND I WERE KNOCKED UNCONSCIOUS — MARY ANN WANDERED AWAY - ETC ~ -
ALL HE WANTS IS A LOCK OF MY HAIR
7-17
! ! !
HERE, POPEYE - HERE'S HOW MUCH I THINK OF YOU
SEGAR

28. July 17, 1932

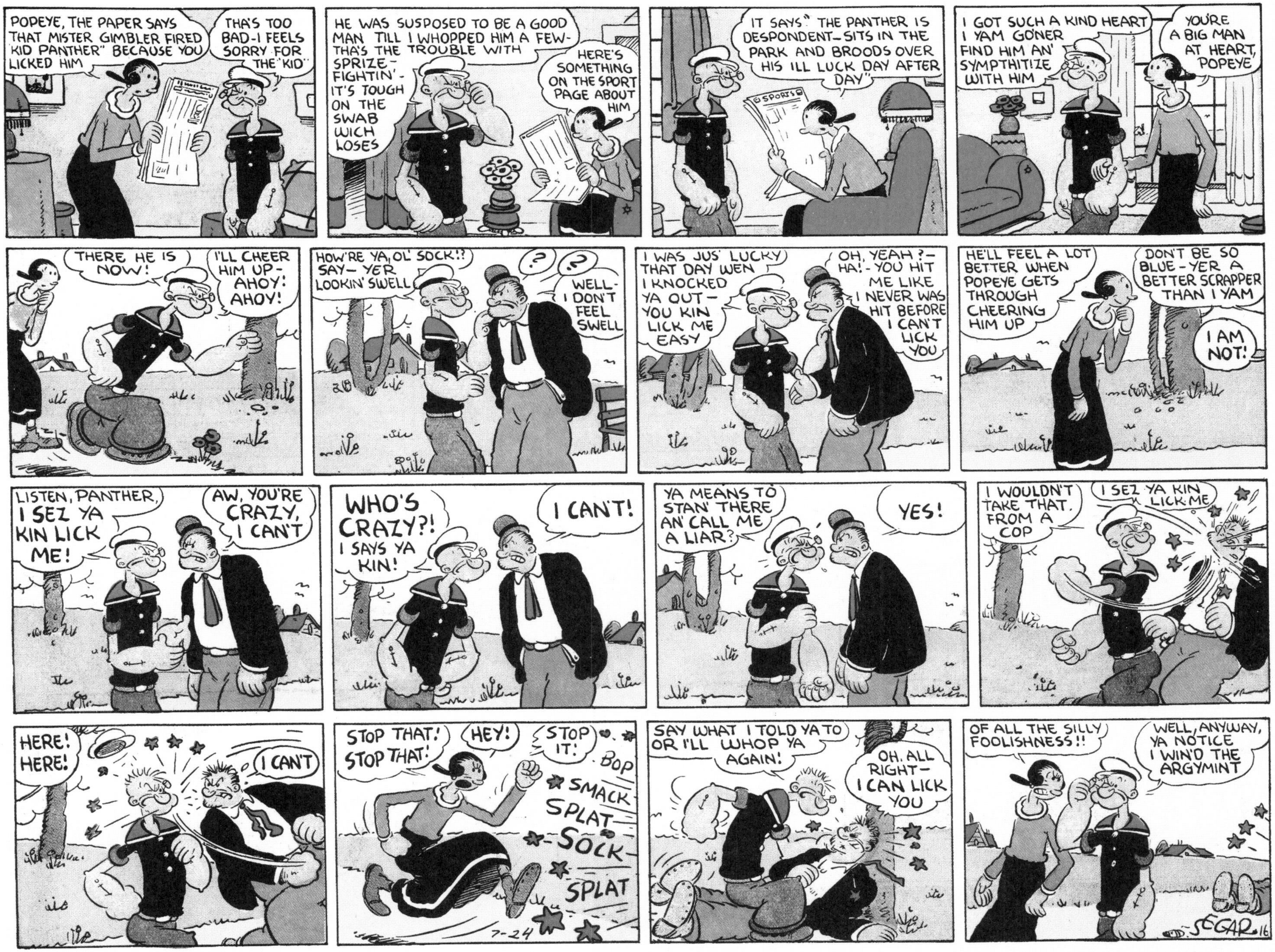
POPEYE, THE PAPER SAYS THAT MISTER GIMBLER FIRED "KID PANTHER" BECAUSE YOU LICKED HIM
THA'S TOO BAD-I FEELS SORRY FOR THE "KID"
HE WAS SUSPOSED TO BE A GOOD MAN TILL I WHOPPED HIM A FEW-THA'S THE TROUBLE WITH SPRIZE-FIGHTIN'-IT'S TOUGH ON THE SWAB WICH LOSES
HERE'S SOMETHING ON THE SPORT PAGE ABOUT HIM
IT SAYS: "THE PANTHER IS DESPONDENT-SITS IN THE PARK AND BROODS OVER HIS ILL LUCK DAY AFTER DAY"
SPORTS
I GOT SUCH A KIND HEART I YAM GONER FIND HIM AN' SYMPTHITIZE WITH HIM
YOU'RE A BIG MAN AT HEART, POPEYE
THERE HE IS NOW!
I'LL CHEER HIM UP-AHOY! AHOY!
HOW'RE YA, OL' SOCK!? SAY-YER LOOKIN' SWELL
?
?
WELL-I DON'T FEEL SWELL
I WAS JUS' LUCKY THAT DAY WEN I KNOCKED YA OUT-YOU KIN LICK ME EASY
OH, YEAH?-HA!-YOU HIT ME LIKE I NEVER WAS HIT BEFORE I CAN'T LICK YOU
HE'LL FEEL A LOT BETTER WHEN POPEYE GETS THROUGH CHEERING HIM UP
DON'T BE SO BLUE-YER A BETTER SCRAPPER THAN I YAM
I AM NOT!
LISTEN, PANTHER, I SEZ YA KIN LICK ME!
AW, YOU'RE CRAZY, I CAN'T
WHO'S CRAZY?! I SAYS YA KIN!
I CAN'T!
YA MEANS TO STAN' THERE AN' CALL ME A LIAR?
YES!
I WOULDN'T TAKE THAT FROM A COP
I SEZ YA KIN LICK ME
HERE! HERE!
I CAN'T
STOP THAT! STOP THAT!
HEY!
STOP IT!
BOP
SMACK
SPLAT
SOCK
SPLAT
7-24
SAY WHAT I TOLD YA TO OR I'LL WHOP YA AGAIN!
OH, ALL RIGHT-I CAN LICK YOU
OF ALL THE SILLY FOOLISHNESS!!
WELL, ANYWAY, YA NOTICE I WIN'D THE ARGYMINT
SEGAR 16

29. July 24, 1932

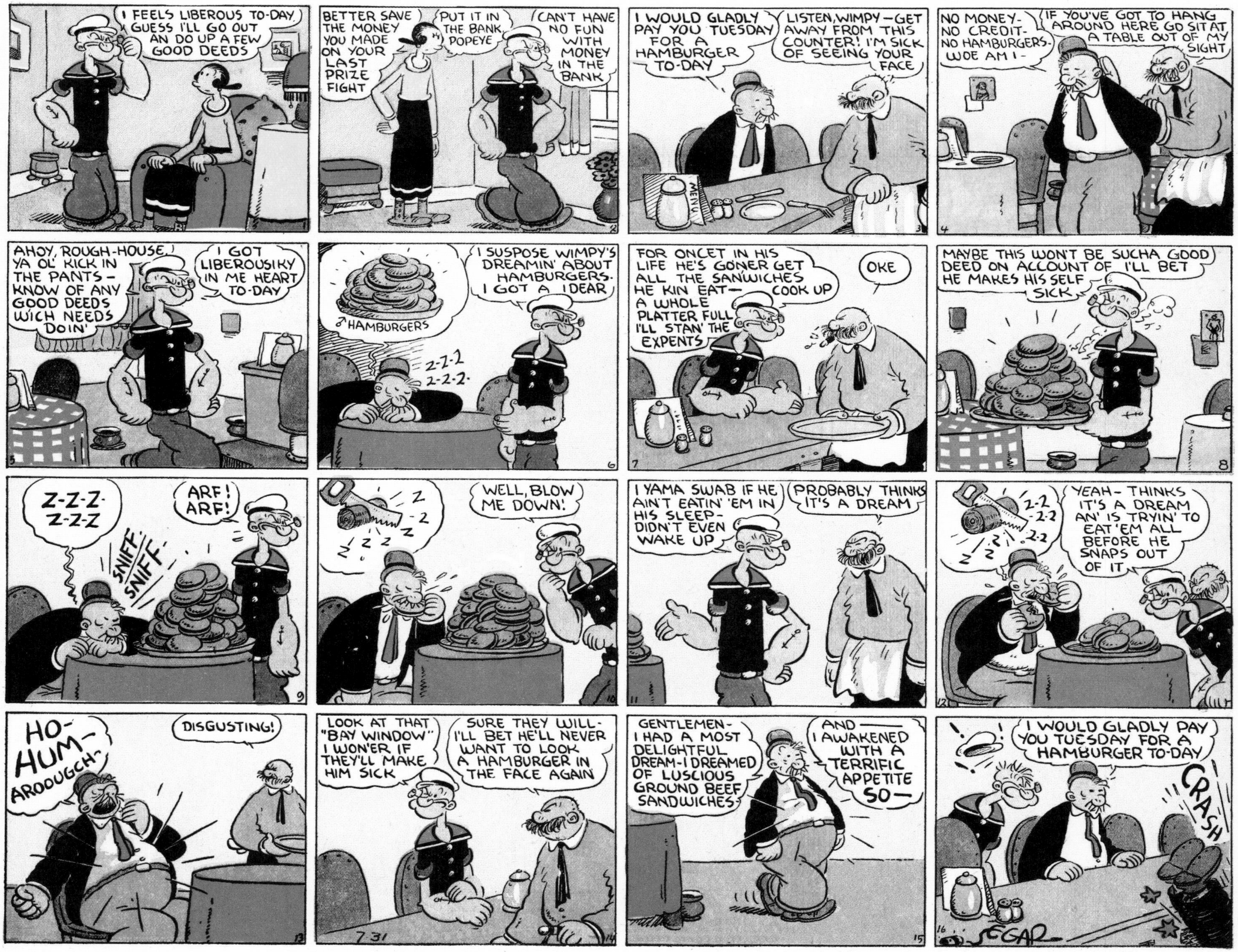
I FEELS LIBEROUS TO-DAY. GUESS I'LL GO OUT AN DO UP A FEW GOOD DEEDS
BETTER SAVE THE MONEY YOU MADE ON YOUR LAST PRIZE FIGHT
PUT IT IN THE BANK, POPEYE
CAN'T HAVE NO FUN WITH MONEY IN THE BANK
I WOULD GLADLY PAY YOU TUESDAY FOR A HAMBURGER TO-DAY
LISTEN, WIMPY—GET AWAY FROM THIS COUNTER! I'M SICK OF SEEING YOUR FACE
MENU
NO MONEY- NO CREDIT- NO HAMBURGERS- WOE AM I-
IF YOU'VE GOT TO HANG AROUND HERE GO SIT AT A TABLE OUT OF MY SIGHT
AHOY, ROUGH-HOUSE, YA OL' KICK IN THE PANTS— KNOW OF ANY GOOD DEEDS WICH NEEDS DOIN'
I GOT LIBEROUSIKY IN ME HEART TO-DAY
HAMBURGERS
I SUSPOSE WIMPY'S DREAMIN' ABOUT HAMBURGERS. I GOT A IDEAR
Z-Z-Z Z-Z-Z.
FOR ONCET IN HIS LIFE HE'S GONER GET ALL THE SANWICHES HE KIN EAT— COOK UP A WHOLE PLATTER FULL I'LL STAN' THE EXPENTS
OKE
MAYBE THIS WON'T BE SUCHA GOOD DEED ON ACCOUNT OF I'LL BET HE MAKES HIS SELF SICK
Z-Z-Z- Z-Z-Z
ARF! ARF!
SNIFF SNIFF
WELL, BLOW ME DOWN!
I YAMA SWAB IF HE AIN'T EATIN' 'EM IN HIS SLEEP- DIDN'T EVEN WAKE UP
PROBABLY THINKS IT'S A DREAM
YEAH- THINKS IT'S A DREAM AN' IS TRYIN' TO EAT 'EM ALL BEFORE HE SNAPS OUT OF IT
HO-HUM-AROOUGCH
DISGUSTING!
LOOK AT THAT "BAY WINDOW" I WON'ER IF THEY'LL MAKE HIM SICK
SURE THEY WILL- I'LL BET HE'LL NEVER WANT TO LOOK A HAMBURGER IN THE FACE AGAIN
7-31
GENTLEMEN- I HAD A MOST DELIGHTFUL DREAM- I DREAMED OF LUSCIOUS GROUND BEEF SANDWICHES
AND— I AWAKENED WITH A TERRIFIC APPETITE SO—
I WOULD GLADLY PAY YOU TUESDAY FOR A HAMBURGER TO-DAY
CRASH
SEGAR

30. July 31, 1932

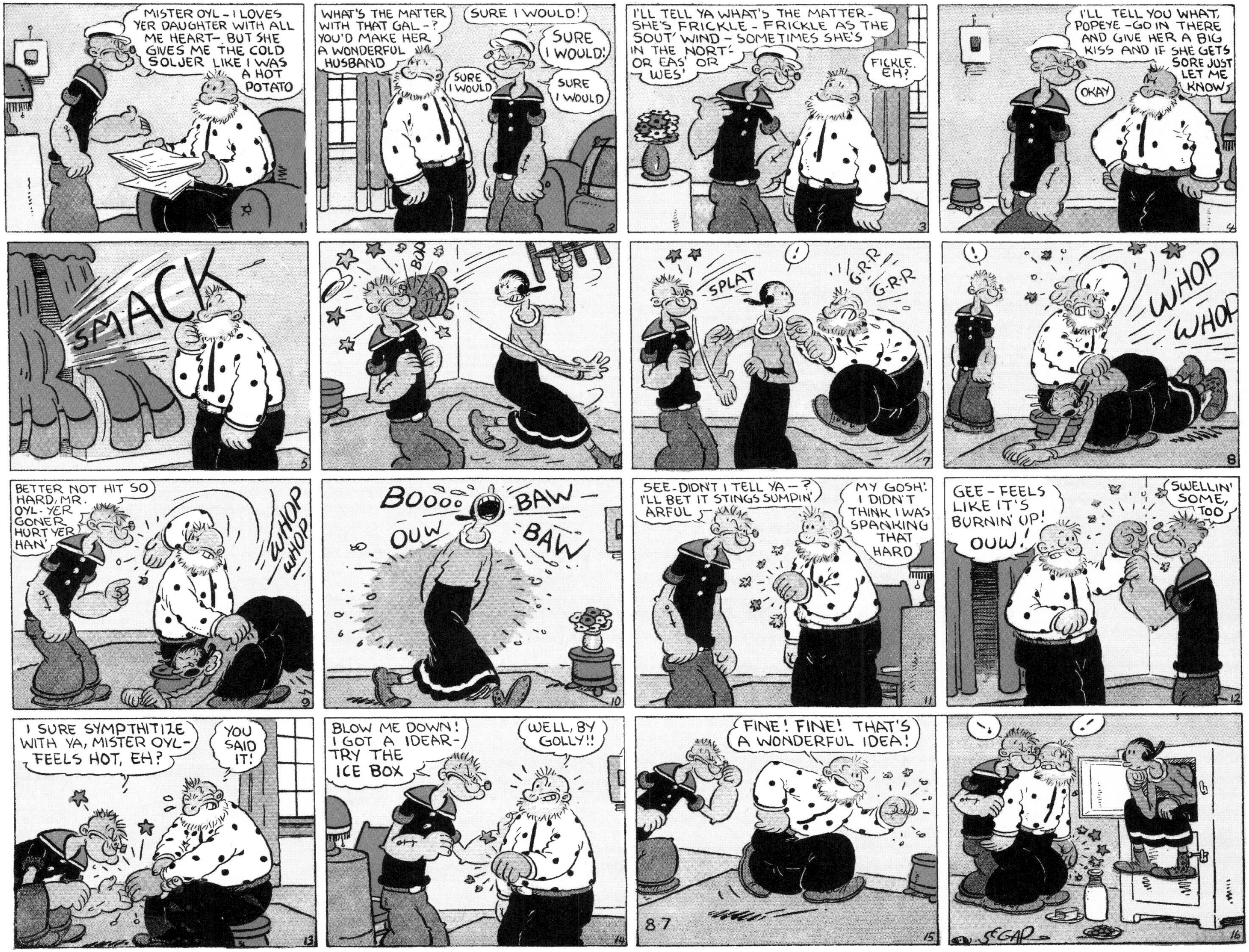
MISTER OYL - I LOVES YER DAUGHTER WITH ALL ME HEART - BUT SHE GIVES ME THE COLD SOLJER LIKE I WAS A HOT POTATO
WHAT'S THE MATTER WITH THAT GAL -? YOU'D MAKE HER A WONDERFUL HUSBAND
SURE I WOULD!
SURE I WOULD!
SURE I WOULD
SURE I WOULD
I'LL TELL YA WHAT'S THE MATTER - SHE'S FRICKLE - FRICKLE AS THE SOUT' WIND - SOMETIMES SHE'S IN THE NORT' OR EAS' OR WES'
FICKLE, EH?
I'LL TELL YOU WHAT, POPEYE - GO IN THERE AND GIVE HER A BIG KISS AND IF SHE GETS SORE JUST LET ME KNOW
OKAY
SMACK
BOP
SPLAT
!
G-R-R
G-R-R
!
WHOP
WHOP
BETTER NOT HIT SO HARD, MR. OYL - YER GONER HURT YER HAN'
WHOP
WHOP
BOOOOO
BAW
OUW
BAW
SEE - DIDN'T I TELL YA --? I'LL BET IT STINGS SUMPIN' ARFUL
MY GOSH! I DIDN'T THINK I WAS SPANKING THAT HARD
GEE - FEELS LIKE IT'S BURNIN' UP!
OUW!
SWELLIN' SOME, TOO
I SURE SYMPTHITIZE WITH YA, MISTER OYL - FEELS HOT, EH?
YOU SAID IT!
BLOW ME DOWN! I GOT A IDEAR - TRY THE ICE BOX
WELL, BY GOLLY!!
FINE! FINE! THAT'S A WONDERFUL IDEA!
8-7
!
!
SEGAR

31. August 7, 1932

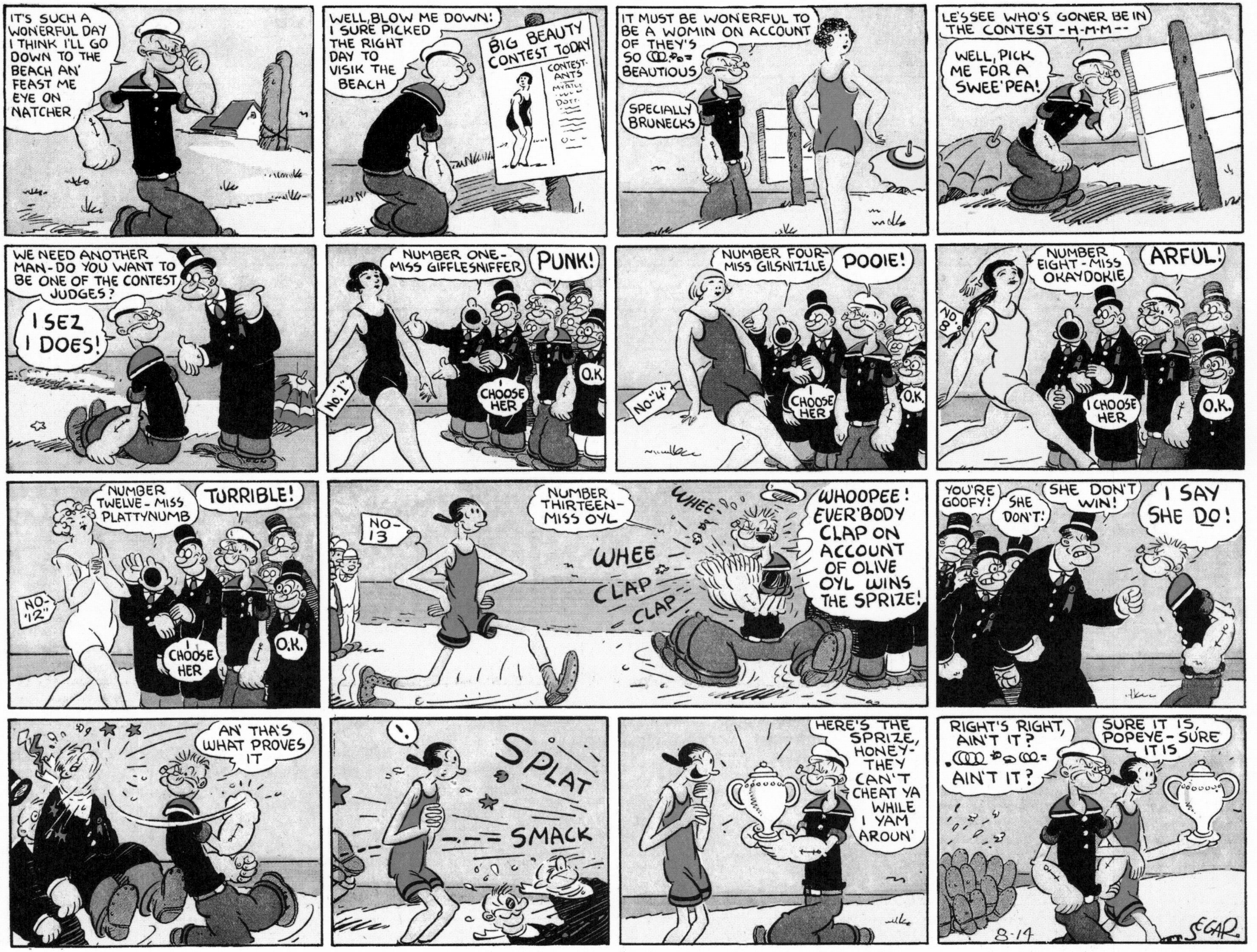
IT'S SUCH A WON'ERFUL DAY I THINK I'LL GO DOWN TO THE BEACH AN' FEAST ME EYE ON NATCHER
WELL, BLOW ME DOWN! I SURE PICKED THE RIGHT DAY TO VISIK THE BEACH
BIG BEAUTY CONTEST TODAY
CONTEST-ANTS
IT MUST BE WON'ERFUL TO BE A WOMIN ON ACCOUNT OF THEY'S SO BEAUTIOUS
SPECIALLY BRUNECKS
LE'SSEE WHO'S GONER BE IN THE CONTEST -H-M-M--
WELL, PICK ME FOR A SWEE'PEA!
WE NEED ANOTHER MAN-DO YOU WANT TO BE ONE OF THE CONTEST JUDGES?
I SEZ I DOES!
NUMBER ONE-MISS GIFFLESNIFFER
PUNK!
NO. "1"
I CHOOSE HER
O.K.
NUMBER FOUR-MISS GILSNIZZLE
POOIE!
NO-"4"
I CHOOSE HER
O.K.
NUMBER EIGHT-MISS OKAYDOKIE
ARFUL!
NO. "8"
I CHOOSE HER
O.K.
NUMBER TWELVE-MISS PLATTYNUMB
TURRIBLE!
NO-"12"
I CHOOSE HER
O.K.
NO-13
NUMBER THIRTEEN-MISS OYL
WHEE
WHEE
CLAP
CLAP
WHOOPEE! EVER'BODY CLAP ON ACCOUNT OF OLIVE OYL WINS THE SPRIZE!
YOU'RE GOOFY!
SHE DON'T!
SHE DON'T WIN!
I SAY SHE DO!
AN' THA'S WHAT PROVES IT
!
SPLAT
SMACK
HERE'S THE SPRIZE, HONEY-THEY CAN'T CHEAT YA WHILE I YAM AROUN'
RIGHT'S RIGHT, AIN'T IT?
AIN'T IT?
SURE IT IS, POPEYE-SURE IT IS
8-14
SEGAR.

32. August 14, 1932

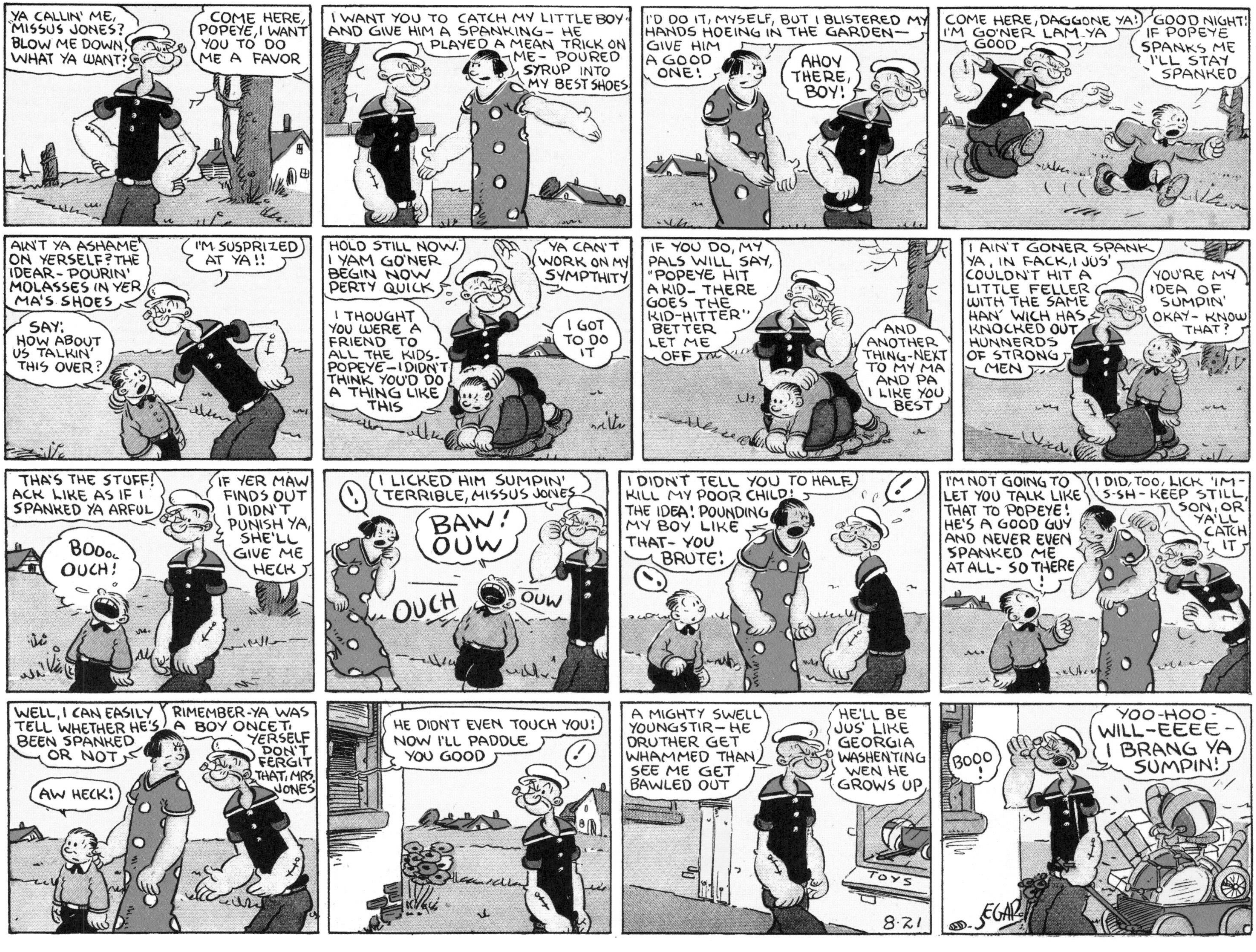

YA CALLIN' ME, MISSUS JONES? BLOW ME DOWN, WHAT YA WANT?
COME HERE, POPEYE, I WANT YOU TO DO ME A FAVOR
I WANT YOU TO CATCH MY LITTLE BOY AND GIVE HIM A SPANKING- HE PLAYED A MEAN TRICK ON ME- POURED SYRUP INTO MY BEST SHOES
I'D DO IT, MYSELF, BUT I BLISTERED MY HANDS HOEING IN THE GARDEN— GIVE HIM A GOOD ONE!
AHOY THERE, BOY!
COME HERE, DAGGONE YA! I'M GO'NER LAM YA GOOD
GOOD NIGHT! IF POPEYE SPANKS ME I'LL STAY SPANKED
AIN'T YA ASHAME ON YERSELF? THE IDEAR - POURIN' MOLASSES IN YER MA'S SHOES
I'M SUSPRIZED AT YA!!
SAY! HOW ABOUT US TALKIN' THIS OVER?
HOLD STILL NOW. I YAM GO'NER BEGIN NOW PERTY QUICK
YA CAN'T WORK ON MY SYMPTHITY
I THOUGHT YOU WERE A FRIEND TO ALL THE KIDS- POPEYE—I DIDN'T THINK YOU'D DO A THING LIKE THIS
I GOT TO DO IT
IF YOU DO, MY PALS WILL SAY, "POPEYE HIT A KID- THERE GOES THE KID-HITTER" BETTER LET ME OFF
AND ANOTHER THING-NEXT TO MY MA AND PA I LIKE YOU BEST
I AIN'T GONER SPANK YA, IN FACK, I JUS' COULDN'T HIT A LITTLE FELLER WITH THE SAME HAN' WICH HAS KNOCKED OUT HUNNERDS OF STRONG MEN
YOU'RE MY IDEA OF SUMPIN' OKAY- KNOW THAT?
THA'S THE STUFF! ACK LIKE AS IF I SPANKED YA ARFUL
IF YER MAW FINDS OUT I DIDN'T PUNISH YA, SHE'LL GIVE ME HECK
BOOOO OUCH!
!
I LICKED HIM SUMPIN' TERRIBLE, MISSUS JONES
BAW! OUW
OUCH
OUW
I DIDN'T TELL YOU TO HALF KILL MY POOR CHILD! THE IDEA! POUNDING MY BOY LIKE THAT- YOU BRUTE!
!
!
I'M NOT GOING TO LET YOU TALK LIKE THAT TO POPEYE! HE'S A GOOD GUY AND NEVER EVEN SPANKED ME AT ALL- SO THERE
I DID, TOO, LICK 'IM - S-SH - KEEP STILL, SON, OR YA'LL CATCH IT
!
WELL, I CAN EASILY TELL WHETHER HE'S BEEN SPANKED OR NOT
RIMEMBER-YA WAS A BOY ONCET, YERSELF DON'T FERGIT THAT, MRS. JONES
AW HECK!
HE DIDN'T EVEN TOUCH YOU! NOW I'LL PADDLE YOU GOOD
!
A MIGHTY SWELL YOUNGSTIR—HE DRUTHER GET WHAMMED THAN SEE ME GET BAWLED OUT
HE'LL BE JUS' LIKE GEORGIA WASHENTING WEN HE GROWS UP
TOYS
8-21
BOOO!
YOO-HOO - WILL-EEEE - I BRANG YA SUMPIN!
SEGAR

33. August 21, 1932

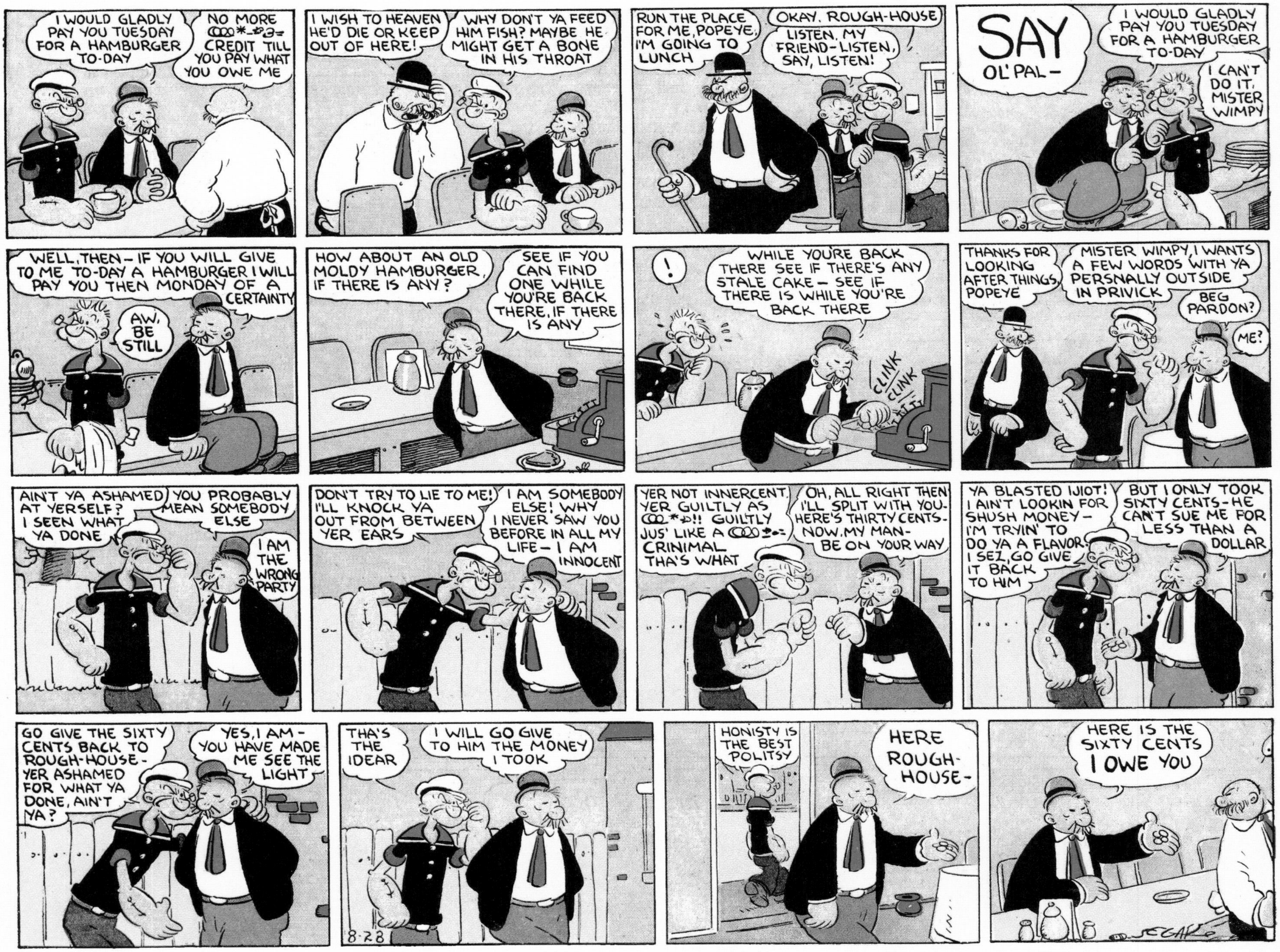

I WOULD GLADLY PAY YOU TUESDAY FOR A HAMBURGER TO-DAY
NO MORE CREDIT TILL YOU PAY WHAT YOU OWE ME
I WISH TO HEAVEN HE'D DIE OR KEEP OUT OF HERE!
WHY DON'T YA FEED HIM FISH? MAYBE HE MIGHT GET A BONE IN HIS THROAT
RUN THE PLACE FOR ME, POPEYE, I'M GOING TO LUNCH
OKAY, ROUGH-HOUSE
LISTEN, MY FRIEND—LISTEN, SAY, LISTEN!
SAY OL' PAL—
I WOULD GLADLY PAY YOU TUESDAY FOR A HAMBURGER TO-DAY
I CAN'T DO IT, MISTER WIMPY
WELL, THEN—IF YOU WILL GIVE TO ME TO-DAY A HAMBURGER I WILL PAY YOU THEN MONDAY OF A CERTAINTY
AW, BE STILL
HOW ABOUT AN OLD MOLDY HAMBURGER, IF THERE IS ANY?
SEE IF YOU CAN FIND ONE WHILE YOU'RE BACK THERE, IF THERE IS ANY
!
WHILE YOU'RE BACK THERE SEE IF THERE'S ANY STALE CAKE—SEE IF THERE IS WHILE YOU'RE BACK THERE
CLINK
CLINK
THANKS FOR LOOKING AFTER THINGS, POPEYE
MISTER WIMPY, I WANTS A FEW WORDS WITH YA PERSNALLY OUTSIDE IN PRIVICK
BEG PARDON?
ME?
AIN'T YA ASHAMED AT YERSELF? I SEEN WHAT YA DONE
YOU PROBABLY MEAN SOMEBODY ELSE
I AM THE WRONG PARTY
DON'T TRY TO LIE TO ME! I'LL KNOCK YA OUT FROM BETWEEN YER EARS
I AM SOMEBODY ELSE! WHY I NEVER SAW YOU BEFORE IN ALL MY LIFE—I AM INNOCENT
YER NOT INNERCENT. YER GUILTLY AS !! GUILTLY JUS' LIKE A CRINIMAL THA'S WHAT
OH, ALL RIGHT THEN I'LL SPLIT WITH YOU. HERE'S THIRTY CENTS. NOW, MY MAN—BE ON YOUR WAY
YA BLASTED IJIOT! I AIN'T LOOKIN FOR SHUSH MONEY—I'M TRYIN' TO DO YA A FLAVOR. I SEZ, GO GIVE IT BACK TO HIM
BUT I ONLY TOOK SIXTY CENTS—HE CAN'T SUE ME FOR LESS THAN A DOLLAR
GO GIVE THE SIXTY CENTS BACK TO ROUGH-HOUSE—YER ASHAMED FOR WHAT YA DONE, AIN'T YA?
YES, I AM—YOU HAVE MADE ME SEE THE LIGHT
THA'S THE IDEAR
I WILL GO GIVE TO HIM THE MONEY I TOOK
8-28
HONISTY IS THE BEST POLITSY
HERE ROUGH-HOUSE—
HERE IS THE SIXTY CENTS I OWE YOU
SEGAR

34. August 28, 1932

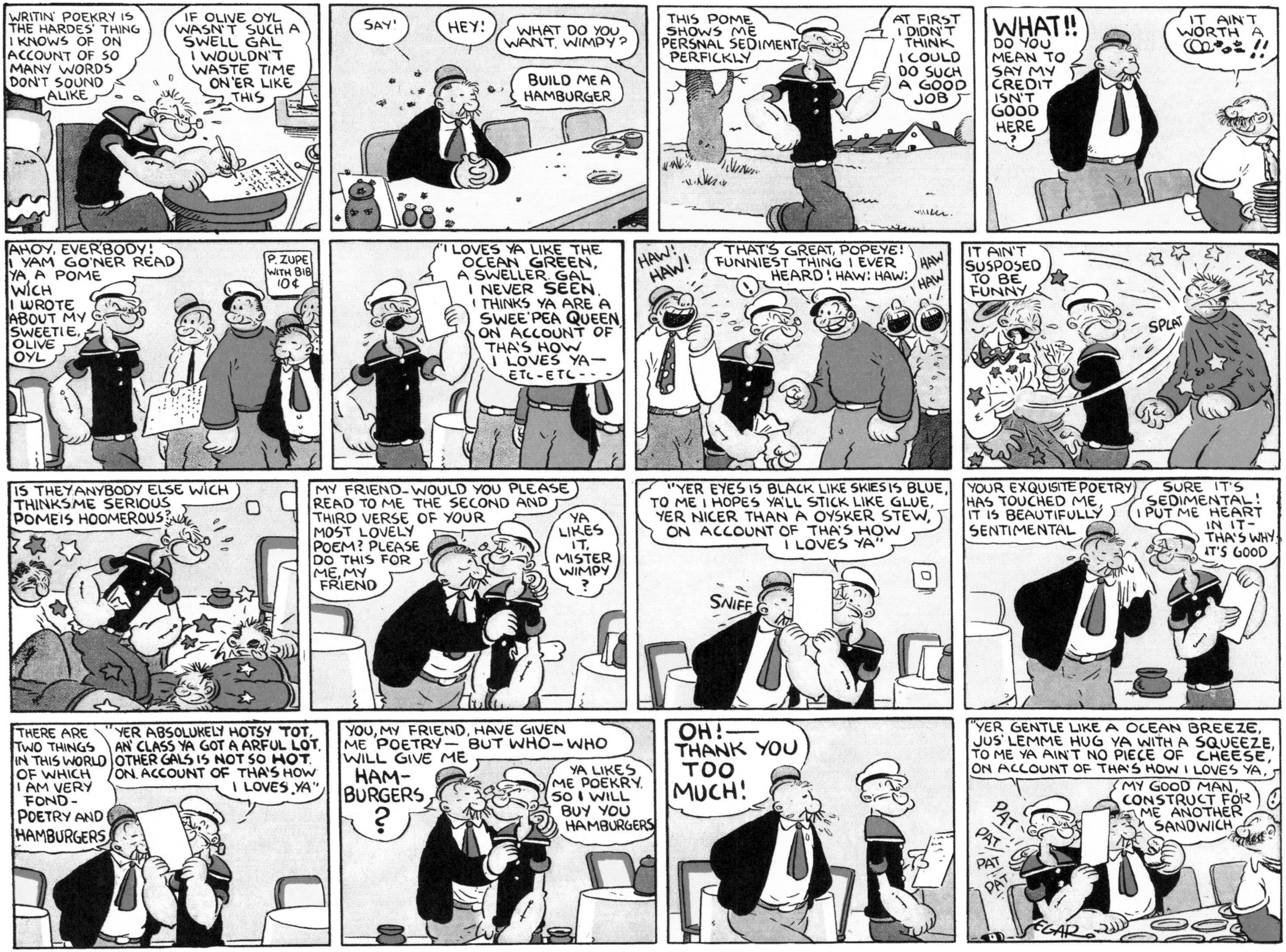
WRITIN' POEKRY IS THE HARDES' THING I KNOWS OF ON ACCOUNT OF SO MANY WORDS DON'T SOUND ALIKE
IF OLIVE OYL WASN'T SUCH A SWELL GAL I WOULDN'T WASTE TIME ON'ER LIKE THIS
SAY!
HEY!
WHAT DO YOU WANT, WIMPY?
BUILD ME A HAMBURGER
THIS POME SHOWS ME PERSNAL SEDIMENT PERFICKLY
AT FIRST I DIDN'T THINK I COULD DO SUCH A GOOD JOB
WHAT!! DO YOU MEAN TO SAY MY CREDIT ISN'T GOOD HERE?
IT AIN'T WORTH A !!
AHOY, EVERBODY! I YAM GO'NER READ YA A POME WICH I WROTE ABOUT MY SWEETIE, OLIVE OYL
P. ZUPE WITH BIB 10¢
"I LOVES YA LIKE THE OCEAN GREEN, A SWELLER GAL I NEVER SEEN. I THINKS YA ARE A SWEE'PEA QUEEN, ON ACCOUNT OF THA'S HOW I LOVES YA— ETC-ETC---
HAW! HAW!
THAT'S GREAT, POPEYE! FUNNIEST THING I EVER HEARD! HAW! HAW!
!
HAW HAW
IT AIN'T SUSPOSED TO BE FUNNY
SPLAT
IS THEY ANYBODY ELSE WICH THINKS ME SERIOUS POME IS HOOMEROUS?
MY FRIEND-WOULD YOU PLEASE READ TO ME THE SECOND AND THIRD VERSE OF YOUR MOST LOVELY POEM? PLEASE DO THIS FOR ME, MY FRIEND
YA LIKES IT, MISTER WIMPY?
"YER EYES IS BLACK LIKE SKIES IS BLUE, TO ME I HOPES YA'LL STICK LIKE GLUE, YER NICER THAN A OYSKER STEW, ON ACCOUNT OF THA'S HOW I LOVES YA"
SNIFF
YOUR EXQUISITE POETRY HAS TOUCHED ME, IT IS BEAUTIFULLY SENTIMENTAL
SURE IT'S SEDIMENTAL! I PUT ME HEART IN IT-THA'S WHY IT'S GOOD
THERE ARE TWO THINGS IN THIS WORLD OF WHICH I AM VERY FOND-POETRY AND HAMBURGERS
"YER ABSOLUKELY HOTSY TOT, AN' CLASS YA GOT A ARFUL LOT, OTHER GALS IS NOT SO HOT. ON ACCOUNT OF THA'S HOW I LOVES YA"
YOU, MY FRIEND, HAVE GIVEN ME POETRY— BUT WHO-WHO WILL GIVE ME HAMBURGERS?
YA LIKES ME POEKRY. SO I WILL BUY YOU HAMBURGERS
OH!— THANK YOU TOO MUCH!
"YER GENTLE LIKE A OCEAN BREEZE, JUS' LEMME HUG YA WITH A SQUEEZE, TO ME YA AIN'T NO PIECE OF CHEESE, ON ACCOUNT OF THA'S HOW I LOVES YA,"
MY GOOD MAN, CONSTRUCT FOR ME ANOTHER SANDWICH
!
PAT PAT PAT PAT
SEGAR

35. September 4, 1932

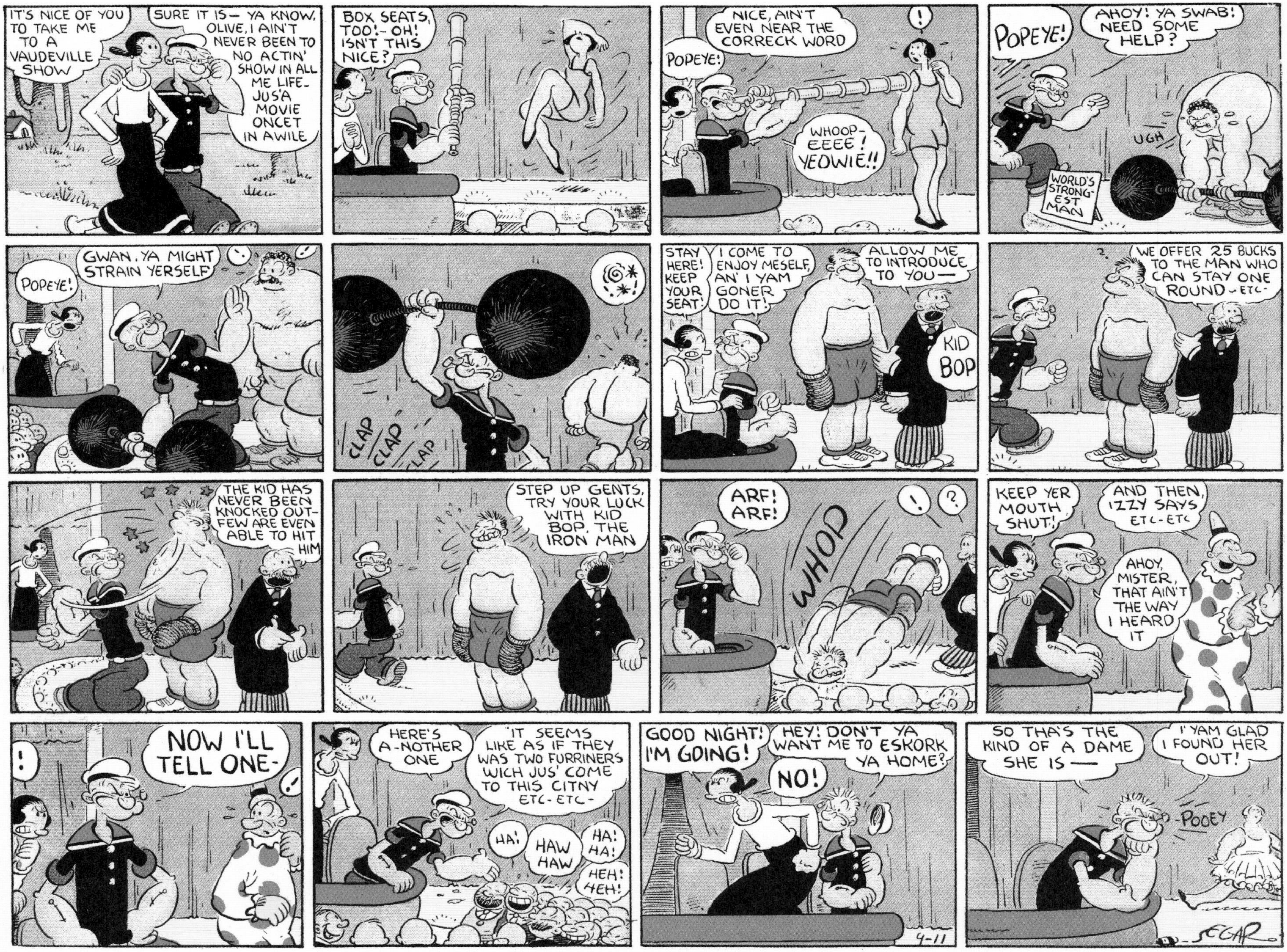
IT'S NICE OF YOU TO TAKE ME TO A VAUDEVILLE SHOW
SURE IT IS— YA KNOW, OLIVE, I AIN'T NEVER BEEN TO NO ACTIN' SHOW IN ALL ME LIFE- JUS'A MOVIE ONCET IN AWILE
BOX SEATS, TOO!- OH! ISN'T THIS NICE?
NICE, AIN'T EVEN NEAR THE CORRECK WORD
!
POPEYE!
WHOOP-EEEE! YEOWIE!!
POPEYE!
AHOY! YA SWAB! NEED SOME HELP?
UGH
WORLD'S STRONG-EST MAN
POPEYE!
GWAN, YA MIGHT STRAIN YERSELF
!
!
CLAP CLAP CLAP
STAY HERE! KEEP YOUR SEAT!
I COME TO ENJOY MESELF, AN' I YAM GONER DO IT!
ALLOW ME TO INTRODUCE TO YOU—
KID BOP
WE OFFER 25 BUCKS TO THE MAN WHO CAN STAY ONE ROUND - ETC -
THE KID HAS NEVER BEEN KNOCKED OUT- FEW ARE EVEN ABLE TO HIT HIM
STEP UP GENTS, TRY YOUR LUCK WITH KID BOP, THE IRON MAN
ARF! ARF!
!
?
WHOP
KEEP YER MOUTH SHUT!
AND THEN, IZZY SAYS ETC - ETC
AHOY, MISTER, THAT AIN'T THE WAY I HEARD IT
!
NOW I'LL TELL ONE-
!
HERE'S A-NOTHER ONE
IT SEEMS LIKE AS IF THEY WAS TWO FURRINERS WICH JUS' COME TO THIS CITNY ETC - ETC -
HA!
HAW HAW
HA! HA!
HEH! HEH!
GOOD NIGHT! I'M GOING!
HEY! DON'T YA WANT ME TO ESKORK YA HOME?
NO!
9-11
SO THA'S THE KIND OF A DAME SHE IS —
I YAM GLAD I FOUND HER OUT!
POOEY
SEGAR

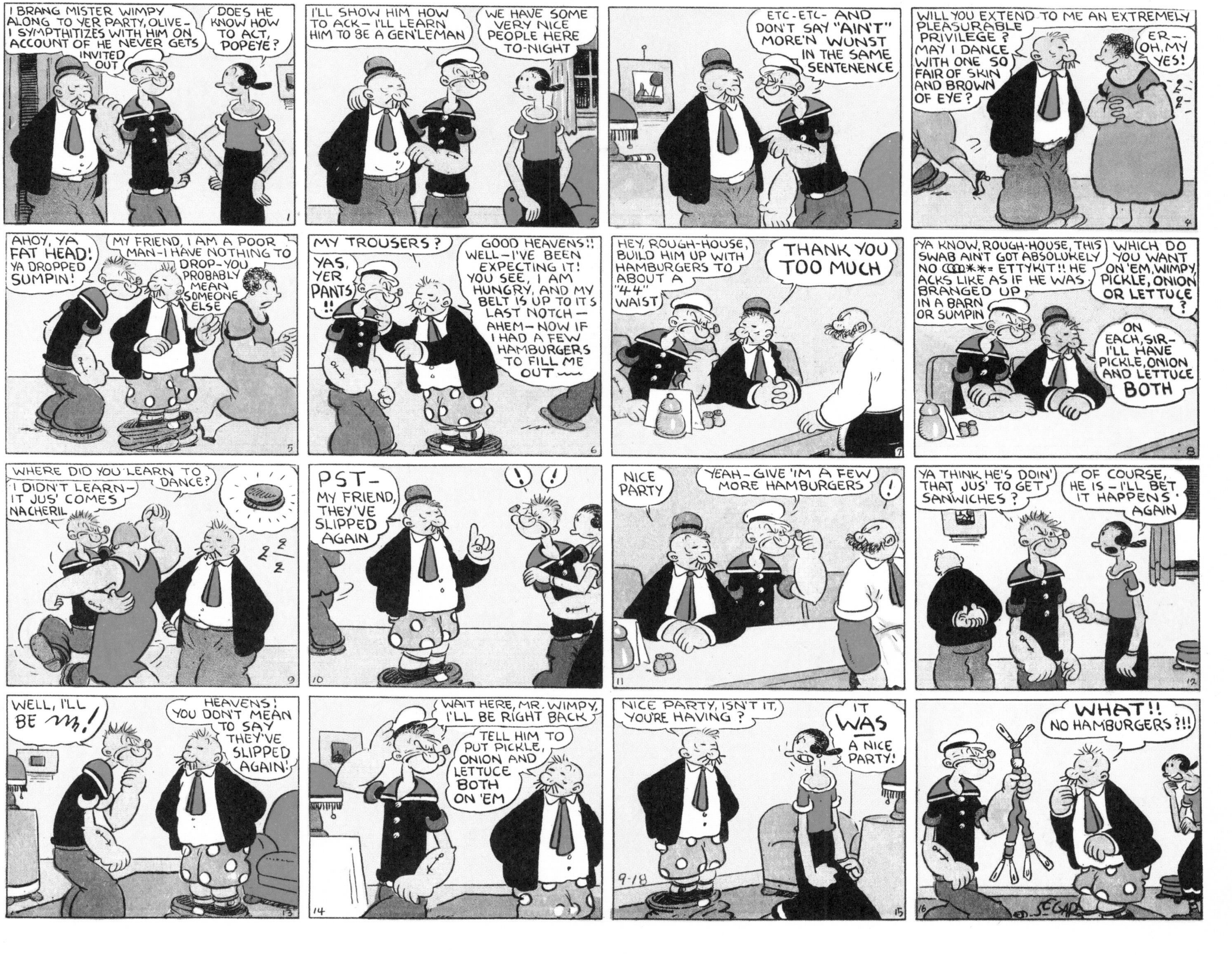
I BRANG MISTER WIMPY ALONG TO YER PARTY, OLIVE– I SYMPTHITIZES WITH HIM ON ACCOUNT OF HE NEVER GETS INVITED OUT
DOES HE KNOW HOW TO ACT, POPEYE?
I'LL SHOW HIM HOW TO ACK – I'LL LEARN HIM TO BE A GEN'LEMAN
WE HAVE SOME VERY NICE PEOPLE HERE TO-NIGHT
ETC-ETC- AND DON'T SAY "AIN'T" MORE'N WUNST IN THE SAME SENTENENCE
WILL YOU EXTEND TO ME AN EXTREMELY PLEASURABLE PRIVILEGE ? MAY I DANCE WITH ONE SO FAIR OF SKIN AND BROWN OF EYE?
ER–. OH, MY YES!
AHOY, YA FAT HEAD! YA DROPPED SUMPIN!
MY FRIEND, I AM A POOR MAN – I HAVE NOTHING TO DROP – YOU PROBABLY MEAN SOMEONE ELSE
MY TROUSERS?
YAS, YER PANTS !!
GOOD HEAVENS!! WELL – I'VE BEEN EXPECTING IT! YOU SEE, I AM HUNGRY, AND MY BELT IS UP TO IT'S LAST NOTCH – AHEM – NOW IF I HAD A FEW HAMBURGERS TO FILL ME OUT
HEY, ROUGH-HOUSE, BUILD HIM UP WITH HAMBURGERS TO ABOUT A "44" WAIST
THANK YOU TOO MUCH
YA KNOW, ROUGH-HOUSE, THIS SWAB AIN'T GOT ABSOLUKELY NO ETTYKIT!! HE ACKS LIKE AS IF HE WAS BRANGED UP IN A BARN OR SUMPIN
WHICH DO YOU WANT ON 'EM, WIMPY, PICKLE, ONION OR LETTUCE ?
ON EACH, SIR – I'LL HAVE PICKLE, ONION AND LETTUCE BOTH
WHERE DID YOU LEARN TO DANCE?
I DIDN'T LEARN – IT JUS' COMES NACHERIL
PST – MY FRIEND, THEY'VE SLIPPED AGAIN
NICE PARTY
YEAH – GIVE 'IM A FEW MORE HAMBURGERS
YA THINK HE'S DOIN' THAT JUS' TO GET SANWICHES?
OF COURSE, HE IS – I'LL BET IT HAPPENS AGAIN
WELL, I'LL BE
HEAVENS! YOU DON'T MEAN TO SAY THEY'VE SLIPPED AGAIN!
WAIT HERE, MR. WIMPY, I'LL BE RIGHT BACK
TELL HIM TO PUT PICKLE, ONION AND LETTUCE BOTH ON 'EM
NICE PARTY, ISN'T IT, YOU'RE HAVING?
IT WAS A NICE PARTY!
9-18
WHAT!! NO HAMBURGERS?!!
E.C. SEGAR

37. September 18, 1932

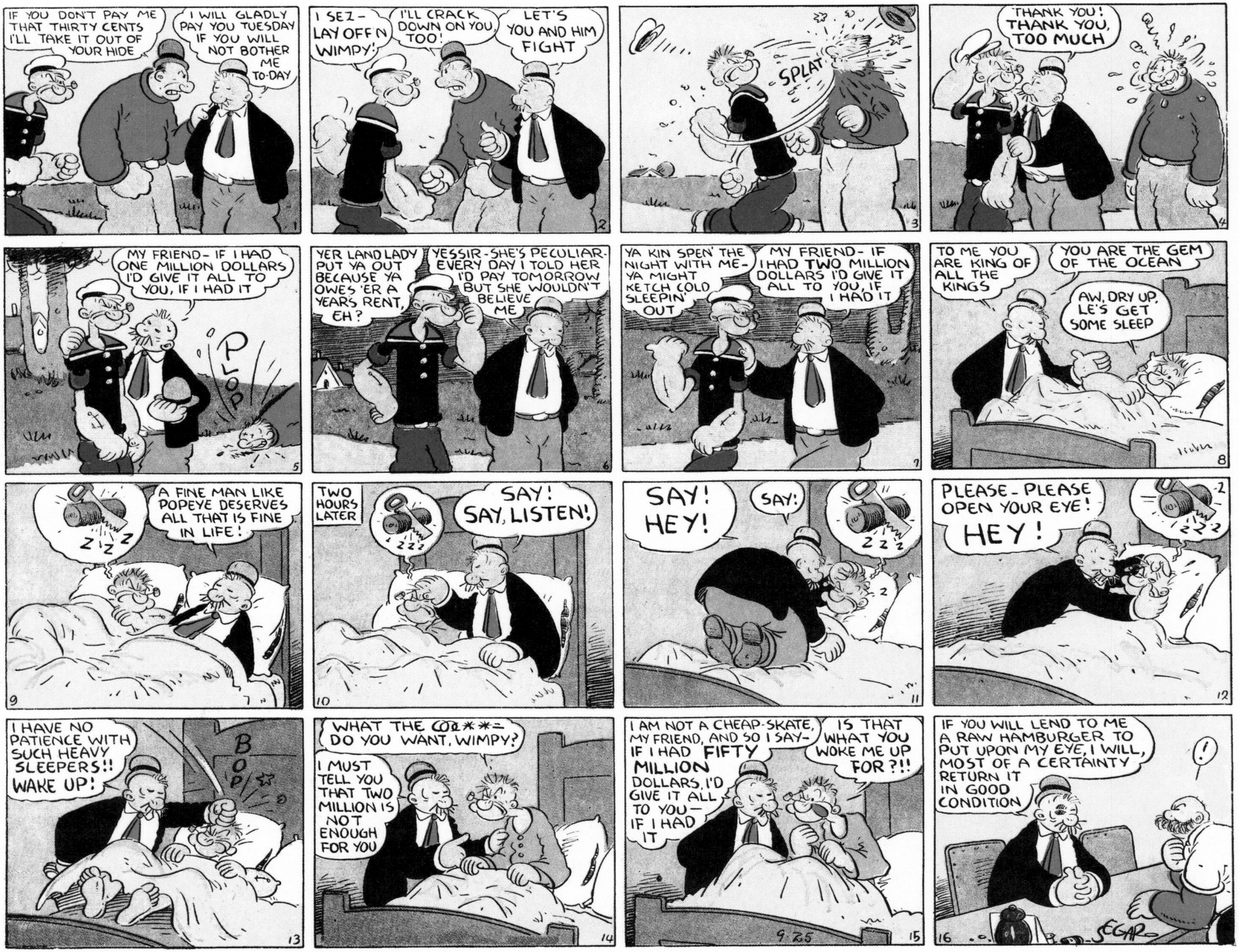
IF YOU DON'T PAY ME THAT THIRTY CENTS I'LL TAKE IT OUT OF YOUR HIDE
I WILL GLADLY PAY YOU TUESDAY IF YOU WILL NOT BOTHER ME TO-DAY
I SEZ - LAY OFF'N WIMPY!
I'LL CRACK DOWN ON YOU, TOO!
LET'S YOU AND HIM FIGHT
SPLAT
THANK YOU! THANK YOU, TOO MUCH
MY FRIEND - IF I HAD ONE MILLION DOLLARS I'D GIVE IT ALL TO YOU, IF I HAD IT
PLOP
YER LAND LADY PUT YA OUT BECAUSE YA OWES 'ER A YEARS RENT, EH?
YESSIR - SHE'S PECULIAR - EVERY DAY I TOLD HER I'D PAY TOMORROW BUT SHE WOULDN'T BELIEVE ME
YA KIN SPEN' THE NIGHT WITH ME - YA MIGHT KETCH COLD SLEEPIN' OUT
MY FRIEND - IF I HAD TWO MILLION DOLLARS I'D GIVE IT ALL TO YOU, IF I HAD IT
TO ME YOU ARE KING OF ALL THE KINGS
YOU ARE THE GEM OF THE OCEAN
AW, DRY UP, LE'S GET SOME SLEEP
A FINE MAN LIKE POPEYE DESERVES ALL THAT IS FINE IN LIFE!
TWO HOURS LATER
SAY! SAY, LISTEN!
SAY! HEY!
SAY!
PLEASE - PLEASE OPEN YOUR EYE! HEY!
I HAVE NO PATIENCE WITH SUCH HEAVY SLEEPERS!! WAKE UP!
BOP
WHAT THE ***- DO YOU WANT, WIMPY?
I MUST TELL YOU THAT TWO MILLION IS NOT ENOUGH FOR YOU
I AM NOT A CHEAP-SKATE, MY FRIEND, AND SO I SAY - IF I HAD FIFTY MILLION DOLLARS, I'D GIVE IT ALL TO YOU - IF I HAD IT
IS THAT WHAT YOU WOKE ME UP FOR?!!
IF YOU WILL LEND TO ME A RAW HAMBURGER TO PUT UPON MY EYE, I WILL, MOST OF A CERTAINTY RETURN IT IN GOOD CONDITION
!
SEGAR

38. September 25, 1932

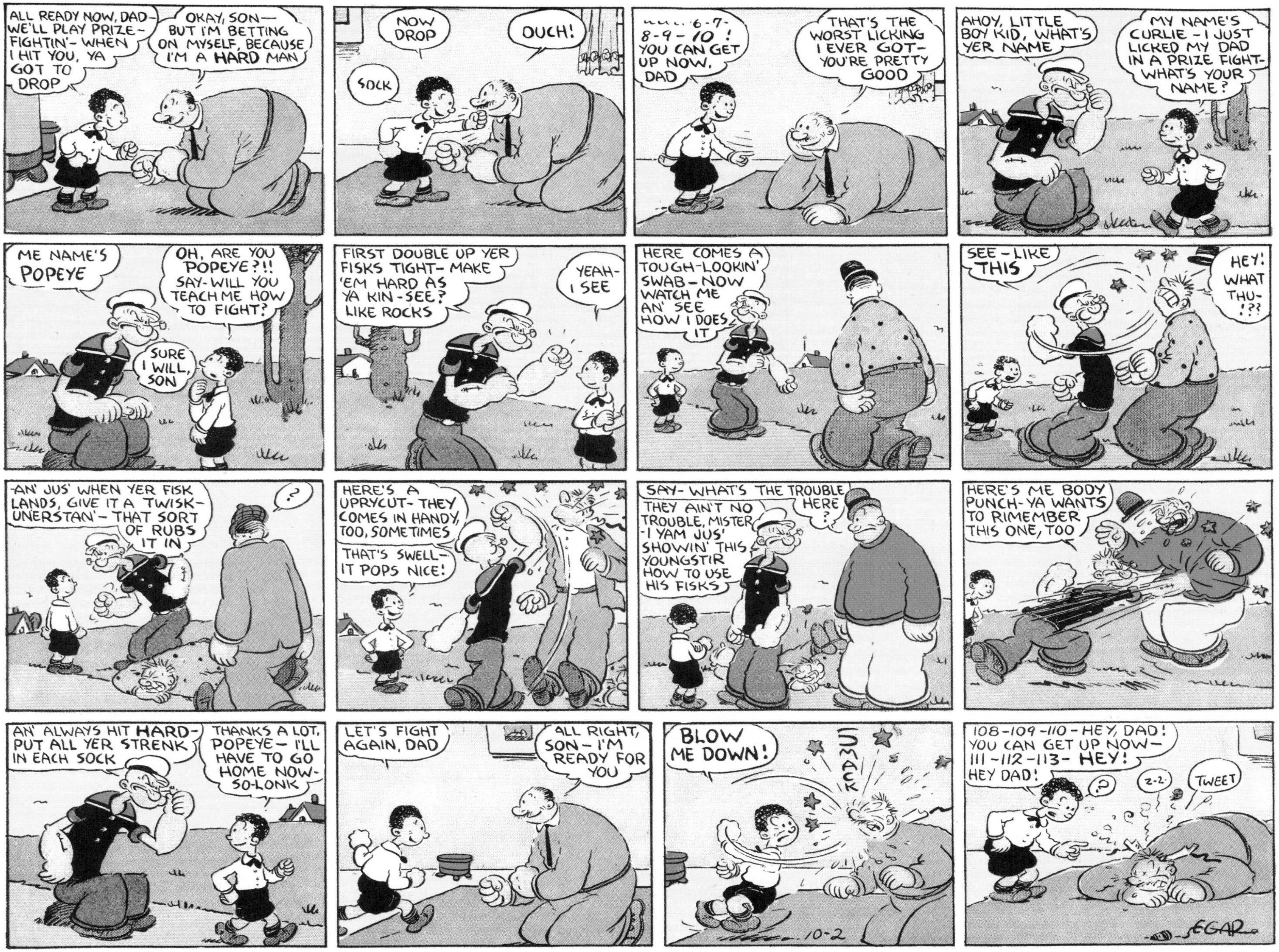
ALL READY NOW, DAD—WE'LL PLAY PRIZE-FIGHTIN'- WHEN I HIT YOU, YA GOT TO DROP
OKAY, SON—BUT I'M BETTING ON MYSELF, BECAUSE I'M A HARD MAN
NOW DROP
SOCK
OUCH!
6-7-8-9-10! YOU CAN GET UP NOW, DAD
THAT'S THE WORST LICKING I EVER GOT-YOU'RE PRETTY GOOD
AHOY, LITTLE BOY KID, WHAT'S YER NAME
MY NAME'S CURLIE - I JUST LICKED MY DAD IN A PRIZE FIGHT-WHAT'S YOUR NAME?
ME NAME'S POPEYE
OH, ARE YOU POPEYE?!! SAY-WILL YOU TEACH ME HOW TO FIGHT?
SURE I WILL, SON
FIRST DOUBLE UP YER FISKS TIGHT- MAKE 'EM HARD AS YA KIN-SEE? LIKE ROCKS
YEAH-I SEE
HERE COMES A TOUGH-LOOKIN' SWAB-NOW WATCH ME AN' SEE HOW I DOES IT
SEE-LIKE THIS
HEY! WHAT THU-!??
-AN' JUS' WHEN YER FISK LANDS, GIVE IT A TWISK-UNERSTAN'-THAT SORT OF RUBS IT IN
?
HERE'S A UPRYCUT- THEY COMES IN HANDY, TOO, SOMETIMES
THAT'S SWELL-IT POPS NICE!
SAY- WHAT'S THE TROUBLE HERE?
THEY AIN'T NO TROUBLE, MISTER -I YAM JUS' SHOWIN' THIS YOUNGSTIR HOW TO USE HIS FISKS
HERE'S ME BODY PUNCH-YA WANTS TO RIMEMBER THIS ONE, TOO
AN' ALWAYS HIT HARD-PUT ALL YER STRENK IN EACH SOCK
THANKS A LOT, POPEYE— I'LL HAVE TO GO HOME NOW-SO-LONK
LET'S FIGHT AGAIN, DAD
ALL RIGHT, SON—I'M READY FOR YOU
BLOW ME DOWN!
SMACK
10-2
108-109-110- HEY, DAD! YOU CAN GET UP NOW—111-112-113- HEY! HEY DAD!
?
Z-Z
TWEET
SEGAR

39. October 2, 1932

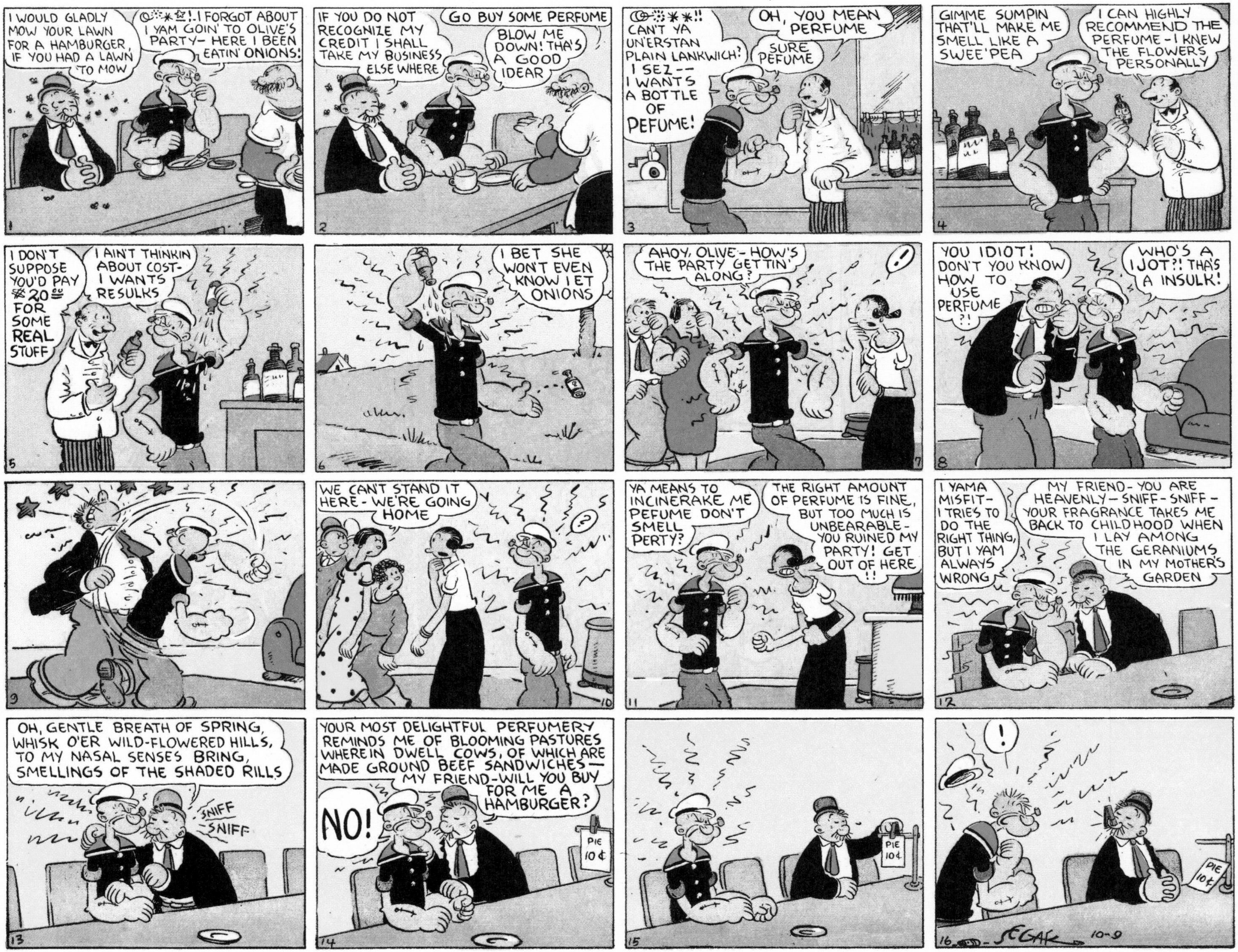

I WOULD GLADLY MOW YOUR LAWN FOR A HAMBURGER, IF YOU HAD A LAWN TO MOW
I FORGOT ABOUT I YAM GOIN' TO OLIVE'S PARTY— HERE I BEEN EATIN' ONIONS!
IF YOU DO NOT RECOGNIZE MY CREDIT I SHALL TAKE MY BUSINESS ELSE WHERE
GO BUY SOME PERFUME
BLOW ME DOWN! THA'S A GOOD IDEAR
CAN'T YA UN'ERSTAN PLAIN LANKWICH? I SEZ -- I WANTS A BOTTLE OF PEFUME!
OH, YOU MEAN PERFUME
SURE PEFUME
GIMME SUMPIN THAT'LL MAKE ME SMELL LIKE A SWEE'PEA
I CAN HIGHLY RECOMMEND THE PERFUME - I KNEW THE FLOWERS PERSONALLY
I DON'T SUPPOSE YOU'D PAY $20.00 FOR SOME REAL STUFF
I AIN'T THINKIN ABOUT COST- I WANTS RESULKS
I BET SHE WON'T EVEN KNOW I ET ONIONS
AHOY, OLIVE - HOW'S THE PARTY GETTIN' ALONG?
!
YOU IDIOT! DON'T YOU KNOW HOW TO USE PERFUME ?!
WHO'S A IJOT?! THA'S A INSULK!
WE CAN'T STAND IT HERE - WE'RE GOING HOME
?
YA MEANS TO INCINERAKE ME PEFUME DON'T SMELL PERTY?
THE RIGHT AMOUNT OF PERFUME IS FINE, BUT TOO MUCH IS UNBEARABLE - YOU RUINED MY PARTY! GET OUT OF HERE !!
I YAMA MISFIT - I TRIES TO DO THE RIGHT THING, BUT I YAM ALWAYS WRONG
MY FRIEND - YOU ARE HEAVENLY — SNIFF — SNIFF — YOUR FRAGRANCE TAKES ME BACK TO CHILDHOOD WHEN I LAY AMONG THE GERANIUMS IN MY MOTHER'S GARDEN
OH, GENTLE BREATH OF SPRING, WHISK O'ER WILD-FLOWERED HILLS, TO MY NASAL SENSES BRING, SMELLINGS OF THE SHADED RILLS
SNIFF SNIFF
YOUR MOST DELIGHTFUL PERFUMERY REMINDS ME OF BLOOMING PASTURES WHEREIN DWELL COWS, OF WHICH ARE MADE GROUND BEEF SANDWICHES— MY FRIEND - WILL YOU BUY FOR ME A HAMBURGER?
NO!
PIE 10¢
PIE 10¢
PIE 10¢
!
SEGAR 10-9

40. October 9, 1932

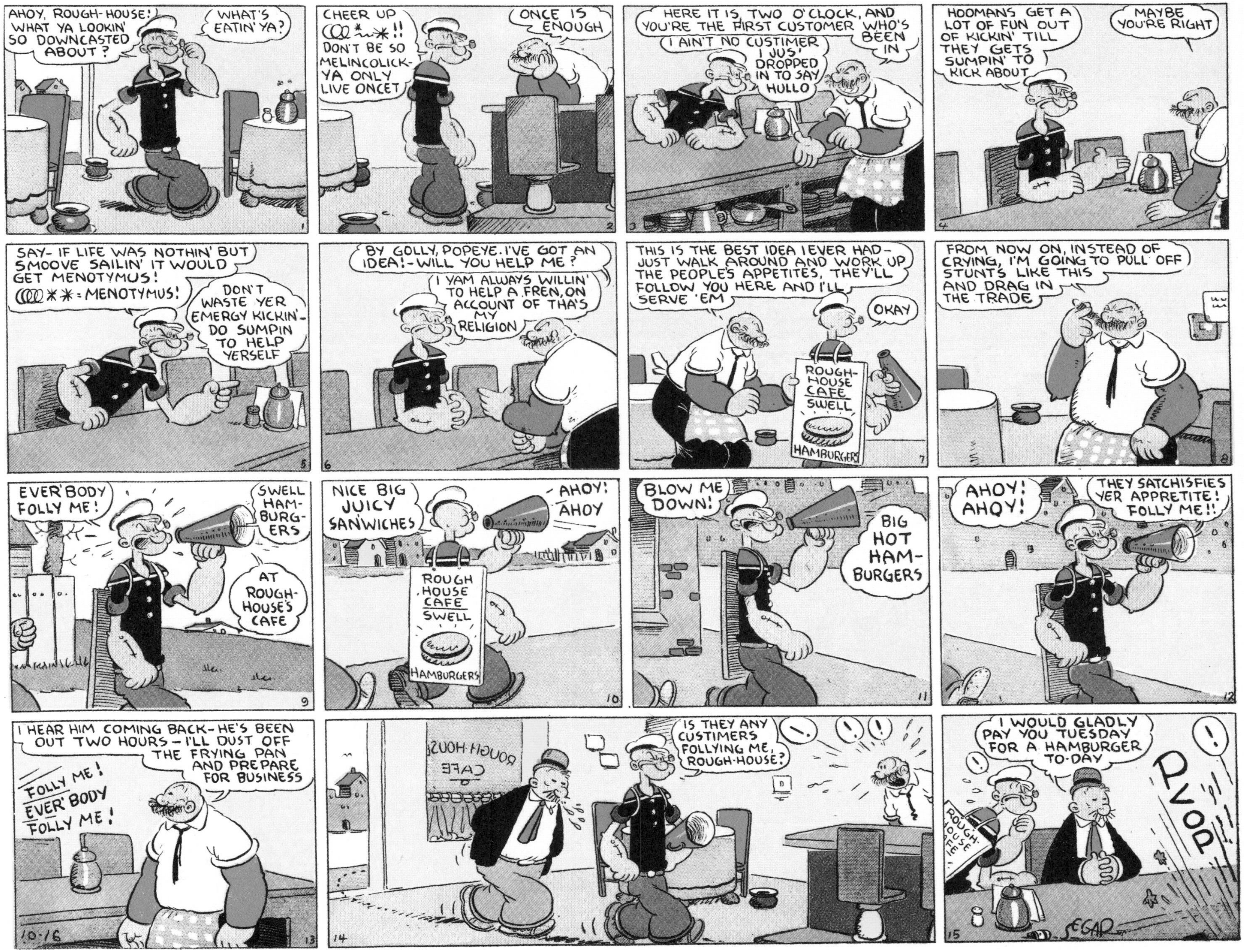
AHOY, ROUGH-HOUSE! WHAT YA LOOKIN' SO DOWNCASTED ABOUT?
WHAT'S EATIN' YA?
CHEER UP
DON'T BE SO MELINCOLICK- YA ONLY LIVE ONCET
ONCE IS ENOUGH
HERE IT IS, TWO O'CLOCK, AND YOU'RE THE FIRST CUSTOMER WHO'S BEEN IN
I AIN'T NO CUSTIMER I JUS' DROPPED IN TO SAY HULLO
HOOMANS GET A LOT OF FUN OUT OF KICKIN' TILL THEY GETS SUMPIN' TO KICK ABOUT
MAYBE YOU'RE RIGHT
SAY- IF LIFE WAS NOTHIN' BUT SMOOVE SAILIN' IT WOULD GET MENOTYMUS!
= MENOTYMUS!
DON'T WASTE YER EMERGY KICKIN'- DO SUMPIN TO HELP YERSELF
BY GOLLY, POPEYE. I'VE GOT AN IDEA! - WILL YOU HELP ME?
I YAM ALWAYS WILLIN' TO HELP A FREN, ON ACCOUNT OF THA'S MY RELIGION
THIS IS THE BEST IDEA I EVER HAD- JUST WALK AROUND AND WORK UP THE PEOPLE'S APPETITES, THEY'LL FOLLOW YOU HERE AND I'LL SERVE 'EM
OKAY
ROUGH-HOUSE CAFE SWELL HAMBURGERS
FROM NOW ON, INSTEAD OF CRYING, I'M GOING TO PULL OFF STUNTS LIKE THIS AND DRAG IN THE TRADE
EVER'BODY FOLLY ME!
SWELL HAM-BURG-ERS
AT ROUGH-HOUSE'S CAFE
NICE BIG JUICY SAN'WICHES
AHOY! AHOY
ROUGH HOUSE CAFE SWELL HAMBURGERS
BLOW ME DOWN!
BIG HOT HAM-BURGERS
AHOY! AHOY!
THEY SATCHISFIES YER APPRETITE! FOLLY ME!!
I HEAR HIM COMING BACK- HE'S BEEN OUT TWO HOURS- I'LL DUST OFF THE FRYING PAN AND PREPARE FOR BUSINESS
FOLLY ME!
EVER' BODY FOLLY ME!
10-16
IS THEY ANY CUSTIMERS FOLLYING ME, ROUGH-HOUSE?
I WOULD GLADLY PAY YOU TUESDAY FOR A HAMBURGER TO-DAY
PLOP
SEGAR

41. October 16, 1932

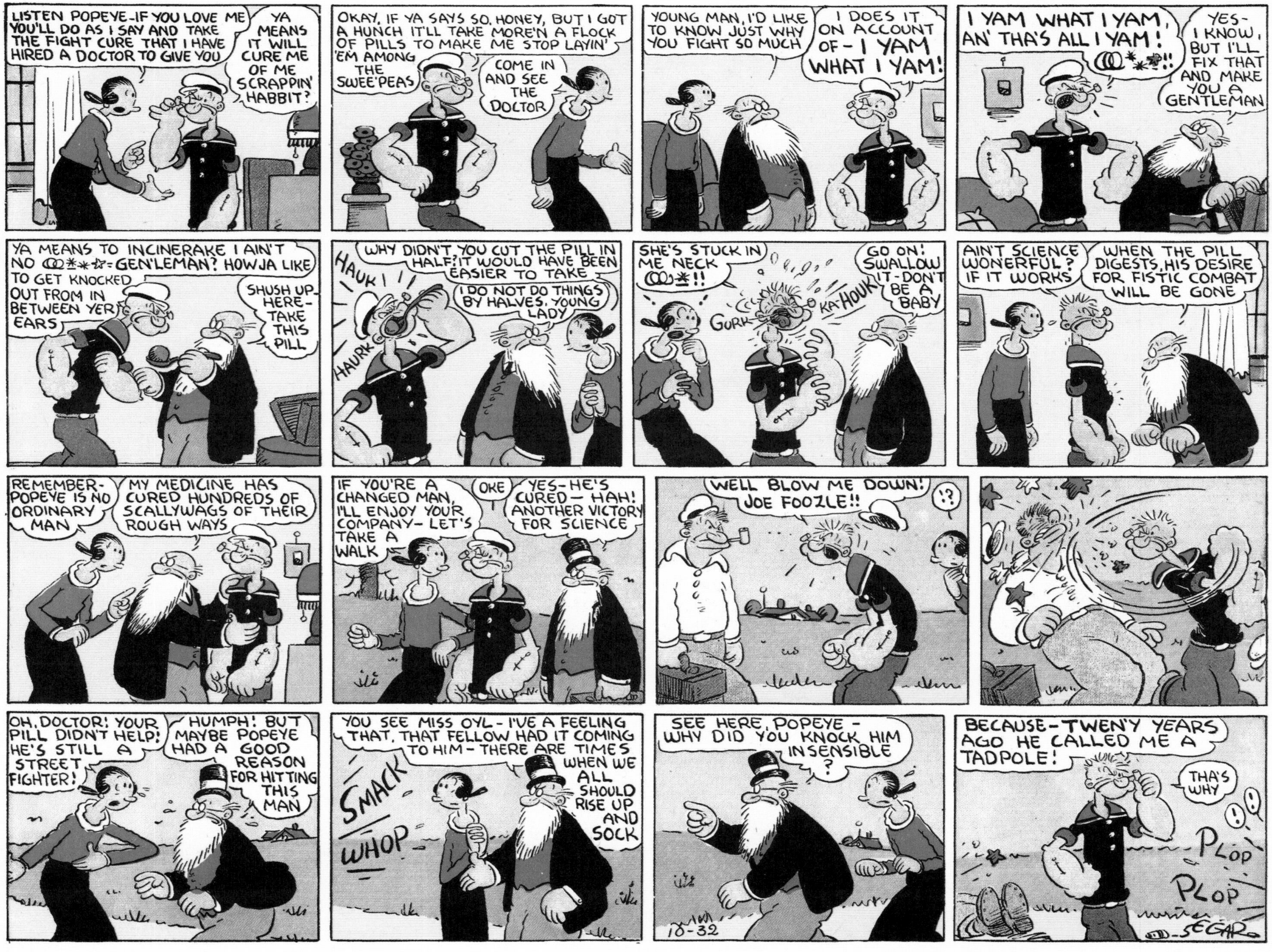

LISTEN POPEYE-IF YOU LOVE ME YOU'LL DO AS I SAY AND TAKE THE FIGHT CURE THAT I HAVE HIRED A DOCTOR TO GIVE YOU
YA MEANS IT WILL CURE ME OF ME SCRAPPIN' HABBIT?
OKAY, IF YA SAYS SO, HONEY, BUT I GOT A HUNCH IT'LL TAKE MORE'N A FLOCK OF PILLS TO MAKE ME STOP LAYIN' 'EM AMONG THE SWEE'PEAS
COME IN AND SEE THE DOCTOR
YOUNG MAN, I'D LIKE TO KNOW JUST WHY YOU FIGHT SO MUCH
I DOES IT ON ACCOUNT OF - I YAM WHAT I YAM!
I YAM WHAT I YAM, AN' THA'S ALL I YAM!
YES- I KNOW, BUT I'LL FIX THAT AND MAKE YOU A GENTLEMAN
YA MEANS TO INCINERAKE I AIN'T NO =GEN'LEMAN? HOWJA LIKE TO GET KNOCKED OUT FROM IN BETWEEN YER EARS
SHUSH UP HERE- TAKE THIS PILL
WHY DIDN'T YOU CUT THE PILL IN HALF? IT WOULD HAVE BEEN EASIER TO TAKE
I DO NOT DO THINGS BY HALVES, YOUNG LADY
HAUK
HAURK
SHE'S STUCK IN ME NECK !!
GO ON! SWALLOW IT-DON'T BE A BABY
GURK
KA-HOUK
AIN'T SCIENCE WONERFUL? IF IT WORKS
WHEN THE PILL DIGESTS, HIS DESIRE FOR FISTIC COMBAT WILL BE GONE
REMEMBER- POPEYE IS NO ORDINARY MAN
MY MEDICINE HAS CURED HUNDREDS OF SCALLYWAGS OF THEIR ROUGH WAYS
IF YOU'RE A CHANGED MAN, I'LL ENJOY YOUR COMPANY- LET'S TAKE A WALK
OKE
YES-HE'S CURED — HAH! ANOTHER VICTORY FOR SCIENCE
WELL BLOW ME DOWN! JOE FOOZLE!!
!?
OH, DOCTOR! YOUR PILL DIDN'T HELP! HE'S STILL A STREET FIGHTER!
HUMPH! BUT MAYBE POPEYE HAD A GOOD REASON FOR HITTING THIS MAN
YOU SEE MISS OYL - I'VE A FEELING THAT, THAT FELLOW HAD IT COMING TO HIM - THERE ARE TIMES WHEN WE ALL SHOULD RISE UP AND SOCK
SMACK
WHOP
SEE HERE, POPEYE - WHY DID YOU KNOCK HIM INSENSIBLE?
10-32
BECAUSE-TWEN'Y YEARS AGO HE CALLED ME A TADPOLE!
THA'S WHY
!
!
PLOP
PLOP
SEGAR

42. October 23, 1932

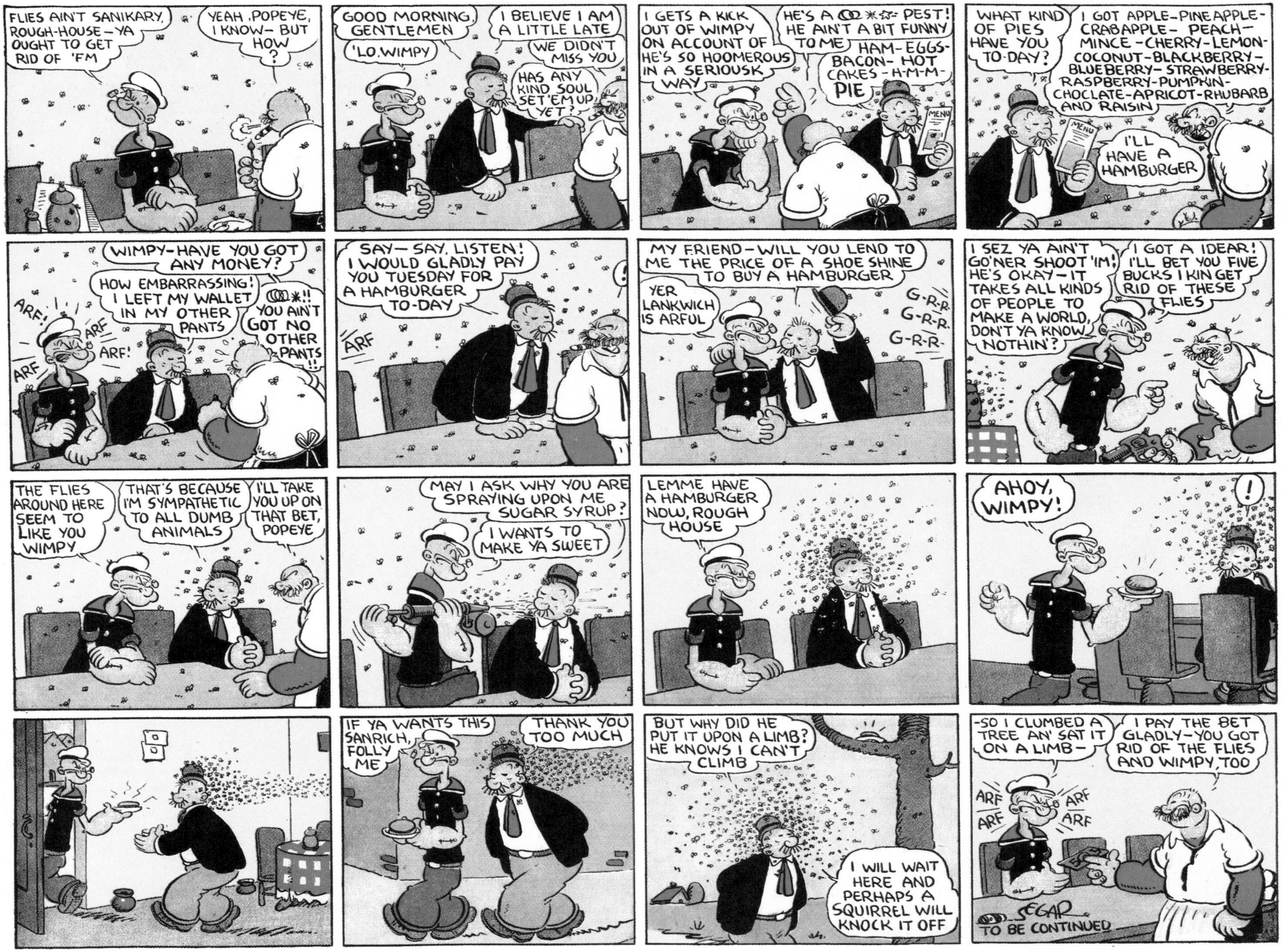
FLIES AIN'T SANIKARY, ROUGH-HOUSE—YA OUGHT TO GET RID OF 'EM
YEAH, POPEYE, I KNOW—BUT HOW ?
GOOD MORNING GENTLEMEN
'LO, WIMPY
I BELIEVE I AM A LITTLE LATE
WE DIDN'T MISS YOU
HAS ANY KIND SOUL SET 'EM UP YET?
I GETS A KICK OUT OF WIMPY ON ACCOUNT OF HE'S SO HOOMEROUS IN A SERIOUSK WAY
HE'S A PEST! HE AIN'T A BIT FUNNY TO ME
HAM-EGGS-BACON-HOT CAKES-H-M-M- PIE
MENU
WHAT KIND OF PIES HAVE YOU TO-DAY?
I GOT APPLE-PINEAPPLE-CRABAPPLE-PEACH-MINCE-CHERRY-LEMON-COCONUT-BLACKBERRY-BLUEBERRY-STRAWBERRY-RASPBERRY-PUMPKIN-CHOCLATE-APRICOT-RHUBARB AND RAISIN
MENU
I'LL HAVE A HAMBURGER
WIMPY—HAVE YOU GOT ANY MONEY?
HOW EMBARRASSING! I LEFT MY WALLET IN MY OTHER PANTS
!! YOU AIN'T GOT NO OTHER PANTS !!
ARF! ARF ARF! ARF
SAY—SAY, LISTEN! I WOULD GLADLY PAY YOU TUESDAY FOR A HAMBURGER TO-DAY
ARF
!
MY FRIEND—WILL YOU LEND TO ME THE PRICE OF A SHOE SHINE TO BUY A HAMBURGER
YER LANKWICH IS ARFUL
G-R-R. G-R-R. G-R-R.
I SEZ YA AIN'T GO'NER SHOOT 'IM! HE'S OKAY—IT TAKES ALL KINDS OF PEOPLE TO MAKE A WORLD, DON'T YA KNOW NOTHIN'?
I GOT A IDEAR! I'LL BET YOU FIVE BUCKS I KIN GET RID OF THESE FLIES
THE FLIES AROUND HERE SEEM TO LIKE YOU WIMPY
THAT'S BECAUSE I'M SYMPATHETIC TO ALL DUMB ANIMALS
I'LL TAKE YOU UP ON THAT BET, POPEYE
MAY I ASK WHY YOU ARE SPRAYING UPON ME SUGAR SYRUP?
I WANTS TO MAKE YA SWEET
LEMME HAVE A HAMBURGER NOW, ROUGH HOUSE
AHOY, WIMPY!
!
IF YA WANTS THIS SANRICH, FOLLY ME
THANK YOU TOO MUCH
BUT WHY DID HE PUT IT UPON A LIMB? HE KNOWS I CAN'T CLIMB
I WILL WAIT HERE AND PERHAPS A SQUIRREL WILL KNOCK IT OFF
-SO I CLUMBED A TREE AN' SAT IT ON A LIMB—
I PAY THE BET GLADLY—YOU GOT RID OF THE FLIES AND WIMPY, TOO
ARF ARF ARF ARF
SEGAR
TO BE CONTINUED

43. October 30, 1932

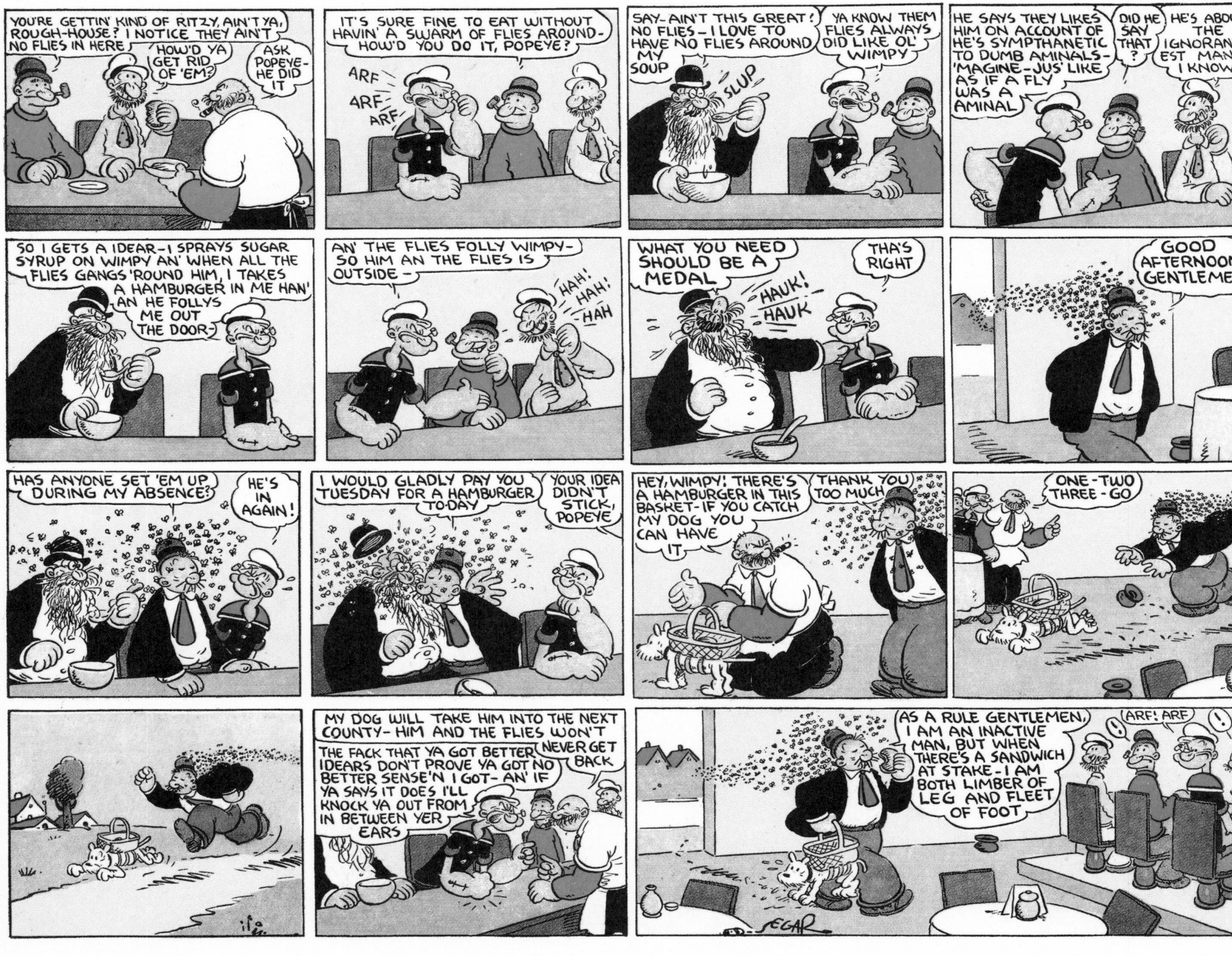
YOU'RE GETTIN' KIND OF RITZY, AIN'T YA, ROUGH-HOUSE? I NOTICE THEY AIN'T NO FLIES IN HERE
HOW'D YA GET RID OF 'EM?
ASK POPEYE- HE DID IT
IT'S SURE FINE TO EAT WITHOUT HAVIN' A SWARM OF FLIES AROUND- HOW'D YOU DO IT, POPEYE?
ARF ARF ARF
SAY- AIN'T THIS GREAT! NO FLIES - I LOVE TO HAVE NO FLIES AROUND MY SOUP
SLUP
YA KNOW THEM FLIES ALWAYS DID LIKE OL' WIMPY
HE SAYS THEY LIKES HIM ON ACCOUNT OF HE'S SYMPTHANETIC TO DUMB AMINALS- 'MAGINE- JUS' LIKE AS IF A FLY WAS A AMINAL
DID HE SAY THAT?
HE'S ABOUT THE IGNORANT-EST MAN I KNOW
SO I GETS A IDEAR- I SPRAYS SUGAR SYRUP ON WIMPY AN' WHEN ALL THE FLIES GANGS 'ROUND HIM, I TAKES A HAMBURGER IN ME HAN' AN HE FOLLYS ME OUT THE DOOR-
AN' THE FLIES FOLLY WIMPY- SO HIM AN THE FLIES IS OUTSIDE-
HAH! HAH! HAH
WHAT YOU NEED SHOULD BE A MEDAL
HAUK! HAUK
THA'S RIGHT
GOOD AFTERNOON, GENTLEMEN
HAS ANYONE SET 'EM UP DURING MY ABSENCE?
HE'S IN AGAIN!
I WOULD GLADLY PAY YOU TUESDAY FOR A HAMBURGER TO-DAY
YOUR IDEA DIDN'T STICK, POPEYE
HEY, WIMPY! THERE'S A HAMBURGER IN THIS BASKET- IF YOU CATCH MY DOG YOU CAN HAVE IT
THANK YOU TOO MUCH
ONE-TWO THREE-GO
MY DOG WILL TAKE HIM INTO THE NEXT COUNTY- HIM AND THE FLIES WON'T NEVER GET BACK
THE FACK THAT YA GOT BETTER IDEARS DON'T PROVE YA GOT NO BETTER SENSE'N I GOT- AN' IF YA SAYS IT DOES I'LL KNOCK YA OUT FROM IN BETWEEN YER EARS
AS A RULE GENTLEMEN, I AM AN INACTIVE MAN, BUT WHEN THERE'S A SANDWICH AT STAKE- I AM BOTH LIMBER OF LEG AND FLEET OF FOOT
ARF! ARF
!
!
SEGAR

44. November 6, 1932

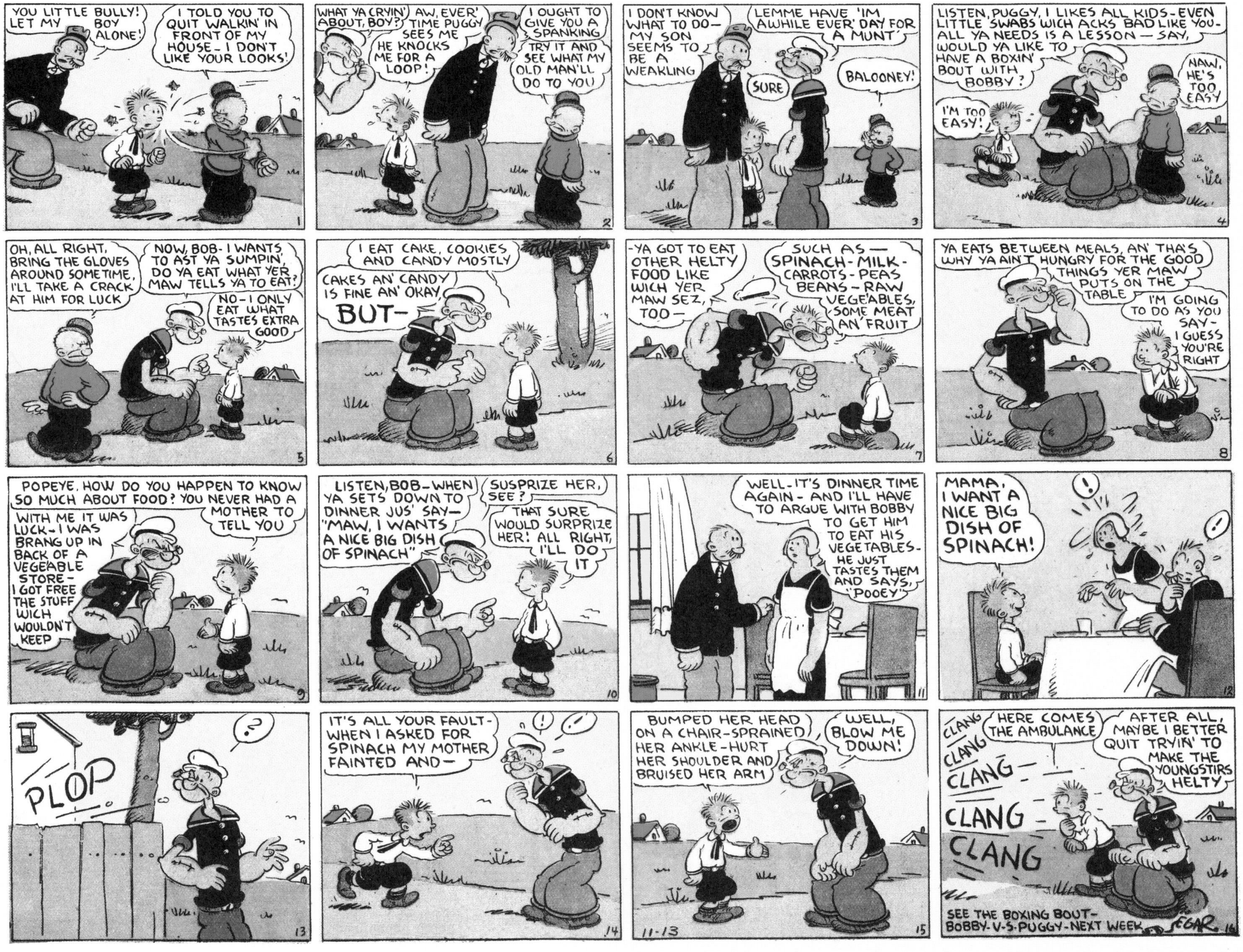
YOU LITTLE BULLY! LET MY BOY ALONE!
I TOLD YOU TO QUIT WALKIN' IN FRONT OF MY HOUSE—I DON'T LIKE YOUR LOOKS!
WHAT YA CRYIN' ABOUT, BOY?
AW, EVER' TIME PUGGY SEES ME HE KNOCKS ME FOR A LOOP!
I OUGHT TO GIVE YOU A SPANKING
TRY IT AND SEE WHAT MY OLD MAN'LL DO TO YOU
I DON'T KNOW WHAT TO DO—MY SON SEEMS TO BE A WEAKLING
LEMME HAVE 'IM AWHILE EVER' DAY FOR A MUNT
SURE
BALOONEY!
LISTEN, PUGGY, I LIKES ALL KIDS—EVEN LITTLE SWABS WICH ACKS BAD LIKE YOU—ALL YA NEEDS IS A LESSON—SAY, WOULD YA LIKE TO HAVE A BOXIN' BOUT WITH BOBBY?
NAW, HE'S TOO EASY
I'M TOO EASY!
OH, ALL RIGHT, BRING THE GLOVES AROUND SOMETIME, I'LL TAKE A CRACK AT HIM FOR LUCK
NOW, BOB—I WANTS TO AST YA SUMPIN', DO YA EAT WHAT YER MAW TELLS YA TO EAT?
NO—I ONLY EAT WHAT TASTES EXTRA GOOD
I EAT CAKE, COOKIES AND CANDY MOSTLY
CAKES AN' CANDY IS FINE AN' OKAY, BUT—
—YA GOT TO EAT OTHER HELTY FOOD LIKE WICH YER MAW SEZ, TOO—
SUCH AS—SPINACH—MILK—CARROTS—PEAS BEANS—RAW VEGE'ABLES, SOME MEAT AN' FRUIT
YA EATS BETWEEN MEALS, AN' THA'S WHY YA AIN'T HUNGRY FOR THE GOOD THINGS YER MAW PUTS ON THE TABLE
I'M GOING TO DO AS YOU SAY—I GUESS YOU'RE RIGHT
POPEYE, HOW DO YOU HAPPEN TO KNOW SO MUCH ABOUT FOOD? YOU NEVER HAD A MOTHER TO TELL YOU
WITH ME IT WAS LUCK—I WAS BRANG UP IN BACK OF A VEGEABLE STORE—I GOT FREE THE STUFF WICH WOULDN'T KEEP
LISTEN, BOB—WHEN YA SETS DOWN TO DINNER JUS' SAY—"MAW, I WANTS A NICE BIG DISH OF SPINACH"
SUSPRIZE HER, SEE?
THAT SURE WOULD SURPRIZE HER! ALL RIGHT, I'LL DO IT
WELL—IT'S DINNER TIME AGAIN—AND I'LL HAVE TO ARGUE WITH BOBBY TO GET HIM TO EAT HIS VEGETABLES—HE JUST TASTES THEM AND SAYS, "POOEY"
MAMA, I WANT A NICE BIG DISH OF SPINACH!
!
!
PLOP
?
IT'S ALL YOUR FAULT—WHEN I ASKED FOR SPINACH MY MOTHER FAINTED AND—
!
!
BUMPED HER HEAD ON A CHAIR—SPRAINED HER ANKLE—HURT HER SHOULDER AND BRUISED HER ARM
WELL, BLOW ME DOWN!
11-13
CLANG
CLANG
CLANG
CLANG
CLANG
HERE COMES THE AMBULANCE
AFTER ALL, MAYBE I BETTER QUIT TRYIN' TO MAKE THE YOUNGSTIRS HELTY
SEE THE BOXING BOUT—BOBBY—V-S—PUGGY—NEXT WEEK
SEGAR

45. November 13, 1932

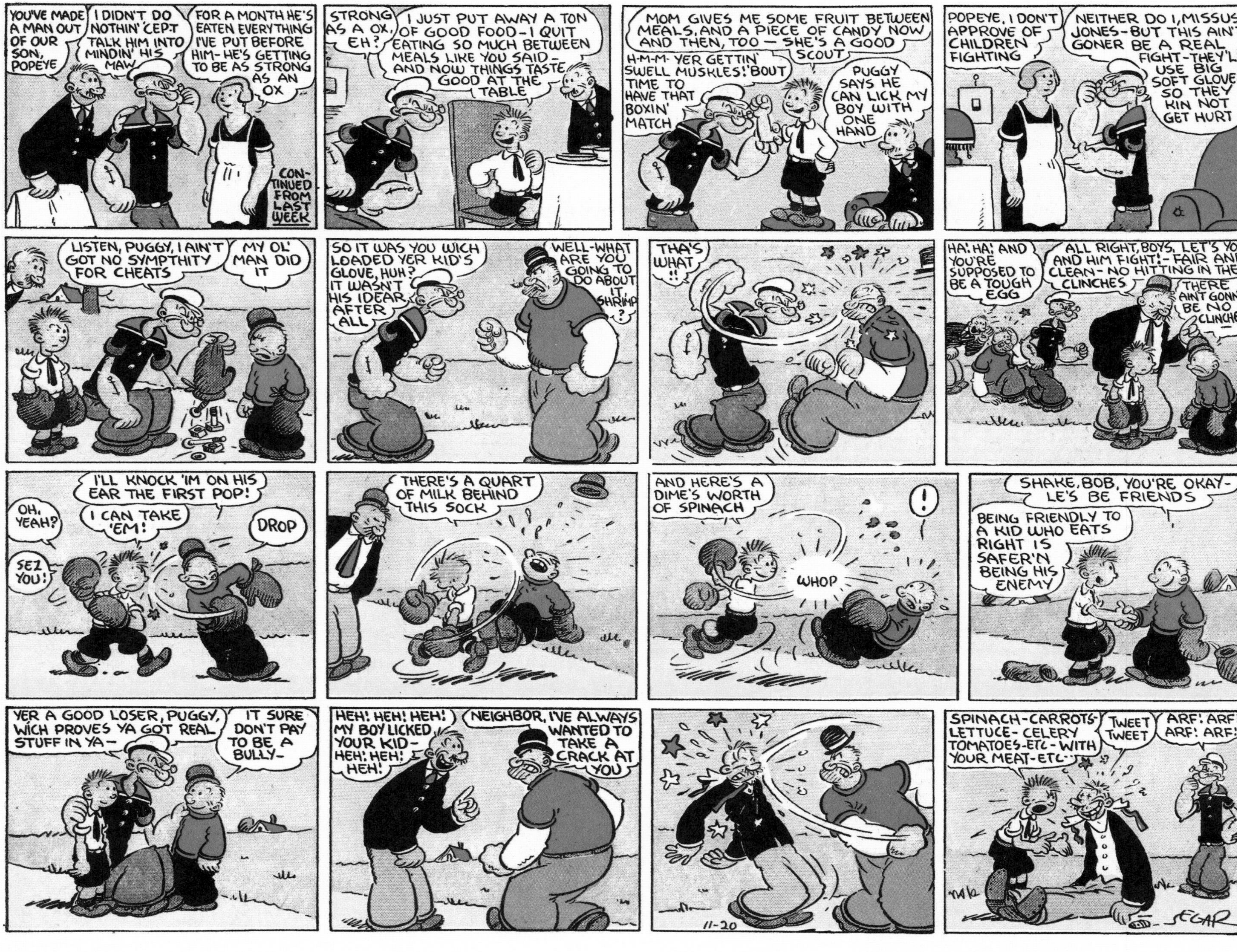

YOU'VE MADE A MAN OUT OF OUR SON, POPEYE
I DIDN'T DO NOTHIN' 'CEP'T TALK HIM INTO MINDIN' HIS MAW
FOR A MONTH HE'S EATEN EVERYTHING I'VE PUT BEFORE HIM- HE'S GETTING TO BE AS STRONG AS AN OX
CONTINUED FROM LAST WEEK
STRONG AS A OX, EH?
I JUST PUT AWAY A TON OF GOOD FOOD-I QUIT EATING SO MUCH BETWEEN MEALS LIKE YOU SAID-AND NOW THINGS TASTE GOOD AT THE TABLE
MOM GIVES ME SOME FRUIT BETWEEN MEALS, AND A PIECE OF CANDY NOW AND THEN, TOO — SHE'S A GOOD SCOUT
H-M-M- YER GETTIN' SWELL MUSKLES! 'BOUT TIME TO HAVE THAT BOXIN' MATCH
PUGGY SAYS HE CAN LICK MY BOY WITH ONE HAND
POPEYE, I DON'T APPROVE OF CHILDREN FIGHTING
NEITHER DO I, MISSUS JONES- BUT THIS AIN'T GONER BE A REAL FIGHT- THEY'LL USE BIG SOFT GLOVES SO THEY KIN NOT GET HURT
LISTEN, PUGGY, I AIN'T GOT NO SYMPTHITY FOR CHEATS
MY OL' MAN DID IT
SO IT WAS YOU WICH LOADED YER KID'S GLOVE, HUH? IT WASN'T HIS IDEAR AFTER ALL
WELL-WHAT ARE YOU GOING TO DO ABOUT IT, SHRIMP?
THA'S WHAT!!
HA! HA! AND YOU'RE SUPPOSED TO BE A TOUGH EGG
ALL RIGHT, BOYS, LET'S YOU AND HIM FIGHT!- FAIR AND CLEAN- NO HITTING IN THE CLINCHES
THERE AIN'T GONNA BE NO CLINCHES
I'LL KNOCK 'IM ON HIS EAR THE FIRST POP!
OH, YEAH?
I CAN TAKE 'EM!
SEZ YOU!
DROP
THERE'S A QUART OF MILK BEHIND THIS SOCK
AND HERE'S A DIME'S WORTH OF SPINACH
!
WHOP
SHAKE, BOB, YOU'RE OKAY- LE'S BE FRIENDS
BEING FRIENDLY TO A KID WHO EATS RIGHT IS SAFER'N BEING HIS ENEMY
YER A GOOD LOSER, PUGGY, WICH PROVES YA GOT REAL STUFF IN YA-
IT SURE DON'T PAY TO BE A BULLY-
HEH! HEH! HEH! MY BOY LICKED YOUR KID- HEH! HEH! HEH!
NEIGHBOR, I'VE ALWAYS WANTED TO TAKE A CRACK AT YOU
11-20
SPINACH-CARROTS-LETTUCE-CELERY TOMATOES-ETC- WITH YOUR MEAT-ETC-
TWEET TWEET
ARF! ARF! ARF! ARF!
SEGAR

46. November 20, 1932

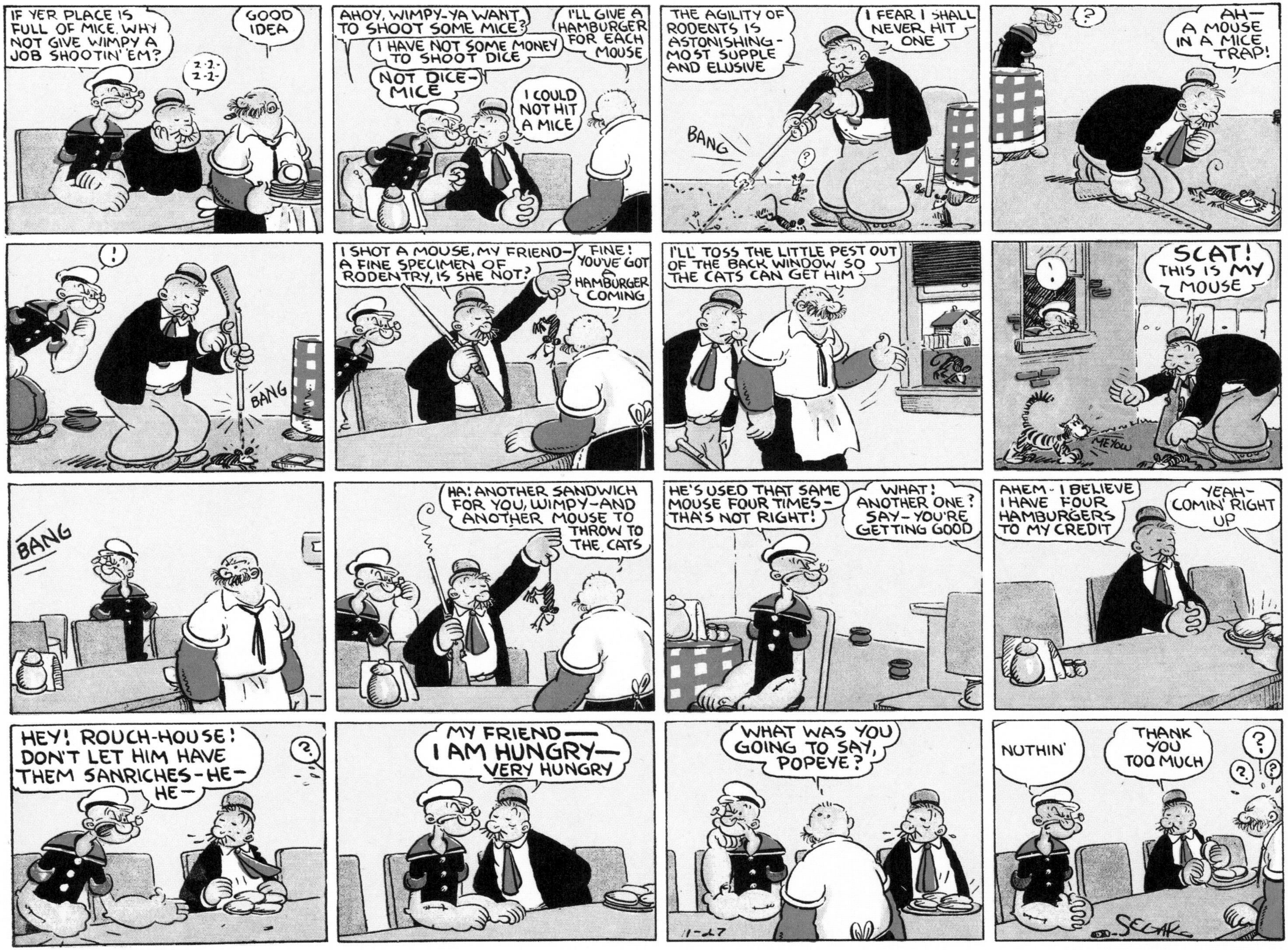
IF YER PLACE IS FULL OF MICE, WHY NOT GIVE WIMPY A JOB SHOOTIN' 'EM?
Z-Z- Z-Z-
GOOD IDEA
AHOY, WIMPY-YA WANT TO SHOOT SOME MICE?
I'LL GIVE A HAMBURGER FOR EACH MOUSE
I HAVE NOT SOME MONEY TO SHOOT DICE
NOT DICE-MICE
I COULD NOT HIT A MICE
THE AGILITY OF RODENTS IS ASTONISHING-MOST SUPPLE AND ELUSIVE
I FEAR I SHALL NEVER HIT ONE
BANG
?
?
AH— A MOUSE IN A MICE TRAP!
!
BANG
I SHOT A MOUSE, MY FRIEND-A FINE SPECIMEN OF RODENTRY, IS SHE NOT?
FINE! YOU'VE GOT A HAMBURGER COMING
I'LL TOSS THE LITTLE PEST OUT OF THE BACK WINDOW SO THE CATS CAN GET HIM
!
SCAT! THIS IS MY MOUSE
MEYOW
BANG
HA! ANOTHER SANDWICH FOR YOU, WIMPY-AND ANOTHER MOUSE TO THROW TO THE CATS
HE'S USED THAT SAME MOUSE FOUR TIMES-THA'S NOT RIGHT!
WHAT! ANOTHER ONE? SAY-YOU'RE GETTING GOOD
AHEM-I BELIEVE I HAVE FOUR HAMBURGERS TO MY CREDIT
YEAH-COMIN' RIGHT UP
HEY! ROUCH-HOUSE! DON'T LET HIM HAVE THEM SANRICHES-HE-HE-
?
MY FRIEND— I AM HUNGRY— VERY HUNGRY
WHAT WAS YOU GOING TO SAY, POPEYE?
11-27
NUTHIN'
THANK YOU TOO MUCH
?
?
?
SEGAR

47. November 27, 1932

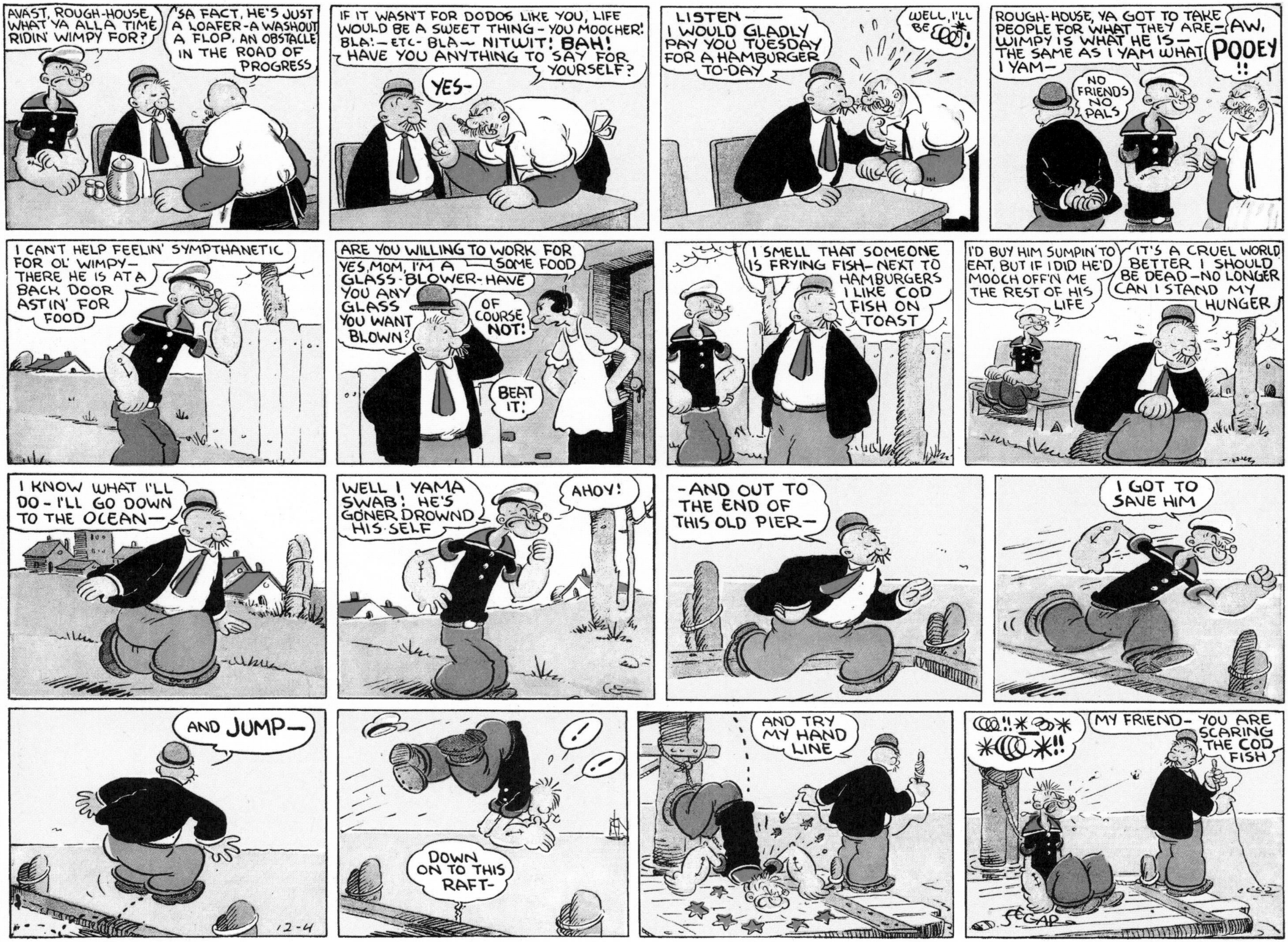
AVAST, ROUGH-HOUSE, WHAT YA ALLA TIME RIDIN' WIMPY FOR?
'SA FACT, HE'S JUST A LOAFER - A WASHOUT A FLOP, AN OBSTACLE IN THE ROAD OF PROGRESS
IF IT WASN'T FOR DODOS LIKE YOU, LIFE WOULD BE A SWEET THING - YOU MOOCHER! BLA! - ETC - BLA ~ NITWIT! BAH! HAVE YOU ANYTHING TO SAY FOR YOURSELF?
YES-
LISTEN —— I WOULD GLADLY PAY YOU TUESDAY FOR A HAMBURGER TO-DAY
WELL, I'LL BE
ROUGH-HOUSE, YA GOT TO TAKE PEOPLE FOR WHAT THEY ARE - WIMPY IS WHAT HE IS - THE SAME AS I YAM WHAT I YAM-
AW, POODEY !!
NO FRIENDS NO PALS
I CAN'T HELP FEELIN' SYMPTHANETIC FOR OL' WIMPY - THERE HE IS AT A BACK DOOR ASTIN' FOR FOOD
ARE YOU WILLING TO WORK FOR SOME FOOD
YES, MOM, I'M A GLASS-BLOWER - HAVE YOU ANY GLASS YOU WANT BLOWN?
OF COURSE NOT!
BEAT IT!
I SMELL THAT SOMEONE IS FRYING FISH - NEXT TO HAMBURGERS I LIKE COD FISH ON TOAST
I'D BUY HIM SUMPIN' TO EAT, BUT IF I DID HE'D MOOCH OFF'N ME THE REST OF HIS LIFE
IT'S A CRUEL WORLD BETTER I SHOULD BE DEAD - NO LONGER CAN I STAND MY HUNGER
I KNOW WHAT I'LL DO - I'LL GO DOWN TO THE OCEAN —
WELL I YAMA SWAB! HE'S GONER DROWND HIS SELF
AHOY!
- AND OUT TO THE END OF THIS OLD PIER -
I GOT TO SAVE HIM
AND JUMP —
!
!
DOWN ON TO THIS RAFT-
12-4
AND TRY MY HAND LINE
MY FRIEND - YOU ARE SCARING THE COD FISH
SEGAR

48. December 4, 1932

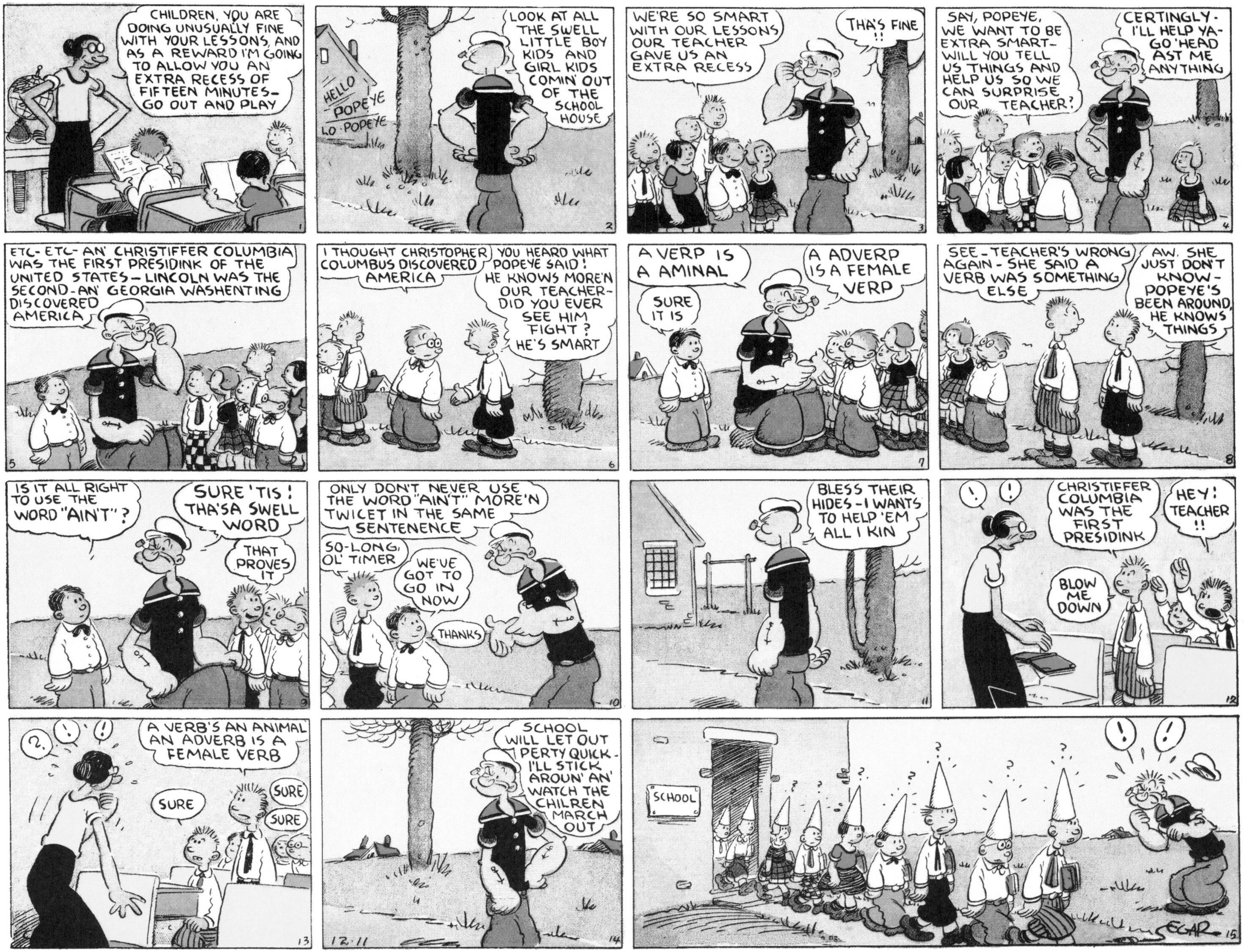
CHILDREN, YOU ARE DOING UNUSUALLY FINE WITH YOUR LESSONS, AND AS A REWARD I'M GOING TO ALLOW YOU AN EXTRA RECESS OF FIFTEEN MINUTES— GO OUT AND PLAY
LOOK AT ALL THE SWELL LITTLE BOY KIDS AND GIRL KIDS COMIN' OUT OF THE SCHOOL HOUSE
HELLO POPEYE
LO-POPEYE
WE'RE SO SMART WITH OUR LESSONS OUR TEACHER GAVE US AN EXTRA RECESS
THA'S FINE !!
SAY, POPEYE, WE WANT TO BE EXTRA SMART— WILL YOU TELL US THINGS AND HELP US SO WE CAN SURPRISE OUR TEACHER?
CERTINGLY— I'LL HELP YA— GO 'HEAD AST ME ANYTHING
ETC—ETC—AN' CHRISTIFFER COLUMBIA WAS THE FIRST PRESIDINK OF THE UNITED STATES—LINCOLN WAS THE SECOND—AN' GEORGIA WASHENTING DISCOVERED AMERICA
I THOUGHT CHRISTOPHER COLUMBUS DISCOVERED AMERICA
YOU HEARD WHAT POPEYE SAID! HE KNOWS MORE'N OUR TEACHER— DID YOU EVER SEE HIM FIGHT? HE'S SMART
A VERP IS A AMINAL
A ADVERP IS A FEMALE VERP
SURE IT IS
SEE—TEACHER'S WRONG AGAIN—SHE SAID A VERB WAS SOMETHING ELSE
AW, SHE JUST DON'T KNOW— POPEYE'S BEEN AROUND, HE KNOWS THINGS
IS IT ALL RIGHT TO USE THE WORD "AIN'T"?
SURE 'TIS! THA'SA SWELL WORD
THAT PROVES IT
ONLY DON'T NEVER USE THE WORD "AIN'T" MORE'N TWICET IN THE SAME SENTENENCE
SO-LONG, OL' TIMER
WE'VE GOT TO GO IN NOW
THANKS
BLESS THEIR HIDES—I WANTS TO HELP 'EM ALL I KIN
! !
CHRISTIFFER COLUMBIA WAS THE FIRST PRESIDINK
HEY! TEACHER !!
BLOW ME DOWN
? ! !
A VERB'S AN ANIMAL AN ADVERB IS A FEMALE VERB
SURE
SURE
SURE
12-11
SCHOOL WILL LET OUT PERTY QUICK— I'LL STICK AROUN' AN' WATCH THE CHILREN MARCH OUT
SCHOOL
! !
SEGAR

49. December 11, 1932

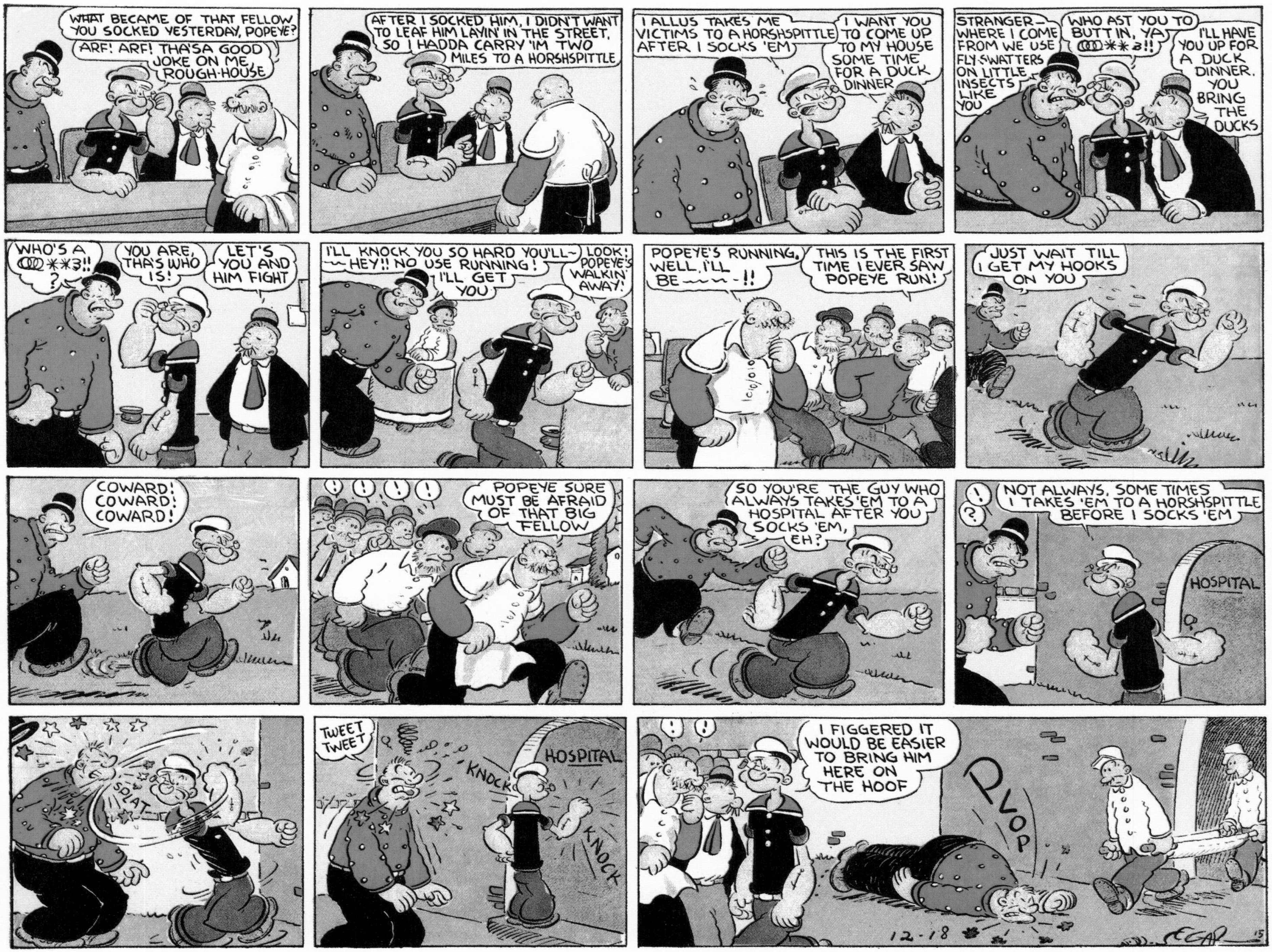

WHAT BECAME OF THAT FELLOW YOU SOCKED YESTERDAY, POPEYE?
ARF! ARF! THA'SA GOOD JOKE ON ME, ROUGH-HOUSE
AFTER I SOCKED HIM, I DIDN'T WANT TO LEAF HIM LAYIN' IN THE STREET, SO I HADDA CARRY 'IM TWO MILES TO A HORSHSPITTLE
I ALLUS TAKES ME VICTIMS TO A HORSHSPITTLE AFTER I SOCKS 'EM
I WANT YOU TO COME UP TO MY HOUSE SOME TIME FOR A DUCK DINNER
STRANGER— WHERE I COME FROM WE USE FLY-SWATTERS ON LITTLE INSECTS LIKE YOU
WHO AST YOU TO BUTT IN, YA
I'LL HAVE YOU UP FOR A DUCK DINNER. YOU BRING THE DUCKS
WHO'S A
?
YOU ARE, THA'S WHO IS!
LET'S YOU AND HIM FIGHT
I'LL KNOCK YOU SO HARD YOU'LL— —HEY!! NO USE RUNNING! I'LL GET YOU
LOOK! POPEYE'S WALKIN' AWAY!
POPEYE'S RUNNING. WELL, I'LL BE——-!!
THIS IS THE FIRST TIME I EVER SAW POPEYE RUN!
JUST WAIT TILL I GET MY HOOKS ON YOU
COWARD! COWARD! COWARD!
! ! ! !
POPEYE SURE MUST BE AFRAID OF THAT BIG FELLOW
SO YOU'RE THE GUY WHO ALWAYS TAKES 'EM TO A HOSPITAL AFTER YOU SOCKS 'EM, EH?
! ?
NOT ALWAYS, SOME TIMES I TAKES 'EM TO A HORSHSPITTLE BEFORE I SOCKS 'EM
HOSPITAL
SPLAT
TWEET TWEET
HOSPITAL
KNOCK
KNOCK
KNOCK
! !
I FIGGERED IT WOULD BE EASIER TO BRING HIM HERE ON THE HOOF
PLOP
12-18
SEGAR

50. December 18, 1932

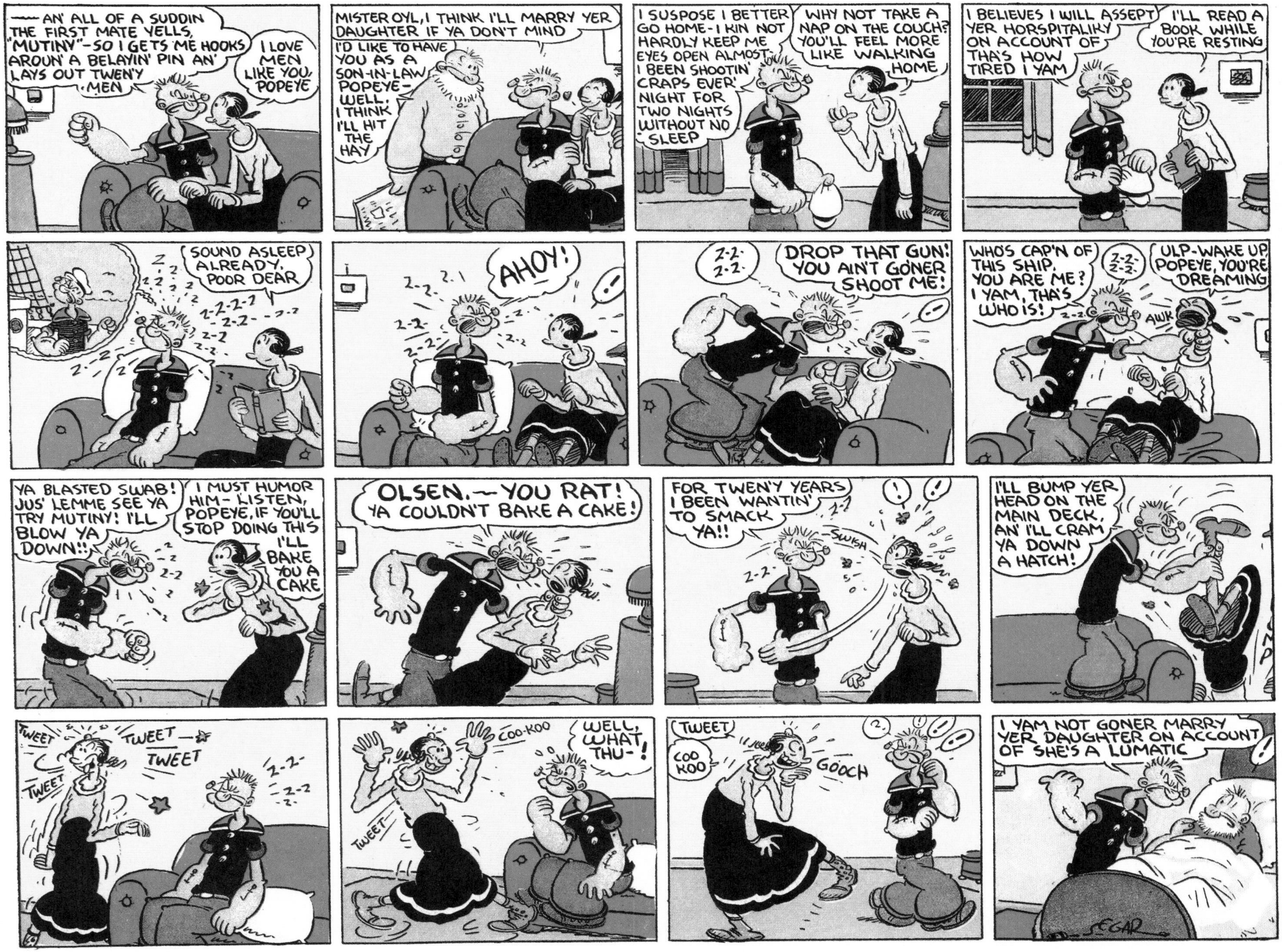
—AN' ALL OF A SUDDIN THE FIRST MATE YELLS, "MUTINY"—SO I GETS ME HOOKS AROUN' A BELAYIN' PIN AN' LAYS OUT TWEN'Y MEN
I LOVE MEN LIKE YOU, POPEYE
MISTER OYL, I THINK I'LL MARRY YER DAUGHTER IF YA DON'T MIND
I'D LIKE TO HAVE YOU AS A SON-IN-LAW, POPEYE—WELL, I THINK I'LL HIT THE HAY
I SUSPOSE I BETTER GO HOME—I KIN NOT HARDLY KEEP ME EYES OPEN ALMOST—I BEEN SHOOTIN' CRAPS EVER' NIGHT FOR TWO NIGHTS WITHOUT NO SLEEP
WHY NOT TAKE A NAP ON THE COUCH? YOU'LL FEEL MORE LIKE WALKING HOME
I BELIEVES I WILL ASSEPT YER HORSPITALIKY ON ACCOUNT OF THA'S HOW TIRED I YAM
I'LL READ A BOOK WHILE YOU'RE RESTING
SOUND ASLEEP ALREADY, POOR DEAR
AHOY!
!
Z-Z- Z-Z-
DROP THAT GUN! YOU AIN'T GONER SHOOT ME!
!
WHO'S CAP'N OF THIS SHIP, YOU ARE ME? I YAM, THA'S WHO IS!
Z-Z- Z-Z-
ULP—WAKE UP POPEYE, YOU'RE DREAMING
AWK
YA BLASTED SWAB! JUS' LEMME SEE YA TRY MUTINY! I'LL BLOW YA DOWN!!
I MUST HUMOR HIM—LISTEN, POPEYE, IF YOU'LL STOP DOING THIS I'LL BAKE YOU A CAKE
OLSEN,—YOU RAT! YA COULDN'T BAKE A CAKE!
FOR TWEN'Y YEARS I BEEN WANTIN' TO SMACK YA!!
! !
SWISH
I'LL BUMP YER HEAD ON THE MAIN DECK, AN' I'LL CRAM YA DOWN A HATCH!
TWEET
TWEET
TWEET
TWEET
Z-Z-
COO-KOO
WELL, WHAT THU-!
TWEET
TWEET
COO KOO
GOOCH
? ! !
I YAM NOT GONER MARRY YER DAUGHTER ON ACCOUNT OF SHE'S A LUMATIC
!
SEGAR

51. December 25, 1932

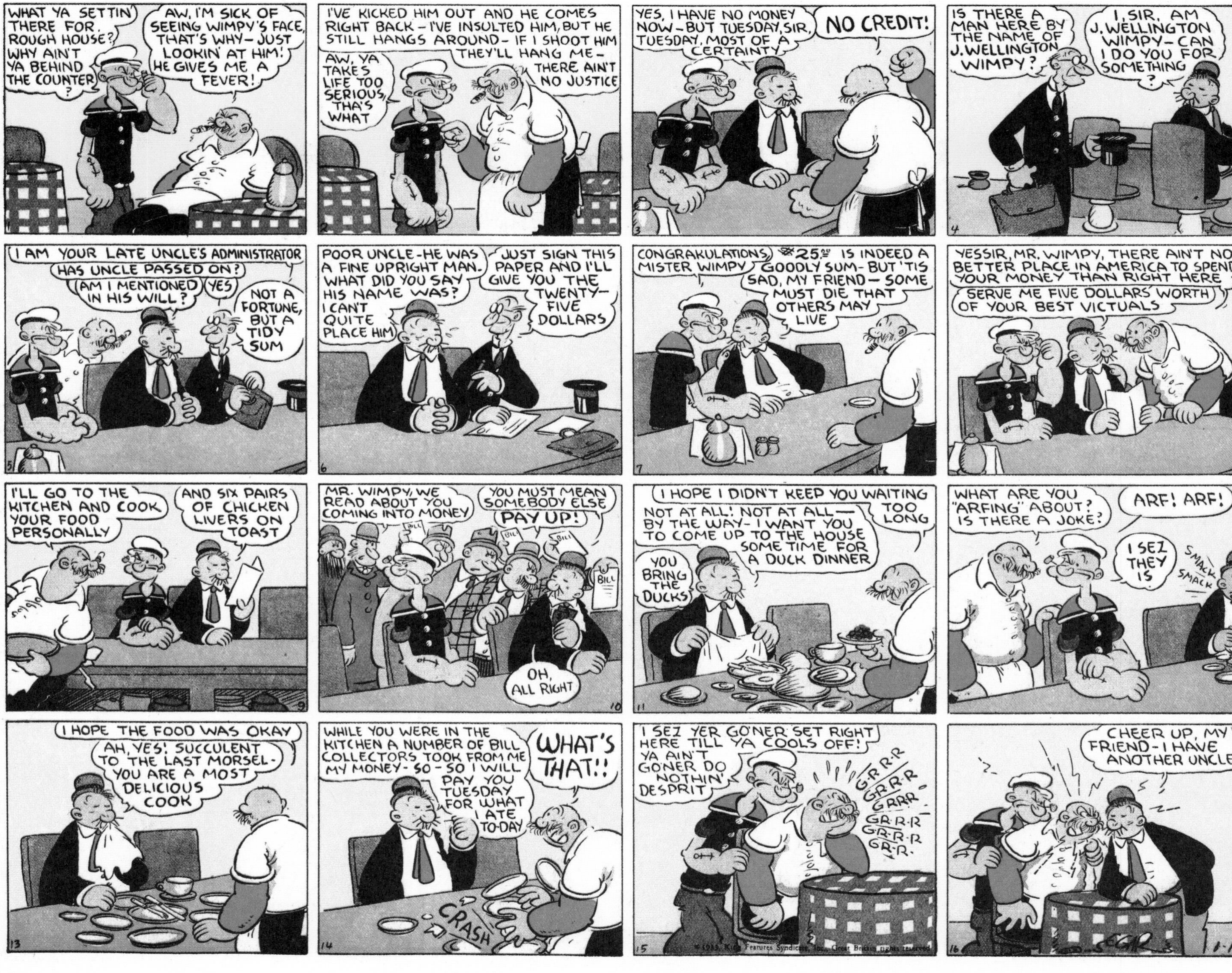
WHAT YA SETTIN' THERE FOR, ROUGH HOUSE? WHY AIN'T YA BEHIND THE COUNTER?
AW, I'M SICK OF SEEING WIMPY'S FACE, THAT'S WHY - JUST LOOKIN' AT HIM! HE GIVES ME A FEVER!
I'VE KICKED HIM OUT AND HE COMES RIGHT BACK - I'VE INSULTED HIM, BUT HE STILL HANGS AROUND - IF I SHOOT HIM THEY'LL HANG ME - THERE AIN'T NO JUSTICE
AW, YA TAKES LIFE TOO SERIOUS, THA'S WHAT
YES, I HAVE NO MONEY NOW - BUT TUESDAY, SIR, TUESDAY, MOST OF A CERTAINTY
NO CREDIT!
IS THERE A MAN HERE BY THE NAME OF J. WELLINGTON WIMPY?
I, SIR, AM J. WELLINGTON WIMPY - CAN I DO YOU FOR SOMETHING?
I AM YOUR LATE UNCLE'S ADMINISTRATOR
HAS UNCLE PASSED ON?
YES
AM I MENTIONED IN HIS WILL?
NOT A FORTUNE, BUT A TIDY SUM
POOR UNCLE - HE WAS A FINE UPRIGHT MAN. WHAT DID YOU SAY HIS NAME WAS? I CAN'T QUITE PLACE HIM
JUST SIGN THIS PAPER AND I'LL GIVE YOU THE TWENTY-FIVE DOLLARS
CONGRAKULATIONS MISTER WIMPY
$25.00 IS INDEED A GOODLY SUM - BUT 'TIS SAD, MY FRIEND - SOME MUST DIE THAT OTHERS MAY LIVE
YESSIR, MR. WIMPY, THERE AIN'T NO BETTER PLACE IN AMERICA TO SPEND YOUR MONEY THAN RIGHT HERE
SERVE ME FIVE DOLLARS WORTH OF YOUR BEST VICTUALS
I'LL GO TO THE KITCHEN AND COOK YOUR FOOD PERSONALLY
AND SIX PAIRS OF CHICKEN LIVERS ON TOAST
MR. WIMPY, WE READ ABOUT YOU COMING INTO MONEY
YOU MUST MEAN SOMEBODY ELSE
PAY UP!
BILL
OH, ALL RIGHT
I HOPE I DIDN'T KEEP YOU WAITING TOO LONG
NOT AT ALL! NOT AT ALL— BY THE WAY - I WANT YOU TO COME UP TO THE HOUSE SOME TIME FOR A DUCK DINNER
YOU BRING THE DUCKS
WHAT ARE YOU "ARFING" ABOUT? IS THERE A JOKE?
ARF! ARF!
I SEZ THEY IS
SMACK SMACK
I HOPE THE FOOD WAS OKAY
AH, YES! SUCCULENT TO THE LAST MORSEL - YOU ARE A MOST DELICIOUS COOK
WHILE YOU WERE IN THE KITCHEN A NUMBER OF BILL COLLECTORS TOOK FROM ME MY MONEY - SO - SO I WILL PAY YOU TUESDAY FOR WHAT I ATE TO-DAY
WHAT'S THAT!!
CRASH
I SEZ YER GO'NER SET RIGHT HERE TILL YA COOLS OFF! YA AIN'T GO'NER DO NOTHIN' DESPRIT
GRRR
CHEER UP, MY FRIEND - I HAVE ANOTHER UNCLE
SEGAR
1-1

52. January 1, 1933

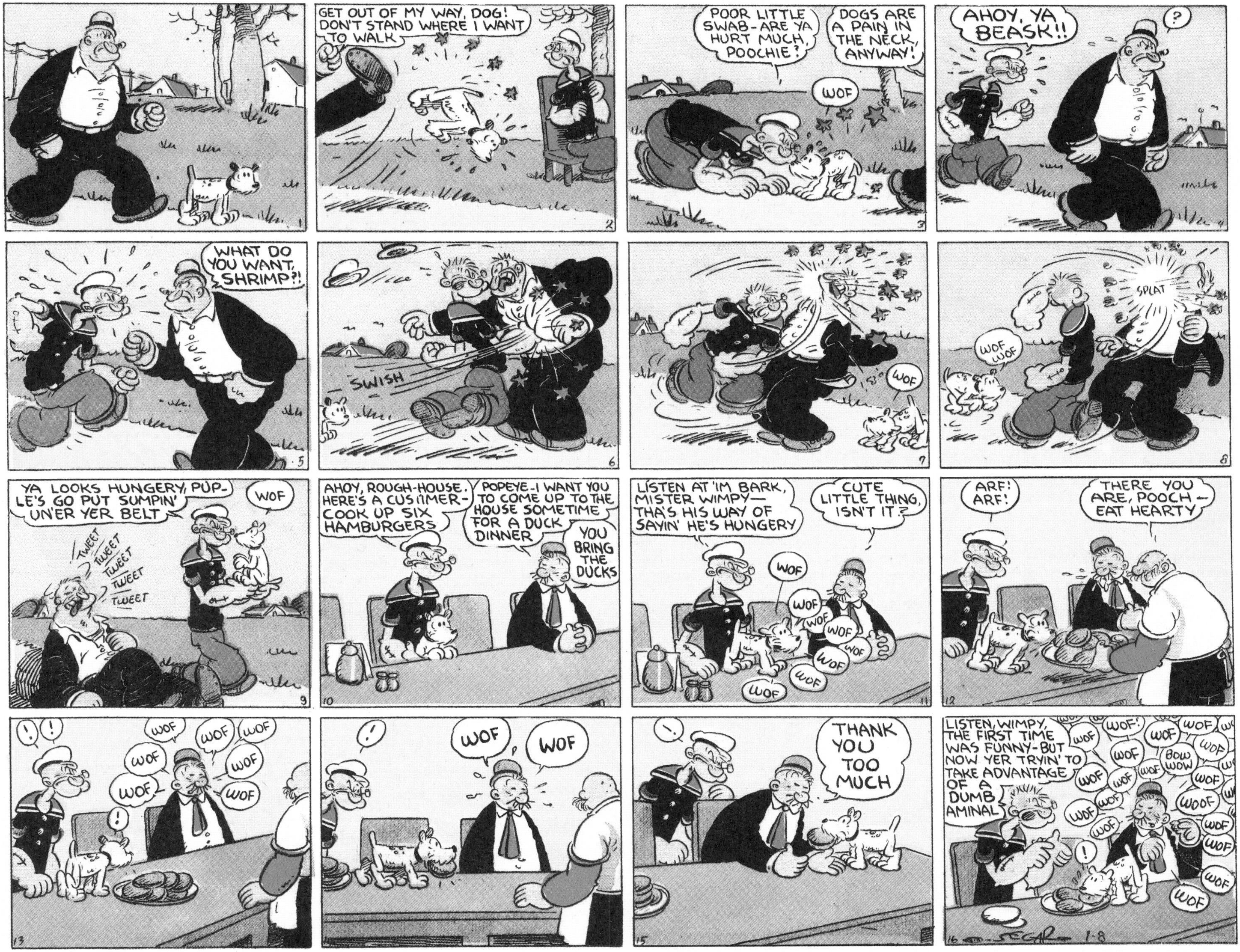
GET OUT OF MY WAY, DOG! DON'T STAND WHERE I WANT TO WALK
POOR LITTLE SWAB-ARE YA HURT MUCH, POOCHIE?
DOGS ARE A PAIN IN THE NECK, ANYWAY!
WOF
AHOY, YA BEASK!!
?
WHAT DO YOU WANT, SHRIMP?!
SWISH
WOF
SPLAT
WOF WOF
YA LOOKS HUNGERY, PUP-LE'S GO PUT SUMPIN' UN'ER YER BELT
WOF
TWEET
TWEET
TWEET
TWEET
TWEET
AHOY, ROUGH-HOUSE. HERE'S A CUS'IMER-COOK UP SIX HAMBURGERS
POPEYE-I WANT YOU TO COME UP TO THE HOUSE SOMETIME FOR A DUCK DINNER
YOU BRING THE DUCKS
LISTEN AT 'IM BARK, MISTER WIMPY—THA'S HIS WAY OF SAYIN' HE'S HUNGERY
CUTE LITTLE THING, ISN'T IT?
WOF
WOF
WOF
WOF
WOF
WOF
WOF
WOF
ARF! ARF!
THERE YOU ARE, POOCH-EAT HEARTY
!
!
WOF
WOF
WOF
WOF
WOF
WOF
!
!
WOF
WOF
!
THANK YOU TOO MUCH
LISTEN, WIMPY, THE FIRST TIME WAS FUNNY-BUT NOW YER TRYIN' TO TAKE ADVANTAGE OF A DUMB AMINAL
WOF!
WOF
WOF
WOF
BOW WOW
WOF
WOF
WOF
WOOF
WOF
WOF
WOF
WOF
WOF
!
SEGAR 1-8

53. January 8, 1933

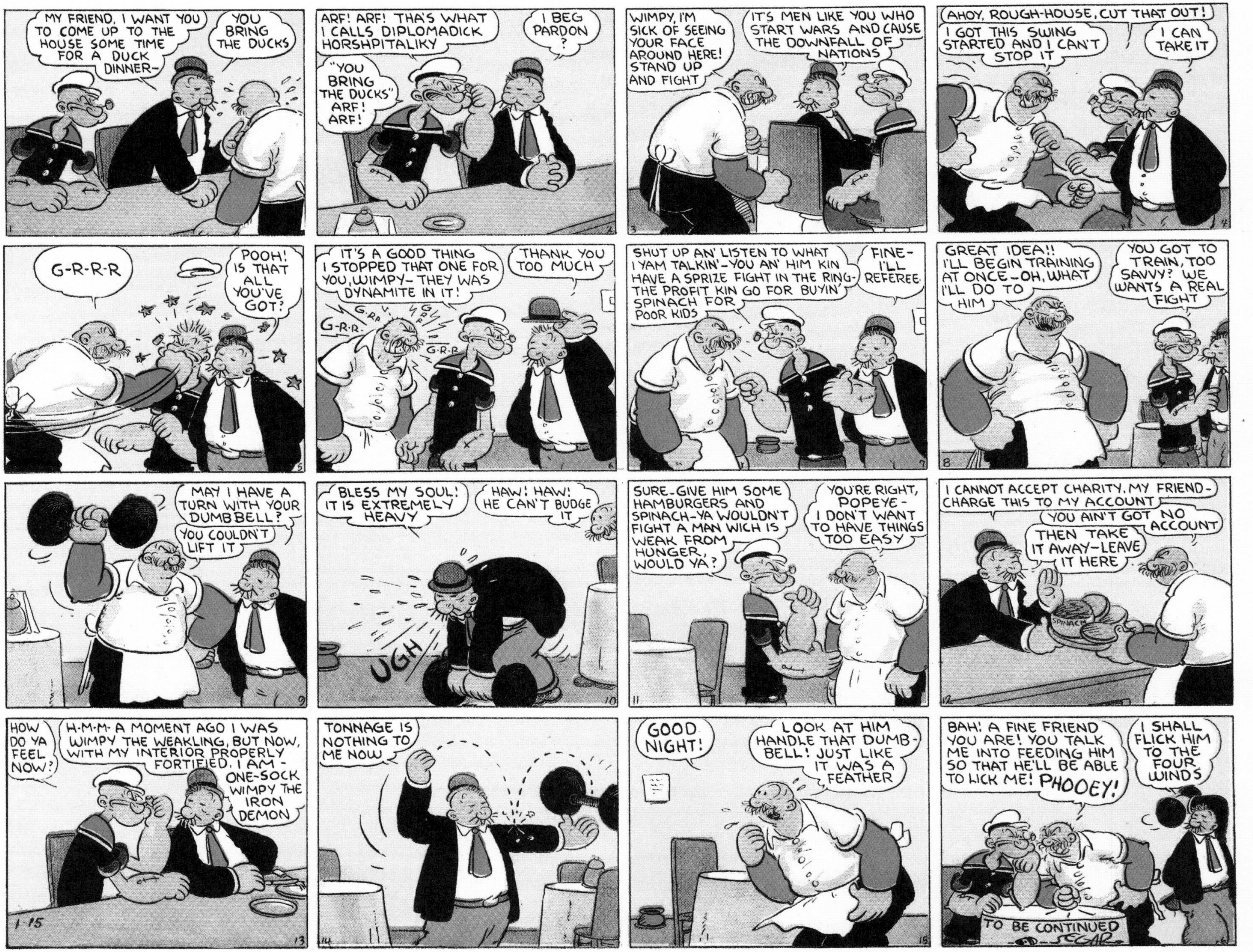
MY FRIEND, I WANT YOU TO COME UP TO THE HOUSE SOME TIME FOR A DUCK DINNER-
YOU BRING THE DUCKS
ARF! ARF! THA'S WHAT I CALLS DIPLOMADICK HORSHPITALIKY
"YOU BRING THE DUCKS" ARF! ARF!
I BEG PARDON ?
WIMPY, I'M SICK OF SEEING YOUR FACE AROUND HERE! STAND UP AND FIGHT
IT'S MEN LIKE YOU WHO START WARS AND CAUSE THE DOWNFALL OF NATIONS
AHOY, ROUGH-HOUSE, CUT THAT OUT!
I GOT THIS SWING STARTED AND I CAN'T STOP IT
I CAN TAKE IT
G-R-R-R
POOH! IS THAT ALL YOU'VE GOT?
IT'S A GOOD THING I STOPPED THAT ONE FOR YOU, WIMPY- THEY WAS DYNAMITE IN IT!
THANK YOU TOO MUCH
SHUT UP AN' LISTEN TO WHAT I YAM TALKIN'-YOU AN' HIM KIN HAVE A SPRIZE FIGHT IN THE RING- THE PROFIT KIN GO FOR BUYIN' SPINACH FOR POOR KIDS
FINE- I'LL REFEREE.
GREAT IDEA!! I'LL BEGIN TRAINING AT ONCE-OH, WHAT I'LL DO TO HIM
YOU GOT TO TRAIN, TOO SAVVY? WE WANTS A REAL FIGHT
MAY I HAVE A TURN WITH YOUR DUMBBELL?
YOU COULDN'T LIFT IT
BLESS MY SOUL! IT IS EXTREMELY HEAVY
HAW! HAW! HE CAN'T BUDGE IT
UGH
SURE-GIVE HIM SOME HAMBURGERS AND SPINACH-YA WOULDN'T FIGHT A MAN WICH IS WEAK FROM HUNGER, WOULD YA?
YOU'RE RIGHT, POPEYE- I DON'T WANT TO HAVE THINGS TOO EASY
I CANNOT ACCEPT CHARITY, MY FRIEND- CHARGE THIS TO MY ACCOUNT
YOU AIN'T GOT NO ACCOUNT
THEN TAKE IT AWAY-LEAVE IT HERE
SPINACH
HOW DO YA FEEL NOW?
H-M-M- A MOMENT AGO I WAS WIMPY THE WEAKLING, BUT NOW, WITH MY INTERIOR PROPERLY FORTIFIED, I AM - ONE-SOCK WIMPY THE IRON DEMON
1-15
TONNAGE IS NOTHING TO ME NOW
GOOD NIGHT!
LOOK AT HIM HANDLE THAT DUMB-BELL! JUST LIKE IT WAS A FEATHER
BAH! A FINE FRIEND YOU ARE! YOU TALK ME INTO FEEDING HIM SO THAT HE'LL BE ABLE TO LICK ME! PHOOEY!
I SHALL FLICK HIM TO THE FOUR WINDS
TO BE CONTINUED
SEGAR

54. January 15, 1933

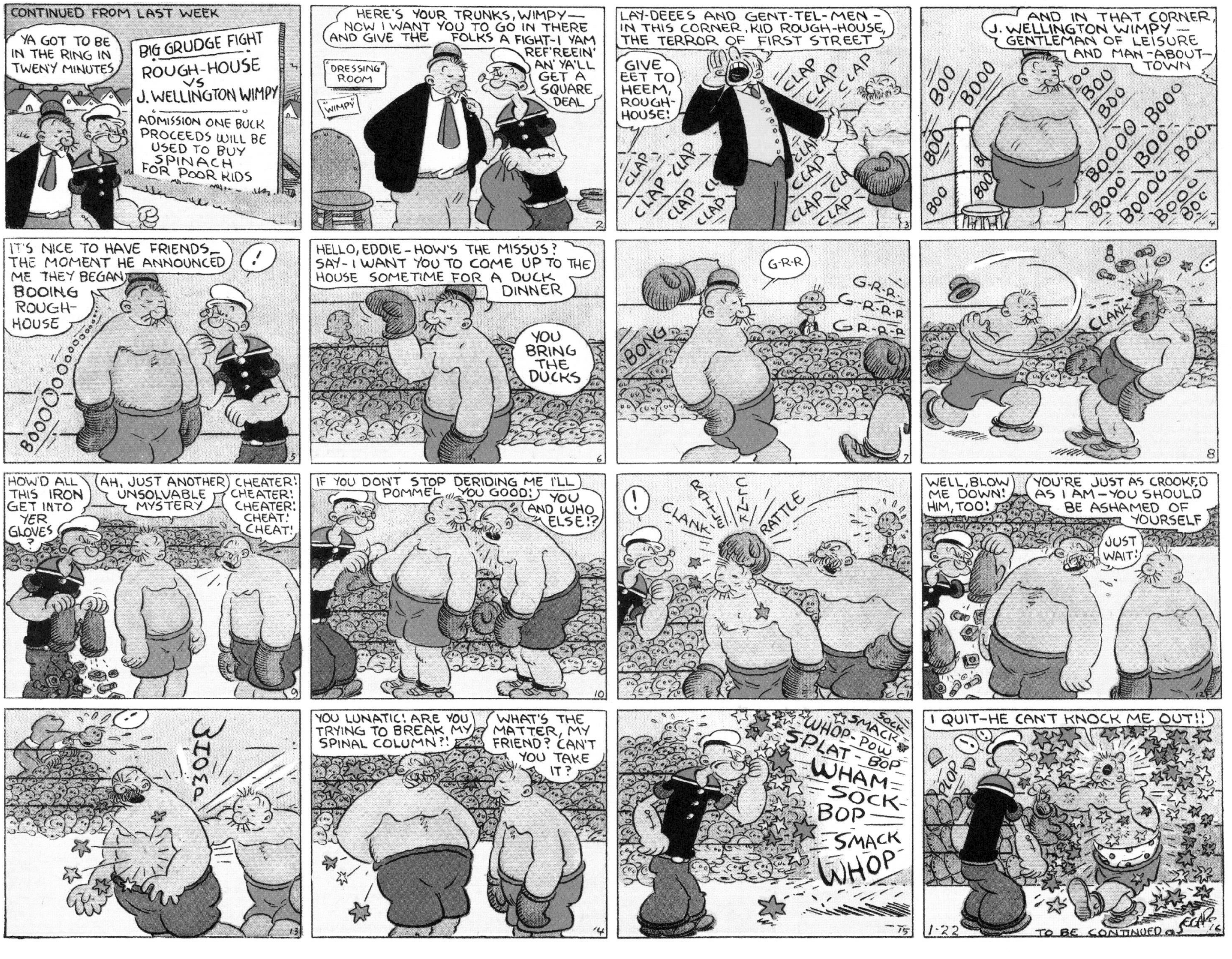

CONTINUED FROM LAST WEEK
YA GOT TO BE IN THE RING IN TWEN'Y MINUTES
BIG GRUDGE FIGHT
ROUGH-HOUSE VS J. WELLINGTON WIMPY
ADMISSION ONE BUCK
PROCEEDS WILL BE USED TO BUY SPINACH FOR POOR KIDS
HERE'S YOUR TRUNKS, WIMPY— NOW I WANT YOU TO GO IN THERE AND GIVE THE FOLKS A FIGHT-I YAM REF'REEIN' AN' YA'LL GET A SQUARE DEAL
"DRESSING" ROOM
"WIMPY"
LAY-DEEES AND GENT-TEL-MEN— IN THIS CORNER, KID ROUGH-HOUSE, THE TERROR OF FIRST STREET
GIVE EET TO HEEM, ROUGH-HOUSE!
CLAP CLAP CLAP
AND IN THAT CORNER, J. WELLINGTON WIMPY— GENTLEMAN OF LEISURE AND MAN-ABOUT-TOWN
BOO BOOO BOOOO
IT'S NICE TO HAVE FRIENDS— THE MOMENT HE ANNOUNCED ME THEY BEGAN BOOING ROUGH-HOUSE
!
BOOOOOOOOO
HELLO, EDDIE-HOW'S THE MISSUS? SAY-I WANT YOU TO COME UP TO THE HOUSE SOMETIME FOR A DUCK DINNER
YOU BRING THE DUCKS
G-R-R
G-R-R- G-R-R-R GR-R-R
BONG
CLANK
HOW'D ALL THIS IRON GET INTO YER GLOVES?
AH, JUST ANOTHER UNSOLVABLE MYSTERY
CHEATER! CHEATER! CHEATER! CHEAT! CHEAT!
IF YOU DON'T STOP DERIDING ME I'LL POMMEL YOU GOOD!
YOU AND WHO ELSE!?
!
CLANK RATTLE CLINK RATTLE
WELL, BLOW ME DOWN! HIM, TOO!
YOU'RE JUST AS CROOKED AS I AM—YOU SHOULD BE ASHAMED OF YOURSELF
JUST WAIT!
WHOMP
YOU LUNATIC! ARE YOU TRYING TO BREAK MY SPINAL COLUMN?!
WHAT'S THE MATTER, MY FRIEND? CAN'T YOU TAKE IT?
SOCK SMACK WHOP-POW SPLAT-BOP WHAM SOCK BOP SMACK WHOP
I QUIT—HE CAN'T KNOCK ME OUT!!
PLOP
1-22
TO BE CONTINUED
SEGAR

55. January 22, 1933

56. January 29, 1933

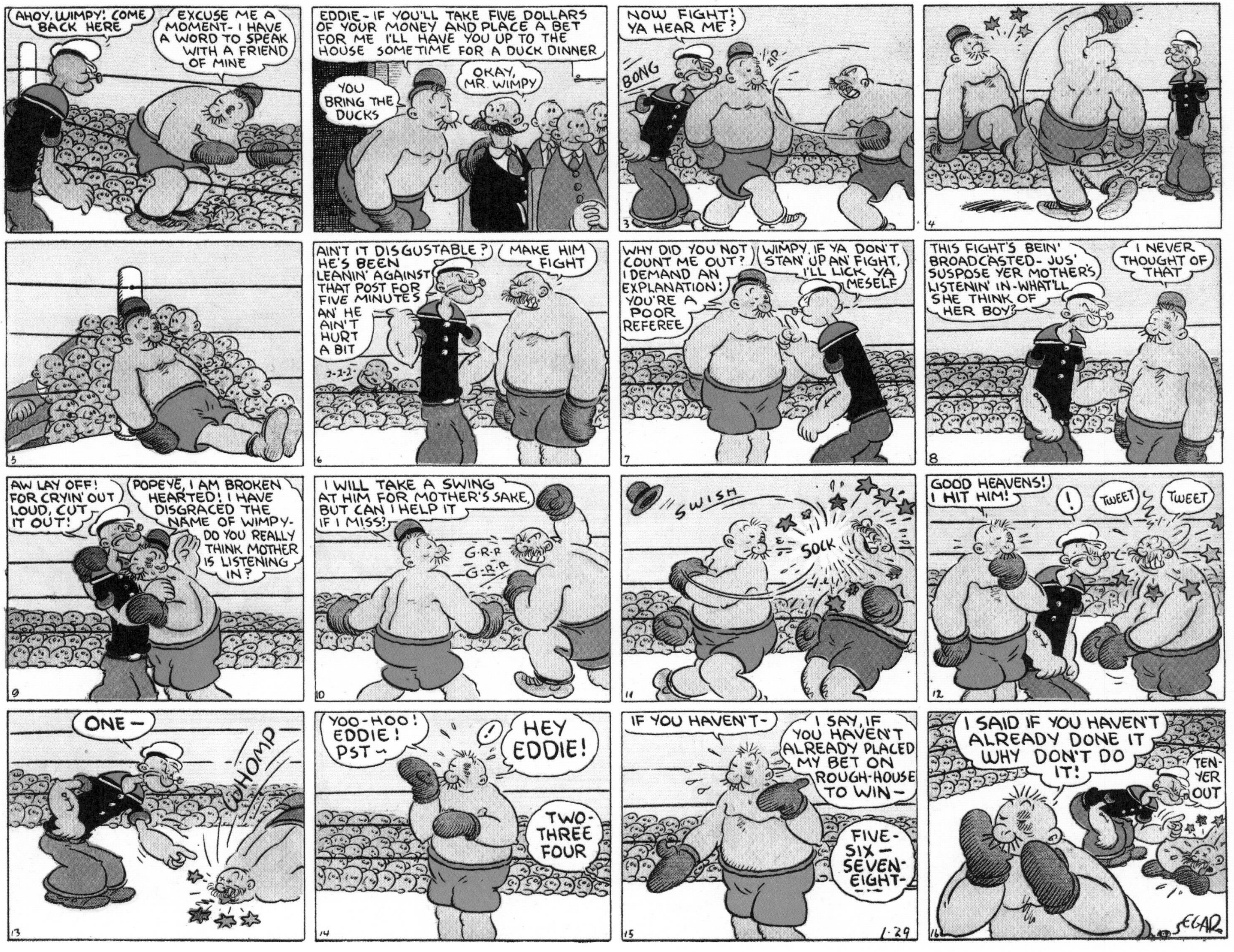

AHOY, WIMPY! COME BACK HERE
EXCUSE ME A MOMENT- I HAVE A WORD TO SPEAK WITH A FRIEND OF MINE
EDDIE - IF YOU'LL TAKE FIVE DOLLARS OF YOUR MONEY AND PLACE A BET FOR ME I'LL HAVE YOU UP TO THE HOUSE SOMETIME FOR A DUCK DINNER
YOU BRING THE DUCKS
OKAY, MR. WIMPY
NOW FIGHT! YA HEAR ME?
BONG
AIN'T IT DISGUSTABLE? HE'S BEEN LEANIN' AGAINST THAT POST FOR FIVE MINUTES AN' HE AIN'T HURT A BIT
MAKE HIM FIGHT
Z-Z-Z
WHY DID YOU NOT COUNT ME OUT? I DEMAND AN EXPLANATION: YOU'RE A POOR REFEREE
WIMPY, IF YA DON'T STAN' UP AN' FIGHT, I'LL LICK YA MESELF
THIS FIGHT'S BEIN' BROADCASTED- JUS' SUSPOSE YER MOTHER'S LISTENIN' IN-WHAT'LL SHE THINK OF HER BOY?
I NEVER THOUGHT OF THAT
AW LAY OFF! FOR CRYIN' OUT LOUD, CUT IT OUT!
POPEYE, I AM BROKEN HEARTED! I HAVE DISGRACED THE NAME OF WIMPY- DO YOU REALLY THINK MOTHER IS LISTENING IN?
I WILL TAKE A SWING AT HIM FOR MOTHER'S SAKE, BUT CAN I HELP IT IF I MISS?
G-R-R
G-R-R
SWISH
SOCK
GOOD HEAVENS! I HIT HIM!
!
TWEET
TWEET
ONE -
WHOMP
YOO-HOO! EDDIE! PST -
!
HEY EDDIE!
TWO- THREE FOUR
IF YOU HAVEN'T-
I SAY, IF YOU HAVEN'T ALREADY PLACED MY BET ON ROUGH-HOUSE TO WIN-
FIVE- SIX- SEVEN- EIGHT-
1-29
I SAID IF YOU HAVEN'T ALREADY DONE IT WHY DON'T DO IT!
TEN- YER OUT
SEGAR

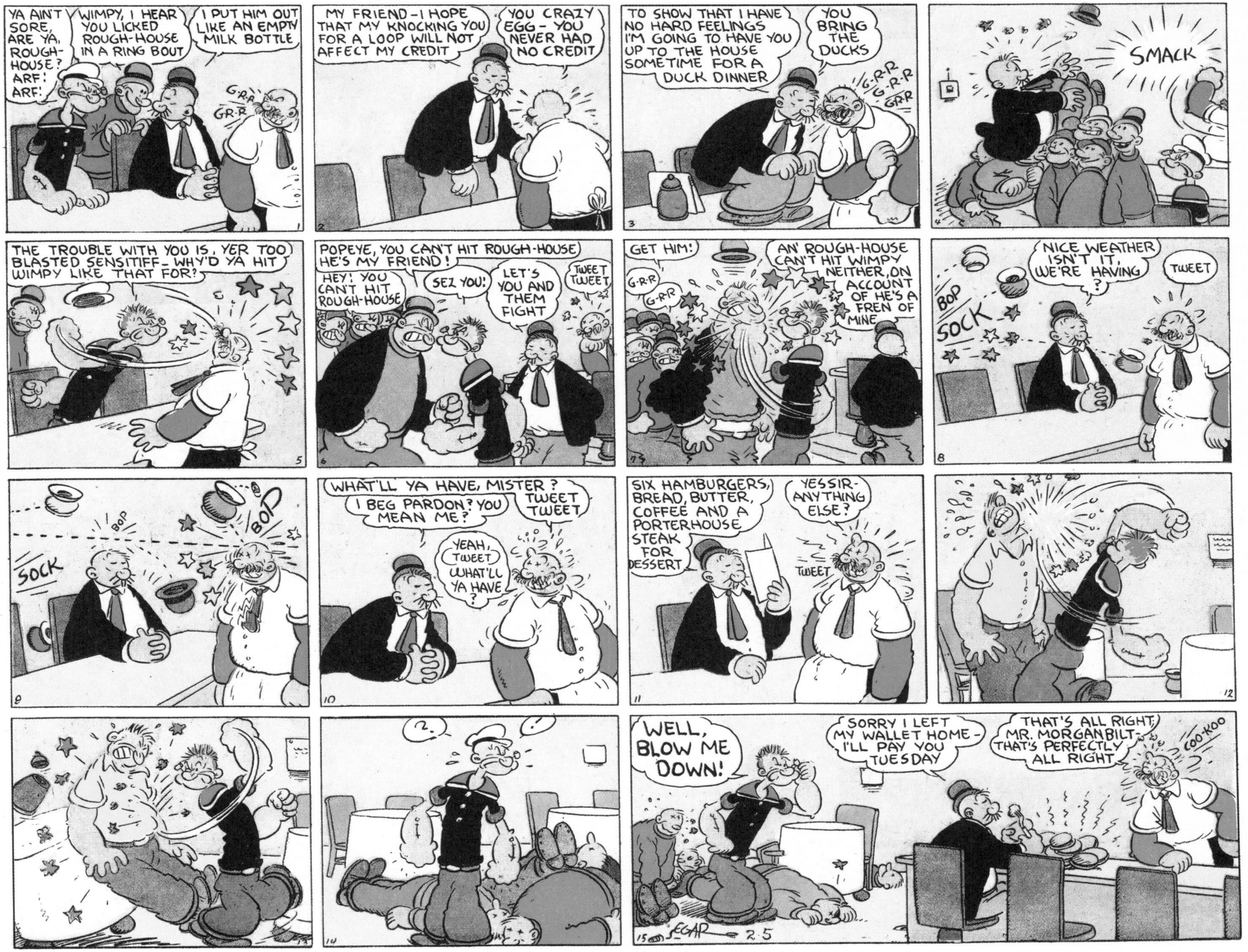
YA AIN'T SORE, ARE YA, ROUGH-HOUSE? ARF! ARF!
WIMPY, I HEAR YOU LICKED ROUGH-HOUSE IN A RING BOUT
I PUT HIM OUT LIKE AN EMPTY MILK BOTTLE
G-R-R
GR-R
MY FRIEND—I HOPE THAT MY KNOCKING YOU FOR A LOOP WILL NOT AFFECT MY CREDIT
YOU CRAZY EGG—YOU NEVER HAD NO CREDIT
TO SHOW THAT I HAVE NO HARD FEELINGS I'M GOING TO HAVE YOU UP TO THE HOUSE SOMETIME FOR A DUCK DINNER
YOU BRING THE DUCKS
G-R-R G-R-R GR-R
SMACK
THE TROUBLE WITH YOU IS, YER TOO BLASTED SENSITIFF— WHY'D YA HIT WIMPY LIKE THAT FOR?
POPEYE, YOU CAN'T HIT ROUGH-HOUSE HE'S MY FRIEND!
HEY! YOU CAN'T HIT ROUGH-HOUSE
SEZ YOU!
LET'S YOU AND THEM FIGHT
TWEET TWEET
GET HIM!
G-R-R
G-R-R
AN' ROUGH-HOUSE CAN'T HIT WIMPY NEITHER, ON ACCOUNT OF HE'S A FREN OF MINE
NICE WEATHER ISN'T IT, WE'RE HAVING?
TWEET
BOP
SOCK
SOCK
BOP
BOP
WHAT'LL YA HAVE, MISTER?
I BEG PARDON? YOU MEAN ME?
TWEET TWEET
YEAH, TWEET WHAT'LL YA HAVE?
SIX HAMBURGERS, BREAD, BUTTER, COFFEE AND A PORTERHOUSE STEAK FOR DESSERT
YESSIR- ANYTHING ELSE?
TWEET
?
!
WELL, BLOW ME DOWN!
SORRY I LEFT MY WALLET HOME— I'LL PAY YOU TUESDAY
THAT'S ALL RIGHT, MR. MORGANBILT— THAT'S PERFECTLY ALL RIGHT
COO-KOO
SEGAR 2.5

57. February 5, 1933

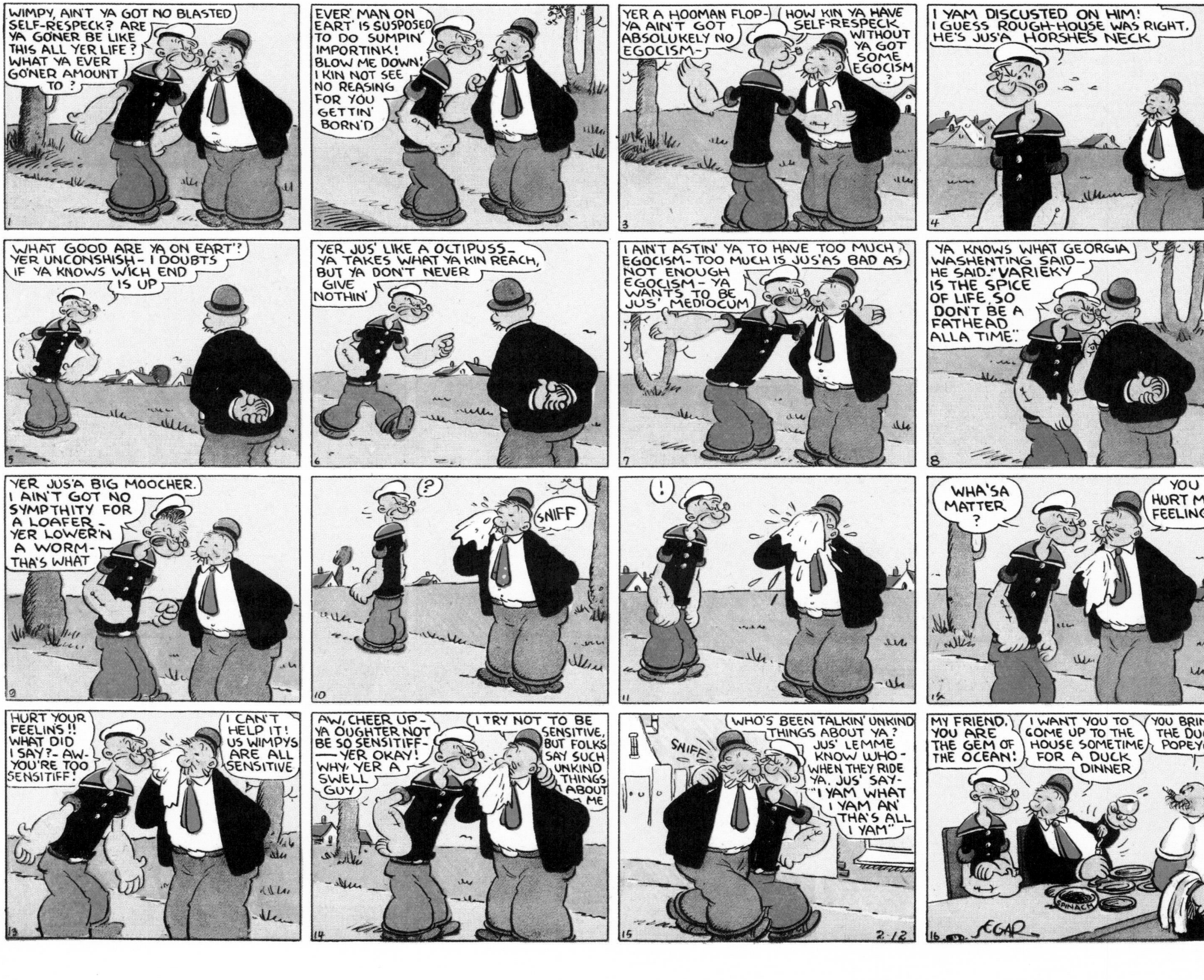
WIMPY, AIN'T YA GOT NO BLASTED SELF-RESPECK? ARE YA GONER BE LIKE THIS ALL YER LIFE? WHAT YA EVER GONER AMOUNT TO?
EVER' MAN ON EART' IS SUSPOSED TO DO SUMPIN' IMPORTINK! BLOW ME DOWN! I KIN NOT SEE NO REASING FOR YOU GETTIN' BORN'D
YER A HOOMAN FLOP- YA AIN'T GOT ABSOLUKELY NO EGOCISM-
HOW KIN YA HAVE SELF-RESPECK WITHOUT YA GOT SOME EGOCISM?
I YAM DISCUSTED ON HIM! I GUESS ROUGH-HOUSE WAS RIGHT. HE'S JUS'A HORSHES NECK
WHAT GOOD ARE YA ON EART'? YER UNCONSHISH- I DOUBTS IF YA KNOWS WICH END IS UP
YER JUS' LIKE A OCTIPUSS- YA TAKES WHAT YA KIN REACH, BUT YA DON'T NEVER GIVE NOTHIN'
I AIN'T ASTIN' YA TO HAVE TOO MUCH EGOCISM- TOO MUCH IS JUS'AS BAD AS NOT ENOUGH EGOCISM- YA WANTS TO BE JUS' MEDIOCUM
YA KNOWS WHAT GEORGIA WASHENTING SAID- HE SAID-"VARIEKY IS THE SPICE OF LIFE, SO DON'T BE A FATHEAD ALLA TIME."
YER JUS'A BIG MOOCHER. I AIN'T GOT NO SYMPTHITY FOR A LOAFER- YER LOWER'N A WORM- THA'S WHAT
?
SNIFF
!
WHA'SA MATTER?
YOU HURT MY FEELINGS
HURT YOUR FEELINS!! WHAT DID I SAY?- AW- YOU'RE TOO SENSITIFF!
I CAN'T HELP IT! US WIMPYS ARE ALL SENSITIVE
AW, CHEER UP- YA OUGHTER NOT BE SO SENSITIFF- —YER OKAY! WHY, YER A SWELL GUY
I TRY NOT TO BE SENSITIVE, BUT FOLKS SAY SUCH UNKIND THINGS ABOUT ME
SNIFF
WHO'S BEEN TALKIN' UNKIND THINGS ABOUT YA? JUS' LEMME KNOW WHO- WHEN THEY RIDE YA. JUS' SAY- "I YAM WHAT I YAM AN' THA'S ALL I YAM"
2-12
MY FRIEND, YOU ARE THE GEM OF THE OCEAN!
I WANT YOU TO COME UP TO THE HOUSE SOMETIME FOR A DUCK DINNER
YOU BRING THE DUCKS POPEYE
SPINACH
SEGAR

58. February 12, 1933

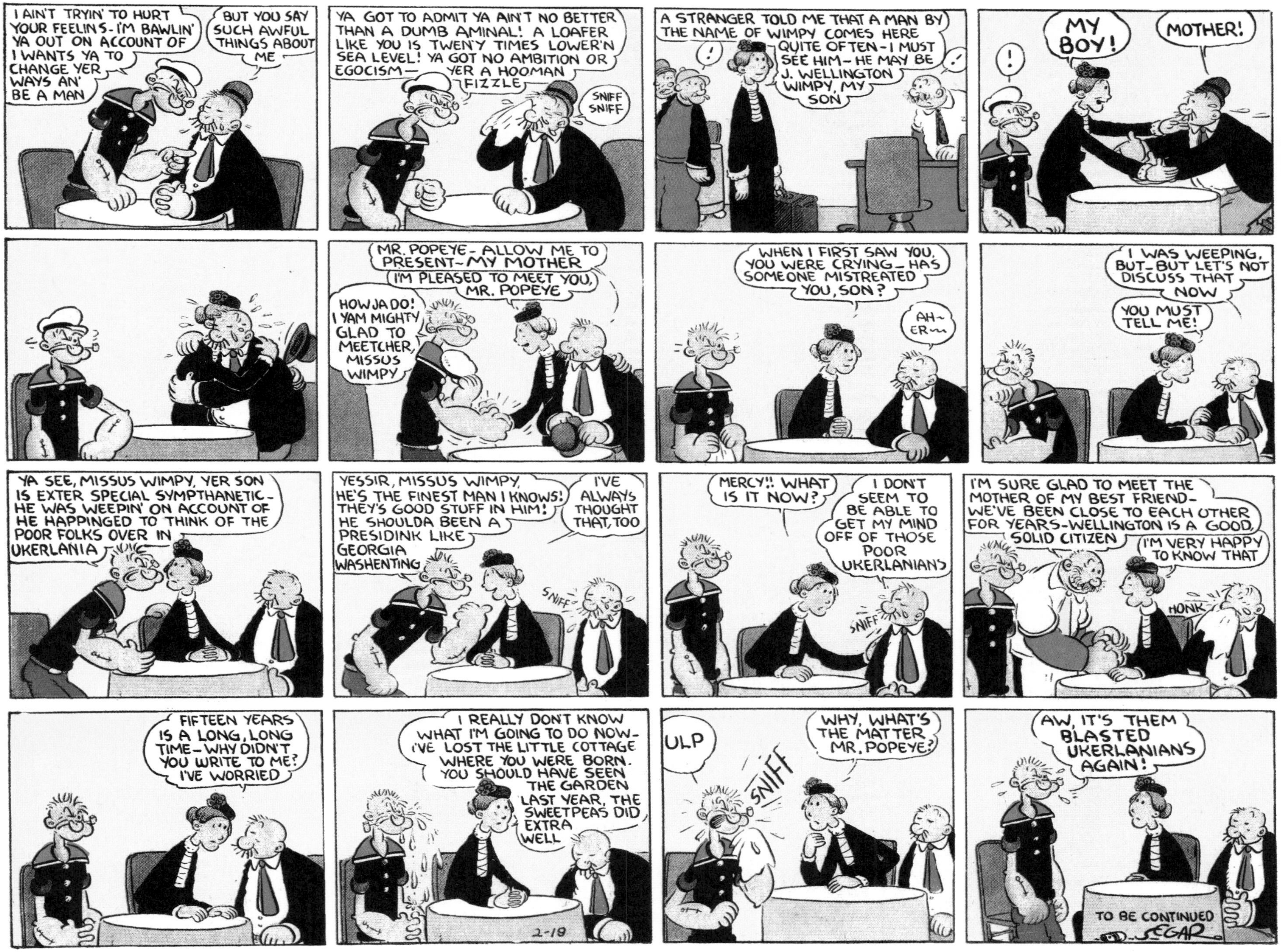
I AIN'T TRYIN' TO HURT YOUR FEELIN'S - I'M BAWLIN' YA OUT ON ACCOUNT OF I WANTS YA TO CHANGE YER WAYS AN' BE A MAN
BUT YOU SAY SUCH AWFUL THINGS ABOUT ME
YA GOT TO ADMIT YA AIN'T NO BETTER THAN A DUMB AMINAL! A LOAFER LIKE YOU IS TWEN'Y TIMES LOWER'N SEA LEVEL! YA GOT NO AMBITION OR EGOCISM — YER A HOOMAN FIZZLE
SNIFF SNIFF
A STRANGER TOLD ME THAT A MAN BY THE NAME OF WIMPY COMES HERE QUITE OFTEN - I MUST SEE HIM - HE MAY BE J. WELLINGTON WIMPY, MY SON
!
!
!
MY BOY!
MOTHER!
MR. POPEYE - ALLOW ME TO PRESENT - MY MOTHER
I'M PLEASED TO MEET YOU, MR. POPEYE
HOWJA DO! I YAM MIGHTY GLAD TO MEETCHER, MISSUS WIMPY
WHEN I FIRST SAW YOU, YOU WERE CRYING - HAS SOMEONE MISTREATED YOU, SON?
AH - ER ~
I WAS WEEPING, BUT - BUT LET'S NOT DISCUSS THAT NOW
YOU MUST TELL ME!
YA SEE, MISSUS WIMPY, YER SON IS EXTER SPECIAL SYMPTHANETIC - HE WAS WEEPIN' ON ACCOUNT OF HE HAPPINGED TO THINK OF THE POOR FOLKS OVER IN UKERLANIA
YESSIR, MISSUS WIMPY, HE'S THE FINEST MAN I KNOWS! THEY'S GOOD STUFF IN HIM! HE SHOULDA BEEN A PRESIDINK LIKE GEORGIA WASHENTING
I'VE ALWAYS THOUGHT THAT, TOO
SNIFF
MERCY!! WHAT IS IT NOW?
I DON'T SEEM TO BE ABLE TO GET MY MIND OFF OF THOSE POOR UKERLANIANS
SNIFF
I'M SURE GLAD TO MEET THE MOTHER OF MY BEST FRIEND - WE'VE BEEN CLOSE TO EACH OTHER FOR YEARS - WELLINGTON IS A GOOD, SOLID CITIZEN
I'M VERY HAPPY TO KNOW THAT
HONK
FIFTEEN YEARS IS A LONG, LONG TIME - WHY DIDN'T YOU WRITE TO ME? I'VE WORRIED
I REALLY DON'T KNOW WHAT I'M GOING TO DO NOW - I'VE LOST THE LITTLE COTTAGE WHERE YOU WERE BORN. YOU SHOULD HAVE SEEN THE GARDEN LAST YEAR, THE SWEETPEAS DID EXTRA WELL
2-18
ULP
SNIFF
WHY, WHAT'S THE MATTER MR. POPEYE?
AW, IT'S THEM BLASTED UKERLANIANS AGAIN!
TO BE CONTINUED
SEGAR

59. February 19, 1933

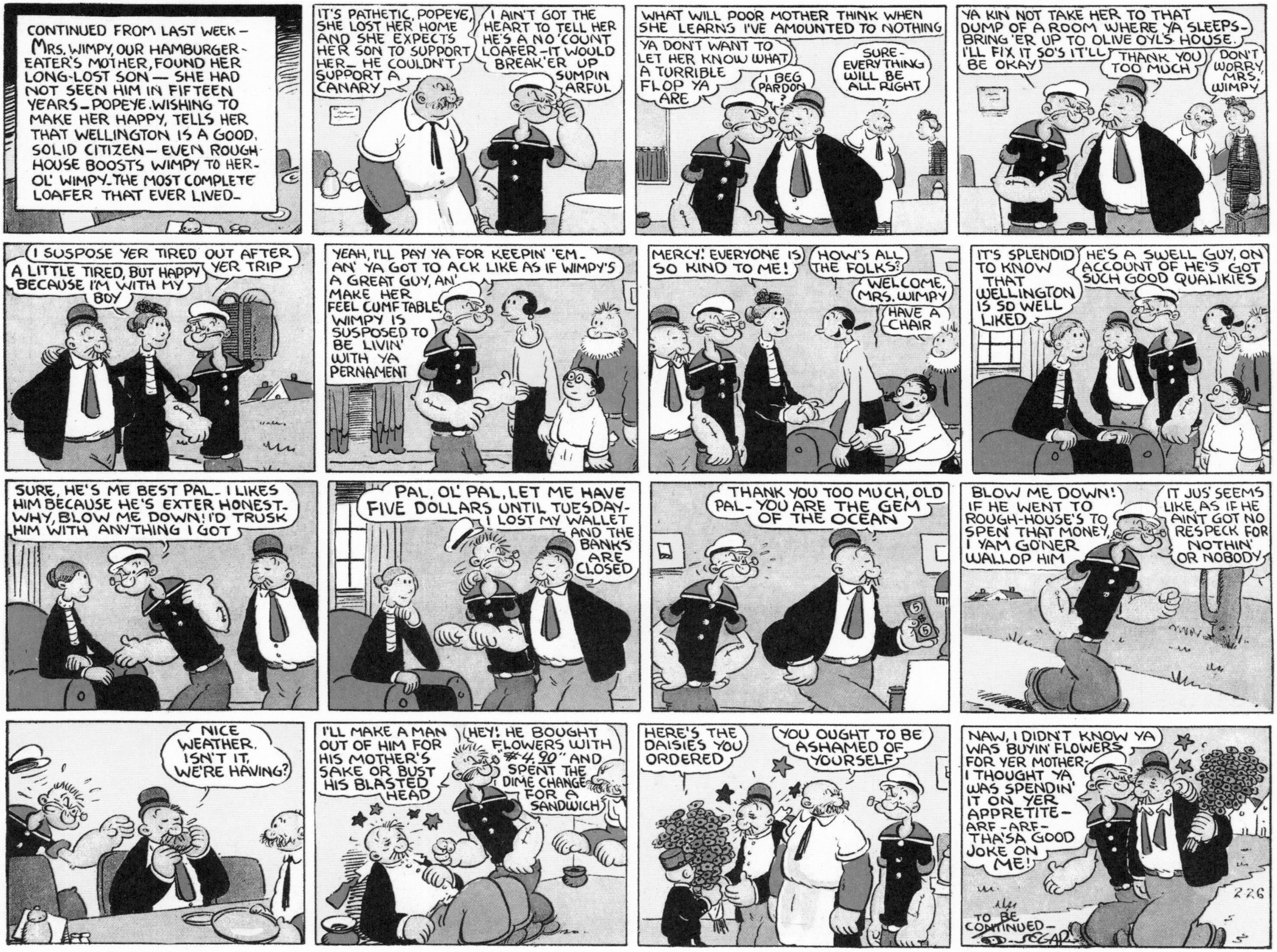
CONTINUED FROM LAST WEEK – MRS. WIMPY, OUR HAMBURGER-EATER'S MOTHER, FOUND HER LONG-LOST SON — SHE HAD NOT SEEN HIM IN FIFTEEN YEARS _ POPEYE, WISHING TO MAKE HER HAPPY, TELLS HER THAT WELLINGTON IS A GOOD, SOLID CITIZEN – EVEN ROUGH-HOUSE BOOSTS WIMPY TO HER-OL' WIMPY_THE MOST COMPLETE LOAFER THAT EVER LIVED–
IT'S PATHETIC, POPEYE, SHE LOST HER HOME AND SHE EXPECTS HER SON TO SUPPORT HER_ HE COULDN'T SUPPORT A CANARY
I AIN'T GOT THE HEART TO TELL HER HE'S A NO 'COUNT LOAFER – IT WOULD BREAK 'ER UP
SUMPIN ARFUL
WHAT WILL POOR MOTHER THINK WHEN SHE LEARNS I'VE AMOUNTED TO NOTHING
YA DON'T WANT TO LET HER KNOW WHAT A TURRIBLE FLOP YA ARE
I BEG PARDON ?
SURE – EVERYTHING WILL BE ALL RIGHT
YA KIN NOT TAKE HER TO THAT DUMP OF A ROOM WHERE YA SLEEPS-BRING 'ER UP TO OLIVE OYL'S HOUSE. I'LL FIX IT SO'S IT'LL BE OKAY
THANK YOU TOO MUCH
DON'T WORRY, MRS. WIMPY
I SUSPOSE YER TIRED OUT AFTER YER TRIP
A LITTLE TIRED, BUT HAPPY BECAUSE I'M WITH MY BOY
YEAH, I'LL PAY YA FOR KEEPIN' 'EM_ AN' YA GOT TO ACK LIKE AS IF WIMPY'S A GREAT GUY, AN' MAKE HER FEEL CUMF'TABLE. WIMPY IS SUSPOSED TO BE LIVIN' WITH YA PERNAMENT
MERCY! EVERYONE IS SO KIND TO ME!
HOW'S ALL THE FOLKS?
WELCOME, MRS. WIMPY
HAVE A CHAIR
IT'S SPLENDID TO KNOW THAT WELLINGTON IS SO WELL LIKED
HE'S A SWELL GUY, ON ACCOUNT OF HE'S GOT SUCH GOOD QUALIKIES
SURE, HE'S ME BEST PAL – I LIKES HIM BECAUSE HE'S EXTER HONEST-WHY, BLOW ME DOWN! I'D TRUSK HIM WITH ANYTHING I GOT
PAL, OL' PAL, LET ME HAVE FIVE DOLLARS UNTIL TUESDAY – I LOST MY WALLET AND THE BANKS ARE CLOSED
THANK YOU TOO MUCH, OLD PAL – YOU ARE THE GEM OF THE OCEAN
BLOW ME DOWN! IF HE WENT TO ROUGH-HOUSE'S TO SPEN' THAT MONEY, I YAM GO'NER WALLOP HIM
IT JUS' SEEMS LIKE, AS IF HE AIN'T GOT NO RESPECK FOR NOTHIN' OR NOBODY
NICE WEATHER, ISN'T IT, WE'RE HAVING?
I'LL MAKE A MAN OUT OF HIM FOR HIS MOTHER'S SAKE OR BUST HIS BLASTED HEAD
HEY! HE BOUGHT FLOWERS WITH "$4.90" AND SPENT THE DIME CHANGE FOR A SANDWICH
HERE'S THE DAISIES YOU ORDERED
YOU OUGHT TO BE ASHAMED OF YOURSELF
NAW, I DIDN'T KNOW YA WAS BUYIN' FLOWERS FOR YER MOTHER – I THOUGHT YA WAS SPENDIN' IT ON YER APPRETITE – ARF-ARF – THA'SA GOOD JOKE ON ME!
2-26
TO BE CONTINUED –
SEGAR

60. February 26, 1933

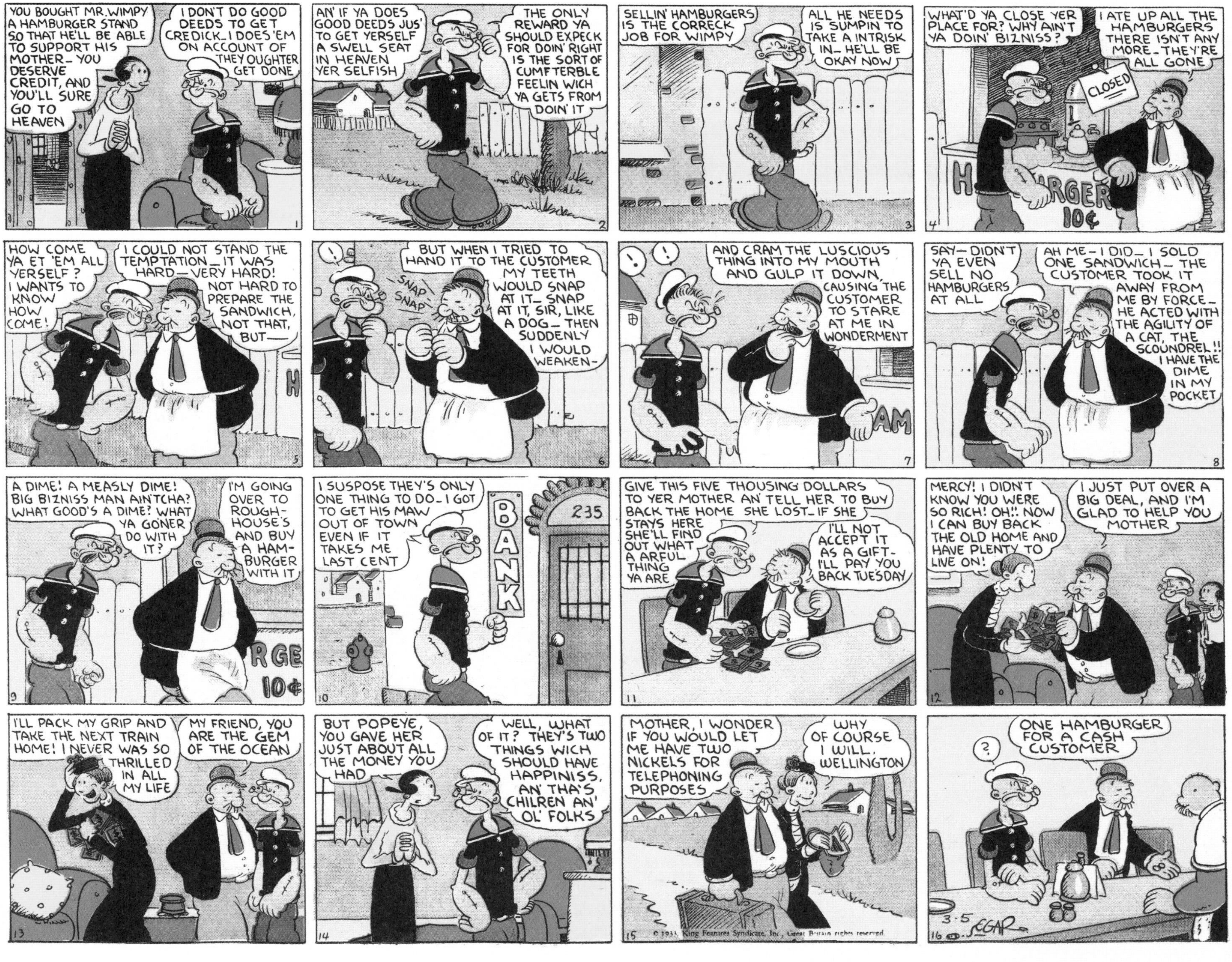
YOU BOUGHT MR. WIMPY A HAMBURGER STAND SO THAT HE'LL BE ABLE TO SUPPORT HIS MOTHER— YOU DESERVE CREDIT, AND YOU'LL SURE GO TO HEAVEN
I DON'T DO GOOD DEEDS TO GET CREDICK_I DOES 'EM ON ACCOUNT OF THEY OUGHTER GET DONE
AN' IF YA DOES GOOD DEEDS JUS' TO GET YERSELF A SWELL SEAT IN HEAVEN YER SELFISH
THE ONLY REWARD YA SHOULD EXPECK FOR DOIN' RIGHT IS THE SORT OF CUMFTERBLE FEELIN WICH YA GETS FROM DOIN' IT
SELLIN' HAMBURGERS IS THE CORRECK JOB FOR WIMPY
ALL HE NEEDS IS SUMPIN TO TAKE A INTRISK IN— HE'LL BE OKAY NOW
WHAT'D YA CLOSE YER PLACE FOR? WHY AIN'T YA DOIN' BIZNISS?
I ATE UP ALL THE HAMBURGERS THERE ISN'T ANY MORE— THEY'RE ALL GONE
CLOSED
HAMBURGER
10¢
HOW COME YA ET 'EM ALL YERSELF? I WANTS TO KNOW HOW COME!
I COULD NOT STAND THE TEMPTATION_IT WAS HARD— VERY HARD! NOT HARD TO PREPARE THE SANDWICH, NOT THAT, BUT—
!
BUT WHEN I TRIED TO HAND IT TO THE CUSTOMER MY TEETH WOULD SNAP AT IT_ SNAP AT IT, SIR, LIKE A DOG— THEN SUDDENLY I WOULD WEAKEN—
SNAP SNAP
! !
AND CRAM THE LUSCIOUS THING INTO MY MOUTH AND GULP IT DOWN, CAUSING THE CUSTOMER TO STARE AT ME IN WONDERMENT
SAY— DIDN'T YA EVEN SELL NO HAMBURGERS AT ALL
AH ME— I DID_ I SOLD ONE SANDWICH— THE CUSTOMER TOOK IT AWAY FROM ME BY FORCE— HE ACTED WITH THE AGILITY OF A CAT, THE SCOUNDREL!! I HAVE THE DIME IN MY POCKET
A DIME! A MEASLY DIME! BIG BIZNISS MAN AIN'TCHA? WHAT GOOD'S A DIME? WHAT YA GONER DO WITH IT?
I'M GOING OVER TO ROUGH-HOUSE'S AND BUY A HAMBURGER WITH IT
I SUSPOSE THEY'S ONLY ONE THING TO DO_I GOT TO GET HIS MAW OUT OF TOWN EVEN IF IT TAKES ME LAST CENT
BANK
235
GIVE THIS FIVE THOUSING DOLLARS TO YER MOTHER AN' TELL HER TO BUY BACK THE HOME SHE LOST_IF SHE STAYS HERE SHE'LL FIND OUT WHAT A AREFUL THING YA ARE
I'LL NOT ACCEPT IT AS A GIFT— I'LL PAY YOU BACK TUESDAY
MERCY! I DIDN'T KNOW YOU WERE SO RICH! OH!! NOW I CAN BUY BACK THE OLD HOME AND HAVE PLENTY TO LIVE ON!
I JUST PUT OVER A BIG DEAL, AND I'M GLAD TO HELP YOU MOTHER
I'LL PACK MY GRIP AND TAKE THE NEXT TRAIN HOME! I NEVER WAS SO THRILLED IN ALL MY LIFE
MY FRIEND, YOU ARE THE GEM OF THE OCEAN
BUT POPEYE, YOU GAVE HER JUST ABOUT ALL THE MONEY YOU HAD
WELL, WHAT OF IT? THEY'S TWO THINGS WICH SHOULD HAVE HAPPINISS, AN' THA'S CHILREN AN' OL' FOLKS
MOTHER, I WONDER IF YOU WOULD LET ME HAVE TWO NICKELS FOR TELEPHONING PURPOSES
WHY OF COURSE I WILL, WELLINGTON
© 1933, King Features Syndicate, Inc., Great Britain rights reserved.
?
ONE HAMBURGER FOR A CASH CUSTOMER
3-5
SEGAR

61. March 5, 1933

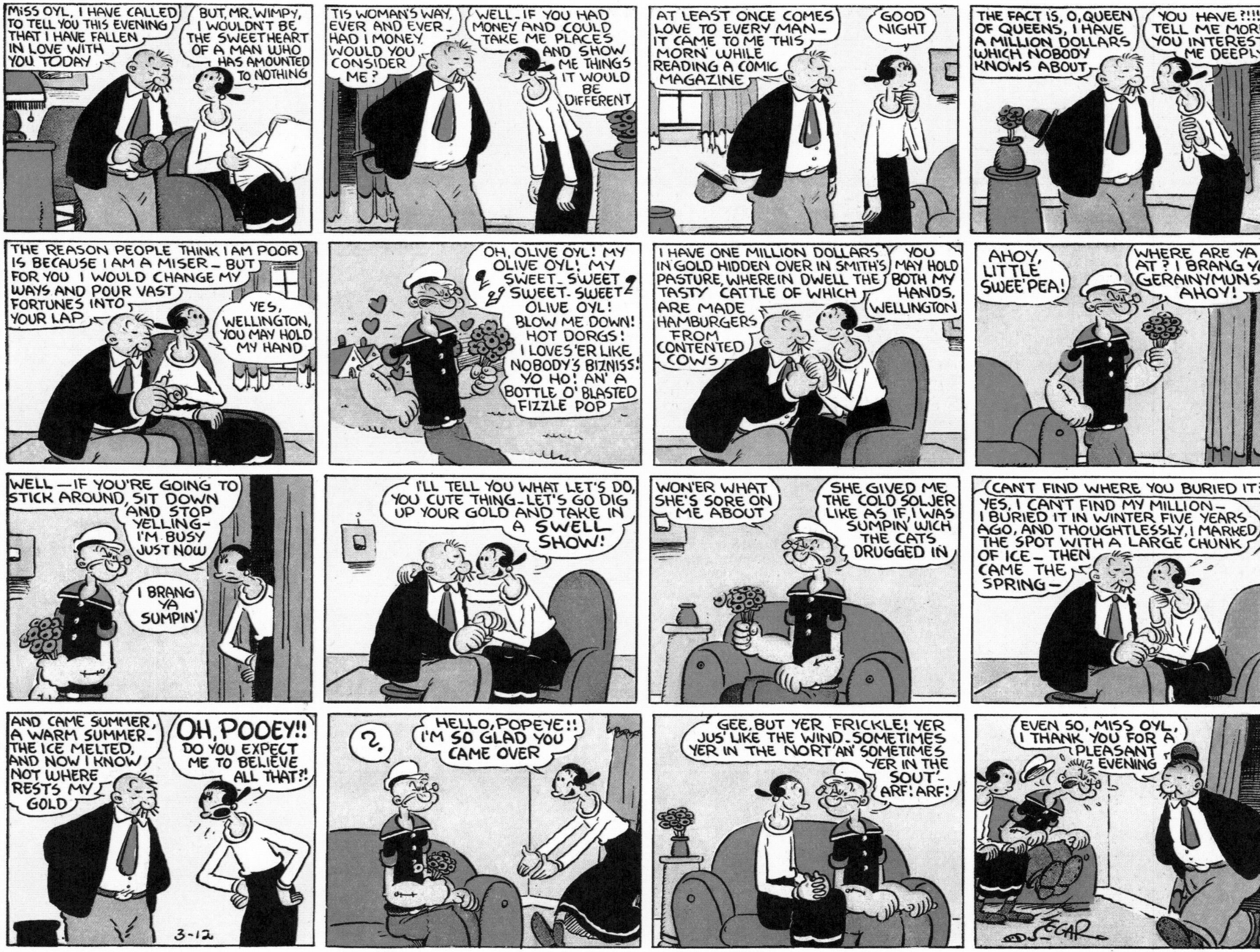
MISS OYL, I HAVE CALLED TO TELL YOU THIS EVENING THAT I HAVE FALLEN IN LOVE WITH YOU TODAY
BUT, MR. WIMPY, I WOULDN'T BE THE SWEETHEART OF A MAN WHO HAS AMOUNTED TO NOTHING
'TIS WOMAN'S WAY, EVER AND EVER - HAD I MONEY, WOULD YOU CONSIDER ME?
WELL - IF YOU HAD MONEY AND COULD TAKE ME PLACES AND SHOW ME THINGS IT WOULD BE DIFFERENT
AT LEAST ONCE COMES LOVE TO EVERY MAN - IT CAME TO ME THIS MORN' WHILE READING A COMIC MAGAZINE
GOOD NIGHT
THE FACT IS, O, QUEEN OF QUEENS, I HAVE A MILLION DOLLARS WHICH NOBODY KNOWS ABOUT
YOU HAVE?!!! TELL ME MORE. YOU INTEREST ME DEEPLY
THE REASON PEOPLE THINK I AM POOR IS BECAUSE I AM A MISER - BUT FOR YOU I WOULD CHANGE MY WAYS AND POUR VAST FORTUNES INTO YOUR LAP
YES, WELLINGTON, YOU MAY HOLD MY HAND
OH, OLIVE OYL! MY OLIVE OYL! MY SWEET - SWEET SWEET - SWEET OLIVE OYL! BLOW ME DOWN! HOT DORGS! I LOVES 'ER LIKE NOBODY'S BIZNISS! YO HO! AN' A BOTTLE O' BLASTED FIZZLE POP
I HAVE ONE MILLION DOLLARS IN GOLD HIDDEN OVER IN SMITH'S PASTURE, WHEREIN DWELL THE TASTY CATTLE OF WHICH ARE MADE HAMBURGERS FROM CONTENTED COWS
YOU MAY HOLD BOTH MY HANDS, WELLINGTON
AHOY, LITTLE SWEE'PEA!
WHERE ARE YA AT? I BRANG YA GERAINYMUNS! AHOY!
WELL - IF YOU'RE GOING TO STICK AROUND, SIT DOWN AND STOP YELLING - I'M BUSY JUST NOW
I BRANG YA SUMPIN'
I'LL TELL YOU WHAT LET'S DO, YOU CUTE THING - LET'S GO DIG UP YOUR GOLD AND TAKE IN A SWELL SHOW!
WON'ER WHAT SHE'S SORE ON ME ABOUT
SHE GIVED ME THE COLD SOLJER LIKE AS IF, I WAS SUMPIN' WICH THE CATS DRUGGED IN
CAN'T FIND WHERE YOU BURIED IT?!!
YES, I CAN'T FIND MY MILLION - I BURIED IT IN WINTER FIVE YEARS AGO, AND THOUGHTLESSLY, I MARKED THE SPOT WITH A LARGE CHUNK OF ICE - THEN CAME THE SPRING -
AND CAME SUMMER, A WARM SUMMER - THE ICE MELTED, AND NOW I KNOW NOT WHERE RESTS MY GOLD
OH, POOEY!! DO YOU EXPECT ME TO BELIEVE ALL THAT?!
3-12
?
HELLO, POPEYE!! I'M SO GLAD YOU CAME OVER
GEE, BUT YER FRICKLE! YER JUS' LIKE THE WIND - SOMETIMES YER IN THE NORT' AN' SOMETIMES YER IN THE SOUT' - ARF! ARF!
EVEN SO, MISS OYL, I THANK YOU FOR A PLEASANT EVENING
SEGAR

62. March 12, 1933

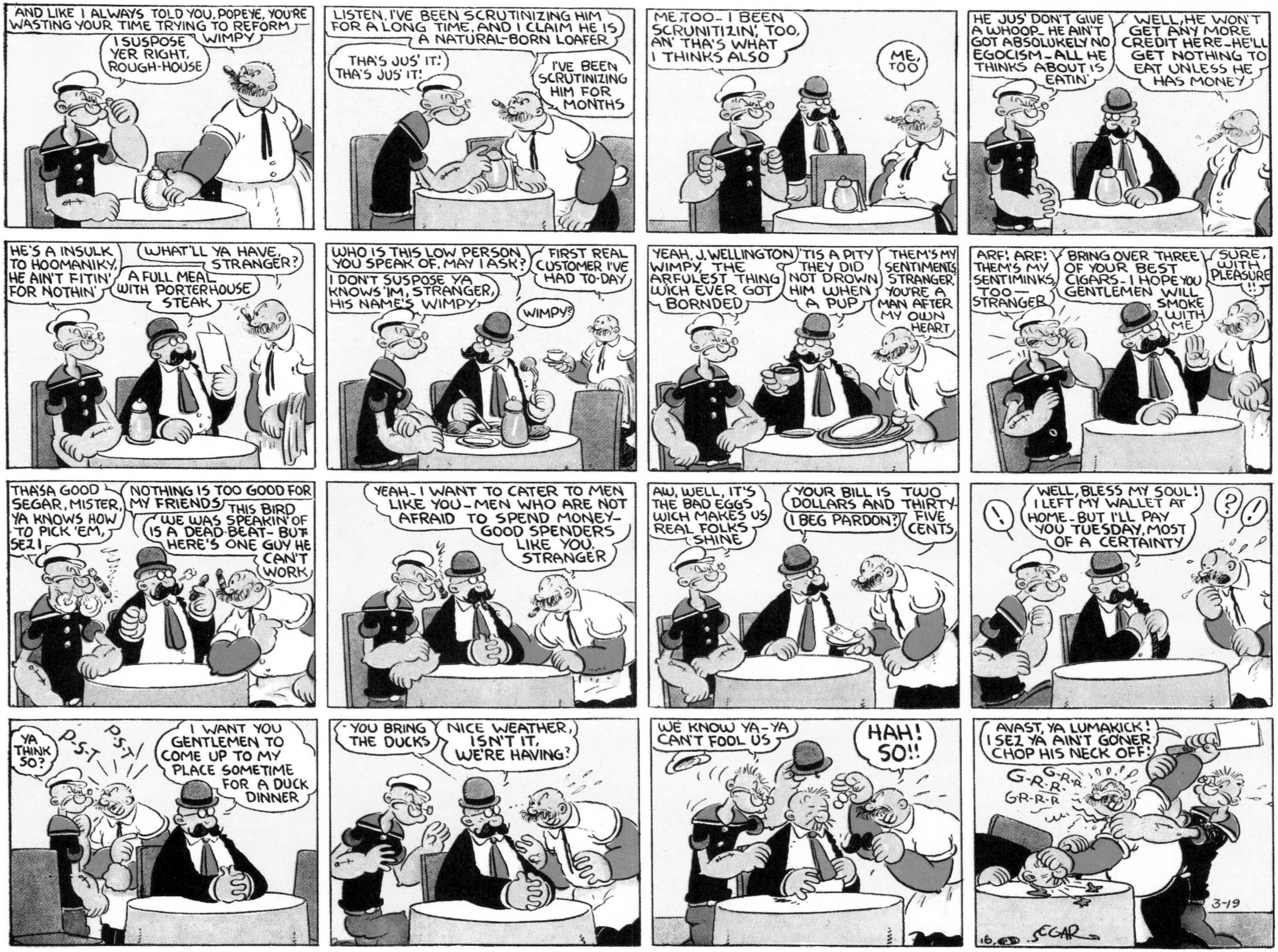
AND LIKE I ALWAYS TOLD YOU, POPEYE, YOU'RE WASTING YOUR TIME TRYING TO REFORM WIMPY
I SUSPOSE YER RIGHT, ROUGH-HOUSE
LISTEN, I'VE BEEN SCRUTINIZING HIM FOR A LONG TIME, AND I CLAIM HE IS A NATURAL-BORN LOAFER
THA'S JUS' IT! THA'S JUS' IT!
I'VE BEEN SCRUTINIZING HIM FOR MONTHS
ME, TOO - I BEEN SCRUNITIZIN', TOO, AN' THA'S WHAT I THINKS ALSO
ME, TOO
HE JUS' DON'T GIVE A WHOOP - HE AIN'T GOT ABSOLUKELY NO EGOCISM - ALL HE THINKS ABOUT IS EATIN'
WELL, HE WON'T GET ANY MORE CREDIT HERE - HE'LL GET NOTHING TO EAT UNLESS HE HAS MONEY
HE'S A INSULK TO HOOMANIKY, HE AIN'T FITIN' FOR NOTHIN'
WHAT'LL YA HAVE, STRANGER?
A FULL MEAL WITH PORTERHOUSE STEAK
WHO IS THIS LOW PERSON YOU SPEAK OF, MAY I ASK?
FIRST REAL CUSTOMER I'VE HAD TO-DAY
I DON'T SUSPOSE YA KNOWS 'IM, STRANGER, HIS NAME'S WIMPY
WIMPY?
YEAH, J. WELLINGTON WIMPY, THE ARFULEST THING WICH EVER GOT BORNDED
'TIS A PITY THEY DID NOT DROWN HIM WHEN A PUP
THEM'S MY SENTIMENTS, STRANGER, YOU'RE A MAN AFTER MY OWN HEART
ARF! ARF! THEM'S MY SENTIMINKS, TOO — STRANGER
BRING OVER THREE OF YOUR BEST CIGARS - I HOPE YOU GENTLEMEN WILL SMOKE WITH ME
SURE, WITH PLEASURE!!
THA'S A GOOD SEGAR, MISTER, YA KNOWS HOW TO PICK 'EM, SEZ I
NOTHING IS TOO GOOD FOR MY FRIENDS
THIS BIRD WE WAS SPEAKIN' OF IS A DEAD-BEAT - BUT HERE'S ONE GUY HE CAN'T WORK
YEAH - I WANT TO CATER TO MEN LIKE YOU - MEN WHO ARE NOT AFRAID TO SPEND MONEY - GOOD SPENDERS LIKE YOU, STRANGER
AW, WELL, IT'S THE BAD EGGS WICH MAKES US REAL FOLKS SHINE
YOUR BILL IS TWO DOLLARS AND THIRTY FIVE CENTS
I BEG PARDON?
!
WELL, BLESS MY SOUL! I LEFT MY WALLET AT HOME - BUT I'LL PAY YOU TUESDAY, MOST OF A CERTAINTY
?!
YA THINK SO?
P-S-T
P-S-T
I WANT YOU GENTLEMEN TO COME UP TO MY PLACE SOMETIME FOR A DUCK DINNER
YOU BRING THE DUCKS
NICE WEATHER, ISN'T IT, WE'RE HAVING?
WE KNOW YA - YA CAN'T FOOL US
HAH! SO!!
AVAST, YA LUMAKICK! I SEZ YA AIN'T GONER CHOP HIS NECK OFF!
G-R-R-R
G-R-R
G-R-R-R
3-19
SEGAR

63. March 19, 1933

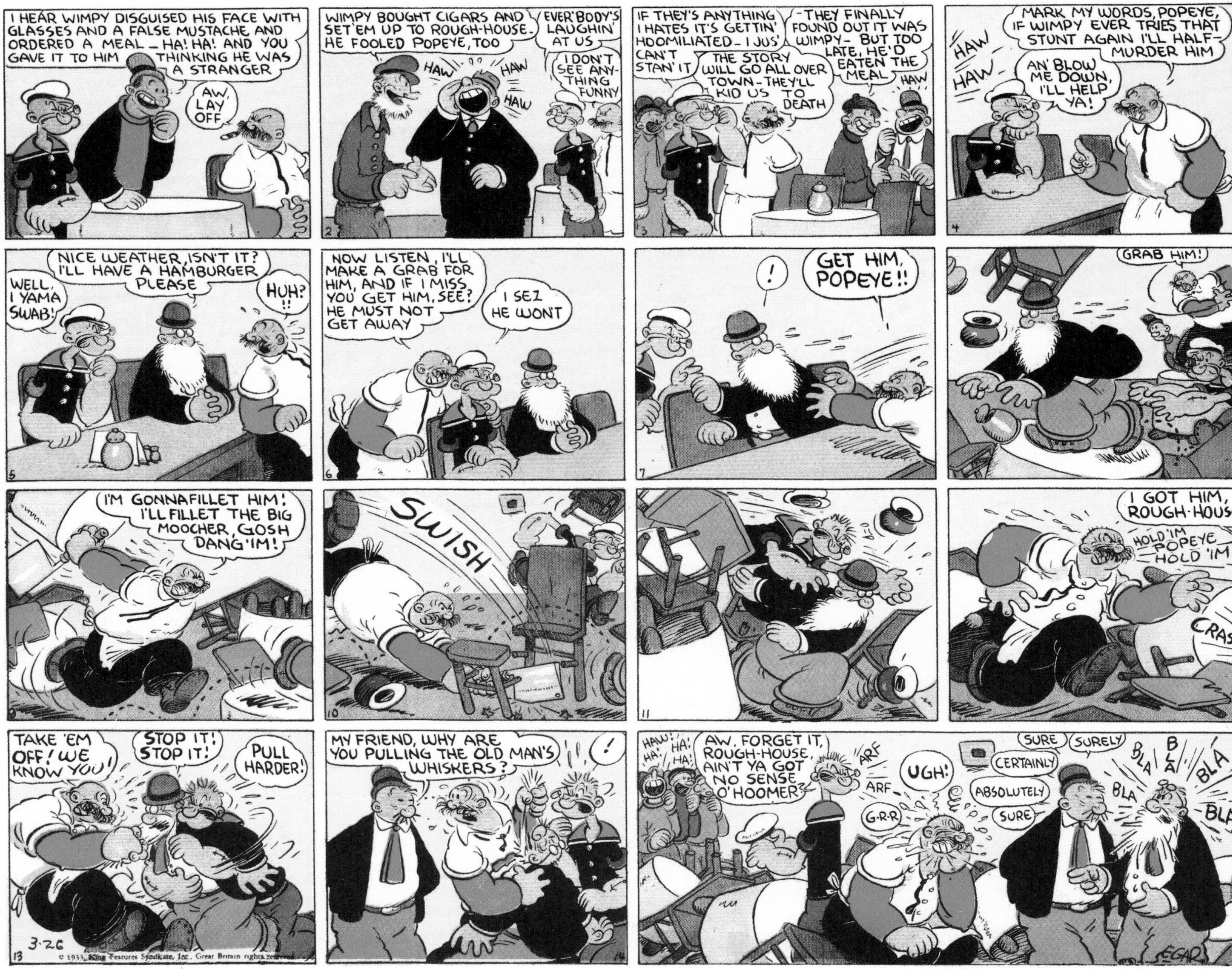

I HEAR WIMPY DISGUISED HIS FACE WITH GLASSES AND A FALSE MUSTACHE AND ORDERED A MEAL - HA! HA! AND YOU GAVE IT TO HIM THINKING HE WAS A STRANGER
AW, LAY OFF
WIMPY BOUGHT CIGARS AND SET 'EM UP TO ROUGH-HOUSE - HE FOOLED POPEYE, TOO
EVER'BODY'S LAUGHIN' AT US
HAW
HAW
HAW
I DON'T SEE ANY-THING FUNNY
IF THEY'S ANYTHING I HATES IT'S GETTIN' HOOMILIATED - I JUS' CAN'T STAN' IT
- THEY FINALLY FOUND OUT IT WAS WIMPY - BUT TOO LATE, HE'D EATEN THE MEAL
THE STORY WILL GO ALL OVER TOWN - THEY'LL KID US TO DEATH
HAW
HAW
HAW
MARK MY WORDS, POPEYE, IF WIMPY EVER TRIES THAT STUNT AGAIN I'LL HALF-MURDER HIM
AN' BLOW ME DOWN, I'LL HELP YA!
WELL, I YAMA SWAB!
NICE WEATHER, ISN'T IT? I'LL HAVE A HAMBURGER PLEASE
HUH? !!
NOW LISTEN, I'LL MAKE A GRAB FOR HIM, AND IF I MISS, YOU GET HIM, SEE? HE MUST NOT GET AWAY
I SEZ HE WON'T
!
GET HIM, POPEYE!!
GRAB HIM!
I'M GONNA FILLET HIM! I'LL FILLET THE BIG MOOCHER, GOSH DANG 'IM!
SWISH
I GOT HIM, ROUGH-HOUSE!
HOLD 'IM POPEYE HOLD 'IM
CRASH
TAKE 'EM OFF! WE KNOW YOU!
STOP IT! STOP IT!
PULL HARDER!
3-26
© 1933, King Features Syndicate, Inc. Great Britain rights reserved
MY FRIEND, WHY ARE YOU PULLING THE OLD MAN'S WHISKERS?
!
HAW! HA!
HA! HA!
AW, FORGET IT, ROUGH-HOUSE, AIN'T YA GOT NO SENSE O' HOOMER?
ARF
ARF
UGH!
G-R-R
SURE
SURELY
CERTAINLY
ABSOLUTELY
SURE
BLA
BLA
BLA
BLA
BLA
E.C. SEGAR

64. March 26, 1933

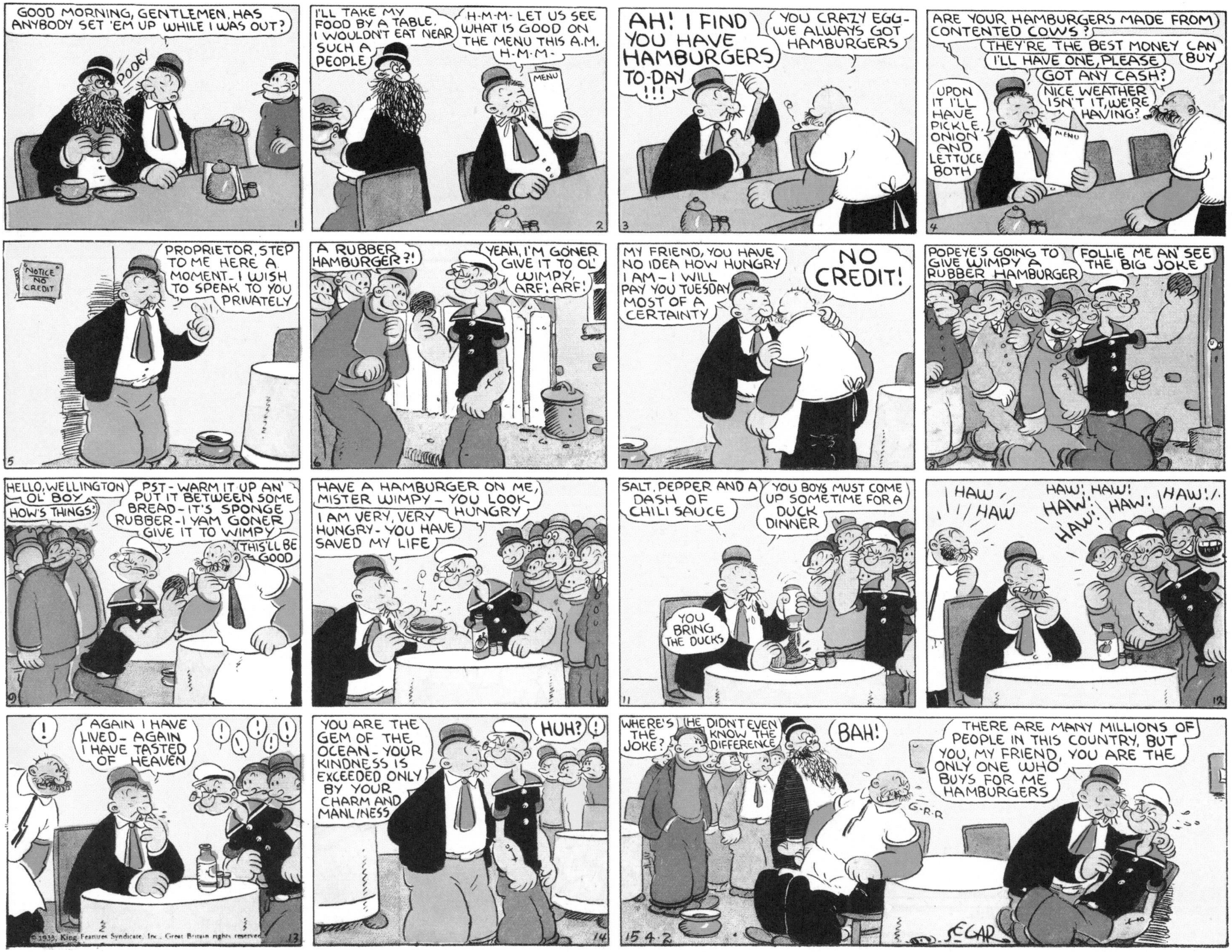
GOOD MORNING, GENTLEMEN. HAS ANYBODY SET 'EM UP WHILE I WAS OUT?
POOEY
I'LL TAKE MY FOOD BY A TABLE. I WOULDN'T EAT NEAR SUCH A PEOPLE
H-M-M- LET US SEE WHAT IS GOOD ON THE MENU THIS A.M. H-M-M-
MENU
AH! I FIND YOU HAVE HAMBURGERS TO-DAY !!!
YOU CRAZY EGG- WE ALWAYS GOT HAMBURGERS
ARE YOUR HAMBURGERS MADE FROM CONTENTED COWS?
THEY'RE THE BEST MONEY CAN BUY
I'LL HAVE ONE, PLEASE
UPON IT I'LL HAVE PICKLE, ONION AND LETTUCE BOTH
GOT ANY CASH?
NICE WEATHER ISN'T IT, WE'RE HAVING?
MENU
"NOTICE" NO CREDIT
PROPRIETOR, STEP TO ME HERE A MOMENT- I WISH TO SPEAK TO YOU PRIVATELY
A RUBBER HAMBURGER?!
YEAH, I'M GONER GIVE IT TO OL' WIMPY, ARF! ARF!
MY FRIEND, YOU HAVE NO IDEA HOW HUNGRY I AM- I WILL PAY YOU TUESDAY MOST OF A CERTAINTY
NO CREDIT!
POPEYE'S GOING TO GIVE WIMPY A RUBBER HAMBURGER
FOLLIE ME AN' SEE THE BIG JOKE
HELLO, WELLINGTON OL' BOY
HOW'S THINGS?
PST- WARM IT UP AN' PUT IT BETWEEN SOME BREAD- IT'S SPONGE RUBBER- I YAM GONER GIVE IT TO WIMPY
THIS'LL BE GOOD
HAVE A HAMBURGER ON ME, MISTER WIMPY- YOU LOOK HUNGRY
I AM VERY, VERY HUNGRY- YOU HAVE SAVED MY LIFE
SALT, PEPPER AND A DASH OF CHILI SAUCE
YOU BOYS MUST COME UP SOMETIME FOR A DUCK DINNER
YOU BRING THE DUCKS
HAW HAW
HAW! HAW! HAW! HAW! HAW! HAW!
!
AGAIN I HAVE LIVED- AGAIN I HAVE TASTED OF HEAVEN
! ! ! ! !
© 1933, King Features Syndicate, Inc., Great Britain rights reserved.
YOU ARE THE GEM OF THE OCEAN- YOUR KINDNESS IS EXCEEDED ONLY BY YOUR CHARM AND MANLINESS
HUH? !
WHERE'S THE JOKE?
HE DIDN'T EVEN KNOW THE DIFFERENCE
BAH!
G-R-R
THERE ARE MANY MILLIONS OF PEOPLE IN THIS COUNTRY, BUT YOU, MY FRIEND, YOU ARE THE ONLY ONE WHO BUYS FOR ME HAMBURGERS
SEGAR

65. April 2, 1933

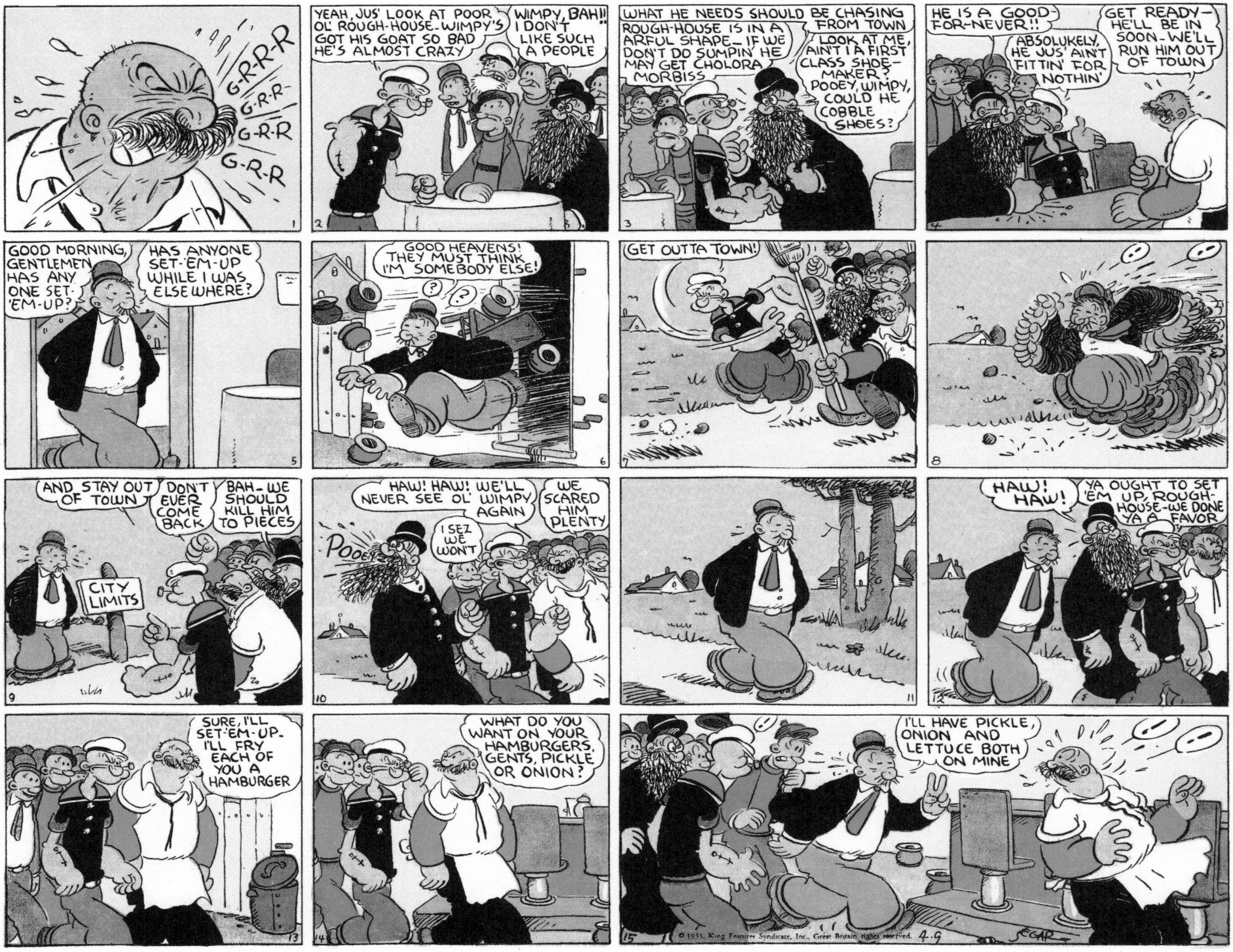
G-R-R-R
G-R-R-
G-R-R
G-R-R
YEAH, JUS' LOOK AT POOR OL' ROUGH-HOUSE - WIMPY'S GOT HIS GOAT SO BAD HE'S ALMOST CRAZY
WIMPY, BAH!! I DON'T LIKE SUCH A PEOPLE
WHAT HE NEEDS SHOULD BE CHASING FROM TOWN
ROUGH-HOUSE IS IN A ARFUL SHAPE - IF WE DON'T DO SUMPIN' HE MAY GET CHOLORA MORBISS
LOOK AT ME, AIN'T I A FIRST CLASS SHOE-MAKER? POOEY, WIMPY, COULD HE COBBLE SHOES?
HE IS A GOOD-FOR-NEVER!!
ABSOLUKELY, HE JUS' AIN'T FITTIN' FOR NOTHIN'
GET READY - HE'LL BE IN SOON - WE'LL RUN HIM OUT OF TOWN
GOOD MORNING, GENTLEMEN HAS ANY ONE SET-'EM-UP?
HAS ANYONE SET-'EM-UP WHILE I WAS ELSEWHERE?
GOOD HEAVENS! THEY MUST THINK I'M SOMEBODY ELSE!
GET OUTTA TOWN!
AND STAY OUT OF TOWN
DON'T EVER COME BACK
BAH - WE SHOULD KILL HIM TO PIECES
CITY LIMITS
HAW! HAW! WE'LL NEVER SEE OL' WIMPY AGAIN
I SEZ WE WON'T
WE SCARED HIM PLENTY
POOEY
HAW! HAW!
YA OUGHT TO SET 'EM UP, ROUGH-HOUSE - WE DONE YA A FAVOR
SURE, I'LL SET-'EM-UP - I'LL FRY EACH OF YOU A HAMBURGER
WHAT DO YOU WANT ON YOUR HAMBURGERS, GENTS, PICKLE OR ONION?
I'LL HAVE PICKLE, ONION AND LETTUCE BOTH ON MINE
© 1933, King Features Syndicate, Inc., Great Britain rights reserved. 4-9
SEGAR

66. April 9, 1933

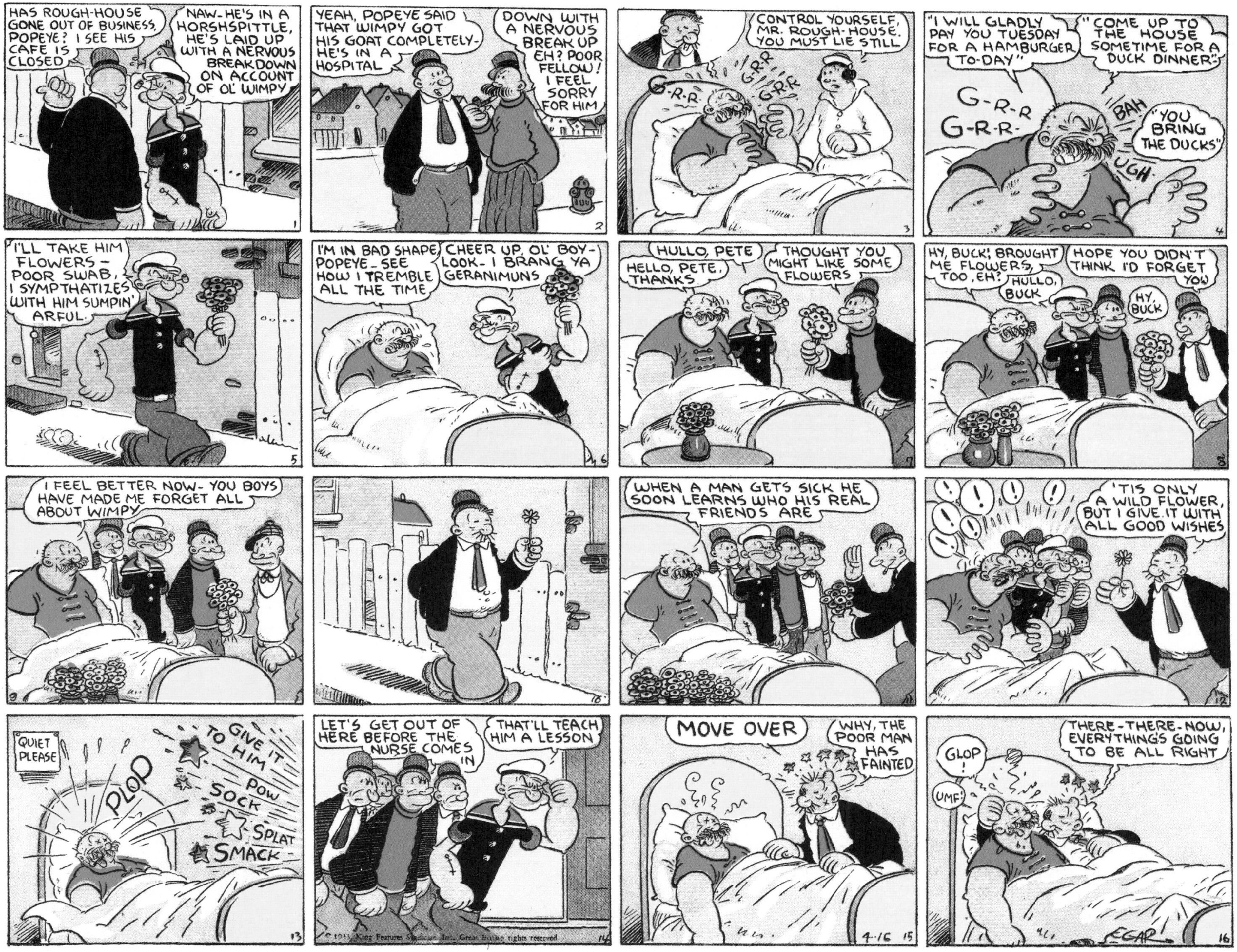
HAS ROUGH-HOUSE GONE OUT OF BUSINESS, POPEYE? I SEE HIS CAFE IS CLOSED
NAW-HE'S IN A HORSHSPITTLE, HE'S LAID UP WITH A NERVOUS BREAKDOWN ON ACCOUNT OF OL' WIMPY
YEAH, POPEYE SAID THAT WIMPY GOT HIS GOAT COMPLETELY-HE'S IN A HOSPITAL
DOWN WITH A NERVOUS BREAK UP EH? POOR FELLOW! I FEEL SORRY FOR HIM
CONTROL YOURSELF, MR. ROUGH-HOUSE. YOU MUST LIE STILL
G-R-R
G-R-R
G-R-R
"I WILL GLADLY PAY YOU TUESDAY FOR A HAMBURGER TO-DAY"
"COME UP TO THE HOUSE SOMETIME FOR A DUCK DINNER"
G-R-R
G-R-R
BAH
"YOU BRING THE DUCKS"
UGH
I'LL TAKE HIM FLOWERS – POOR SWAB, I SYMPTHATIZES WITH HIM SUMPIN' ARFUL.
I'M IN BAD SHAPE POPEYE_SEE HOW I TREMBLE ALL THE TIME
CHEER UP, OL' BOY-LOOK- I BRANG YA GERANIMUNS
HULLO, PETE
HELLO, PETE, THANKS
THOUGHT YOU MIGHT LIKE SOME FLOWERS
HY, BUCK; BROUGHT ME FLOWERS, TOO, EH?
HULLO, BUCK
HY, BUCK
HOPE YOU DIDN'T THINK I'D FORGET YOU
I FEEL BETTER NOW- YOU BOYS HAVE MADE ME FORGET ALL ABOUT WIMPY
WHEN A MAN GETS SICK HE SOON LEARNS WHO HIS REAL FRIENDS ARE
!
'TIS ONLY A WILD FLOWER, BUT I GIVE IT WITH ALL GOOD WISHES
QUIET PLEASE
GIVE IT TO HIM
PLOP
POW
SOCK
SPLAT
SMACK
LET'S GET OUT OF HERE BEFORE THE NURSE COMES IN
THAT'LL TEACH HIM A LESSON
© 1933, King Features Syndicate, Inc., Great Britain rights reserved
MOVE OVER
WHY, THE POOR MAN HAS FAINTED
4-16
GLOP!
UMF!
THERE-THERE-NOW, EVERYTHING'S GOING TO BE ALL RIGHT
SEGAR

67. April 16, 1933

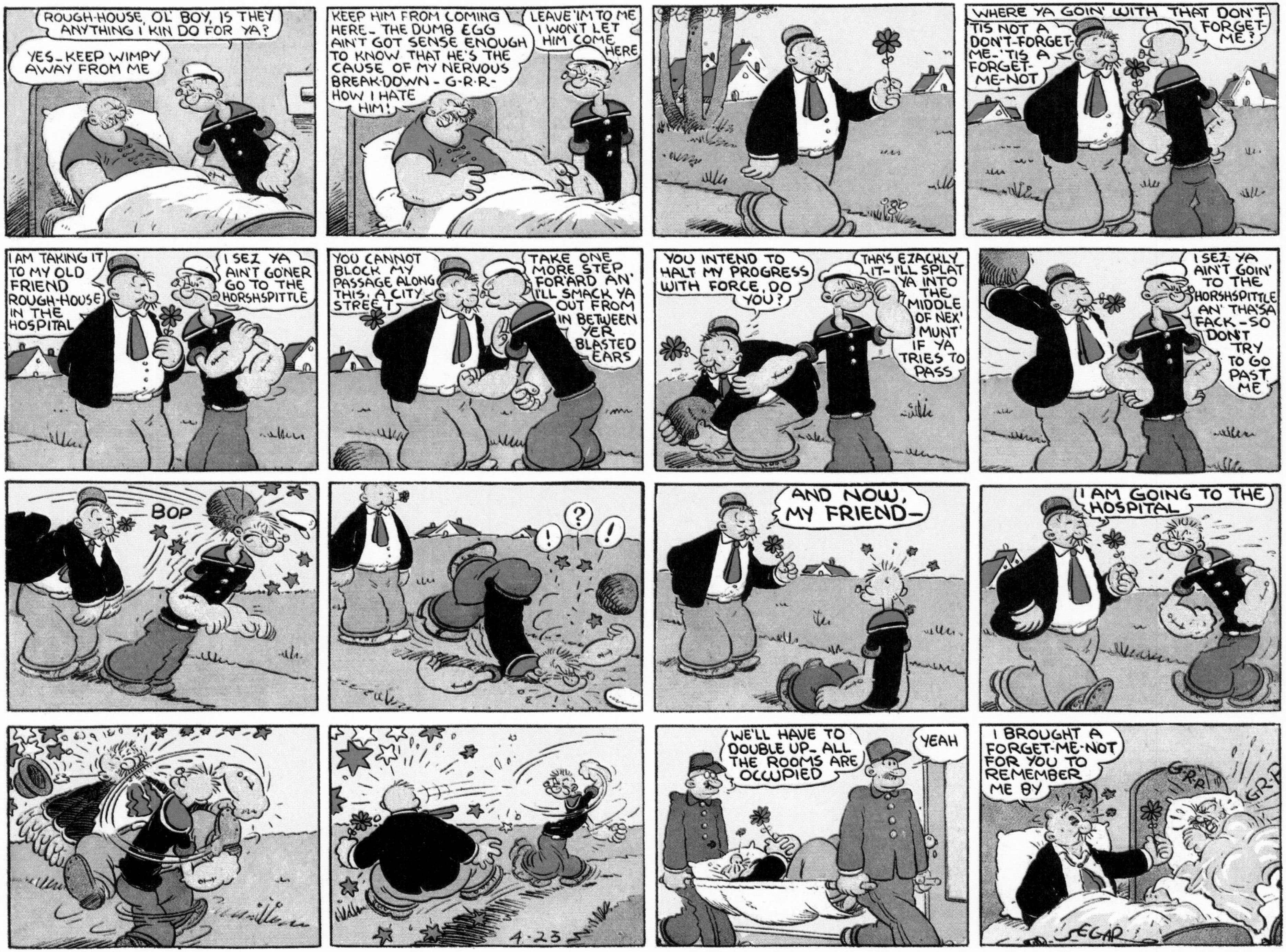
ROUGH-HOUSE, OL' BOY, IS THEY ANYTHING I KIN DO FOR YA?
YES_KEEP WIMPY AWAY FROM ME
KEEP HIM FROM COMING HERE_ THE DUMB EGG AIN'T GOT SENSE ENOUGH TO KNOW THAT HE'S THE CAUSE OF MY NERVOUS BREAK-DOWN - G-R-R- HOW I HATE HIM!
LEAVE 'IM TO ME I WON'T LET HIM COME HERE
WHERE YA GOIN' WITH THAT DON'T-FORGET-ME?
'TIS NOT A DON'T-FORGET-ME-'TIS A FORGET-ME-NOT
I AM TAKING IT TO MY OLD FRIEND ROUGH-HOUSE IN THE HOSPITAL
I SEZ YA AIN'T GO'NER GO TO THE HORSHSPITTLE
YOU CANNOT BLOCK MY PASSAGE ALONG THIS, A CITY STREET
TAKE ONE MORE STEP FOR'ARD AN' I'LL SMACK YA OUT FROM IN BETWEEN YER BLASTED EARS
YOU INTEND TO HALT MY PROGRESS WITH FORCE, DO YOU?
THA'S EZACKLY IT- I'LL SPLAT YA INTO THE MIDDLE OF NEX' MUNT' IF YA TRIES TO PASS
I SEZ YA AIN'T GOIN' TO THE HORSHSPITTLE AN' THA'SA FACK-SO DON'T TRY TO GO PAST ME
BOP
!
?
!
AND NOW, MY FRIEND-
I AM GOING TO THE HOSPITAL
4-23
WE'LL HAVE TO DOUBLE UP- ALL THE ROOMS ARE OCCUPIED
YEAH
I BROUGHT A FORGET-ME-NOT FOR YOU TO REMEMBER ME BY
G-R-R
GR-R
SEGAR

68. April 23, 1933

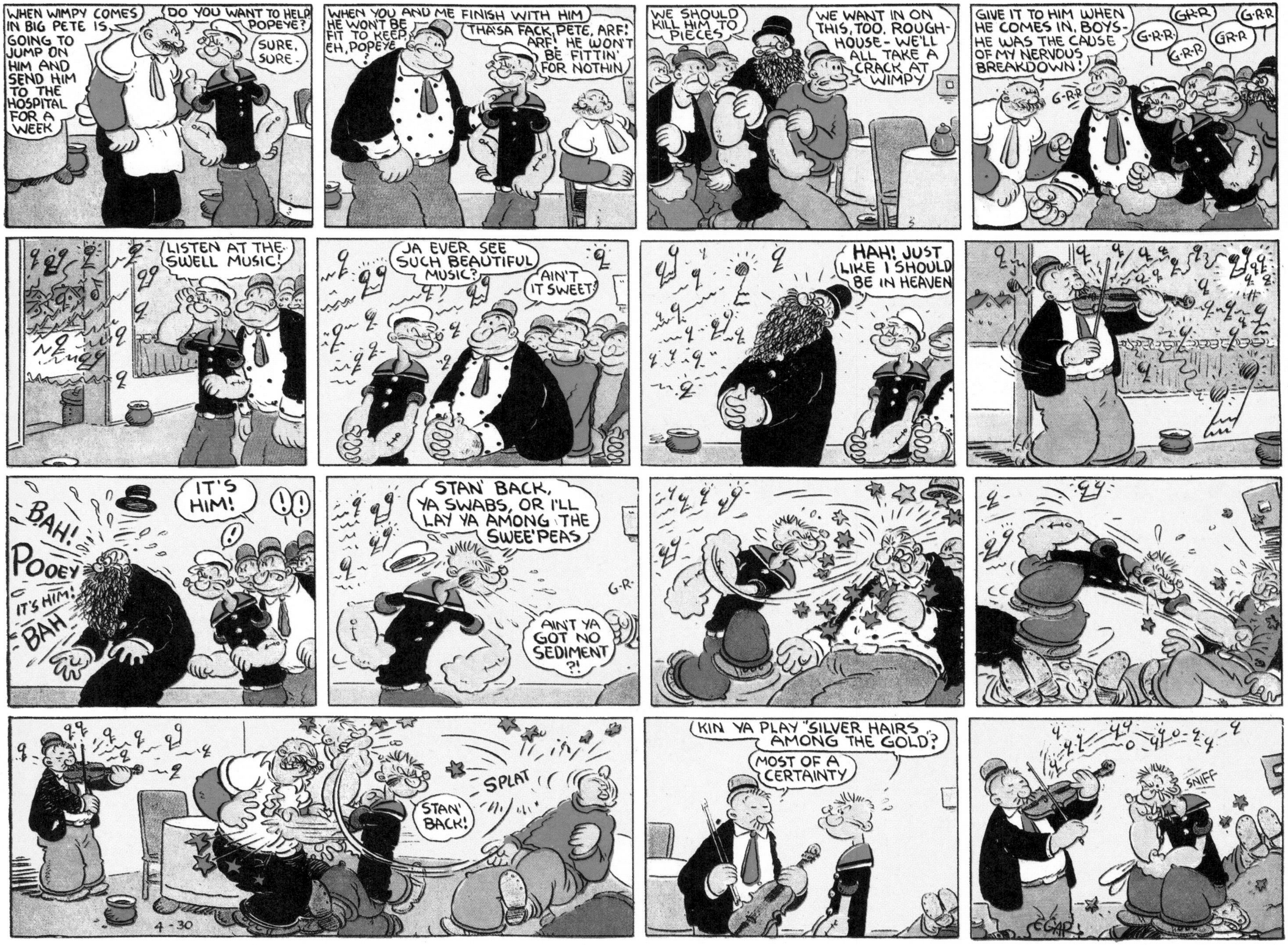
WHEN WIMPY COMES IN BIG PETE IS GOING TO JUMP ON HIM AND SEND HIM TO THE HOSPITAL FOR A WEEK
DO YOU WANT TO HELP POPEYE?
SURE, SURE-
WHEN YOU AND ME FINISH WITH HIM HE WON'T BE FIT TO KEEP, EH, POPEYE?
THA'SA FACK, PETE, ARF! ARF! HE WON'T BE FITTIN' FOR NOTHIN'
WE SHOULD KILL HIM TO PIECES
WE WANT IN ON THIS, TOO, ROUGH-HOUSE- WE'LL ALL TAKE A CRACK AT WIMPY
GIVE IT TO HIM WHEN HE COMES IN, BOYS- HE WAS THE CAUSE OF MY NERVOUS BREAKDOWN!
GR-R
G-R-R
G-R-R
GR-R
G-R-R
G-R-R
LISTEN AT THE SWELL MUSIC!
JA EVER SEE SUCH BEAUTIFUL MUSIC?
AIN'T IT SWEET?
HAH! JUST LIKE I SHOULD BE IN HEAVEN
BAH!
POOEY
IT'S HIM!
BAH
IT'S HIM!
!!
!
STAN' BACK, YA SWABS, OR I'LL LAY YA AMONG THE SWEE'PEAS
G-R-
AIN'T YA GOT NO SEDIMENT ?!
SPLAT
STAN' BACK!
4-30
KIN YA PLAY "SILVER HAIRS AMONG THE GOLD"?
MOST OF A CERTAINTY
SNIFF

69. April 30, 1933

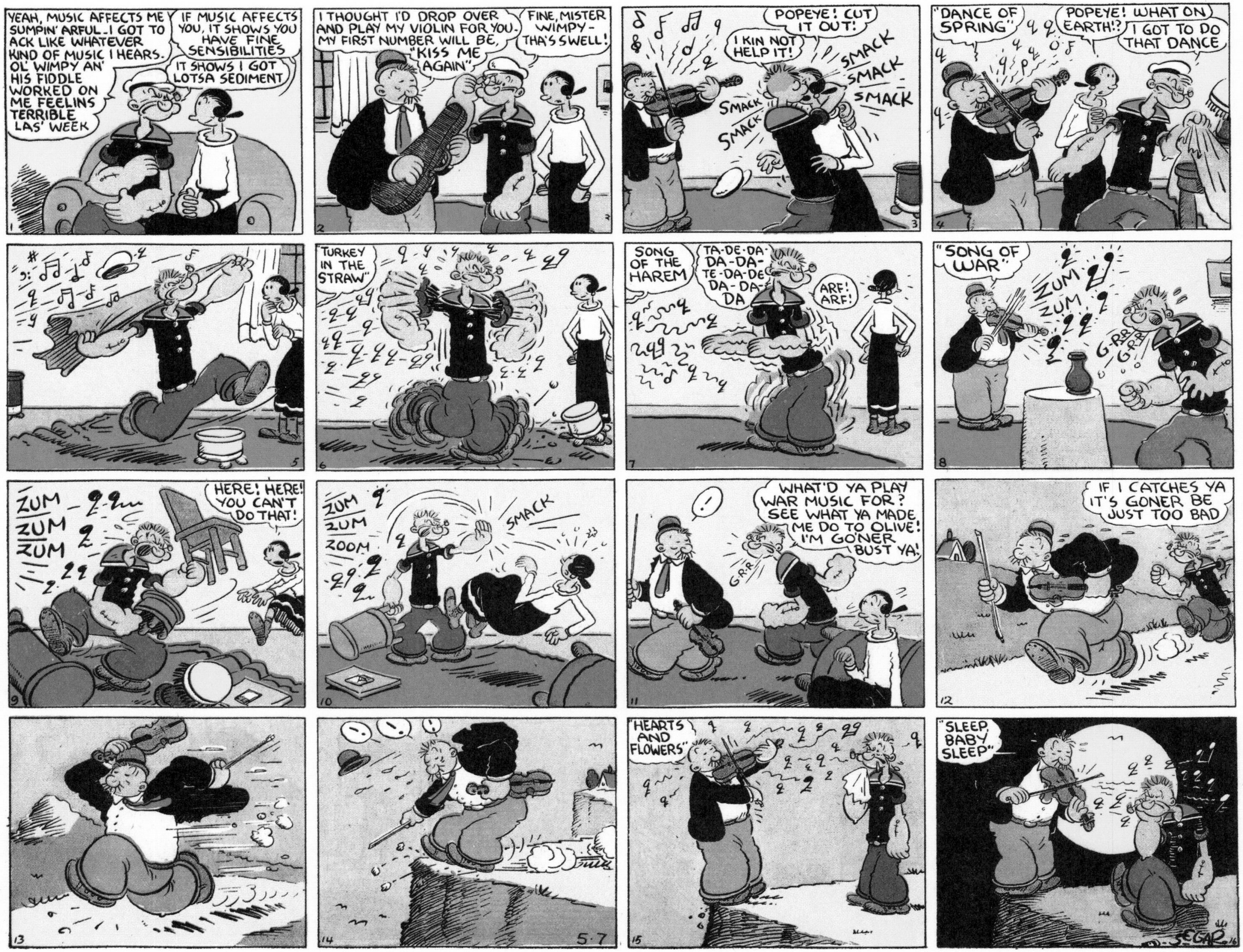
YEAH, MUSIC AFFECTS ME SUMPIN' ARFUL_I GOT TO ACK LIKE WHATEVER KIND OF MUSIC I HEARS. OL' WIMPY AN' HIS FIDDLE WORKED ON ME FEELINS TERRIBLE LAS' WEEK
IF MUSIC AFFECTS YOU, IT SHOWS YOU HAVE FINE SENSIBILITIES
IT SHOWS I GOT LOTSA SEDIMENT
I THOUGHT I'D DROP OVER AND PLAY MY VIOLIN FOR YOU. MY FIRST NUMBER WILL BE, "KISS ME AGAIN"
FINE, MISTER WIMPY-THA'S SWELL!
POPEYE! CUT IT OUT!
I KIN NOT HELP IT!
SMACK
SMACK
SMACK
SMACK
SMACK
"DANCE OF SPRING"
POPEYE! WHAT ON EARTH!?
I GOT TO DO THAT DANCE
"TURKEY IN THE STRAW"
SONG OF THE HAREM
TA-DE-DA DA-DA-TE-DA-DE DA-DA-DA
ARF! ARF!
"SONG OF WAR"
ZUM
ZUM
G-RR
ZUM
ZUM
ZUM
HERE! HERE! YOU CAN'T DO THAT!
ZUM
ZUM
ZOOM
SMACK
!
WHAT'D YA PLAY WAR MUSIC FOR? SEE WHAT YA MADE ME DO TO OLIVE! I'M GO'NER BUST YA!
G-R-R
IF I CATCHES YA IT'S GONER BE JUST TOO BAD
5-7
"HEARTS AND FLOWERS"
"SLEEP BABY SLEEP"
SEGAR

70. May 7, 1933

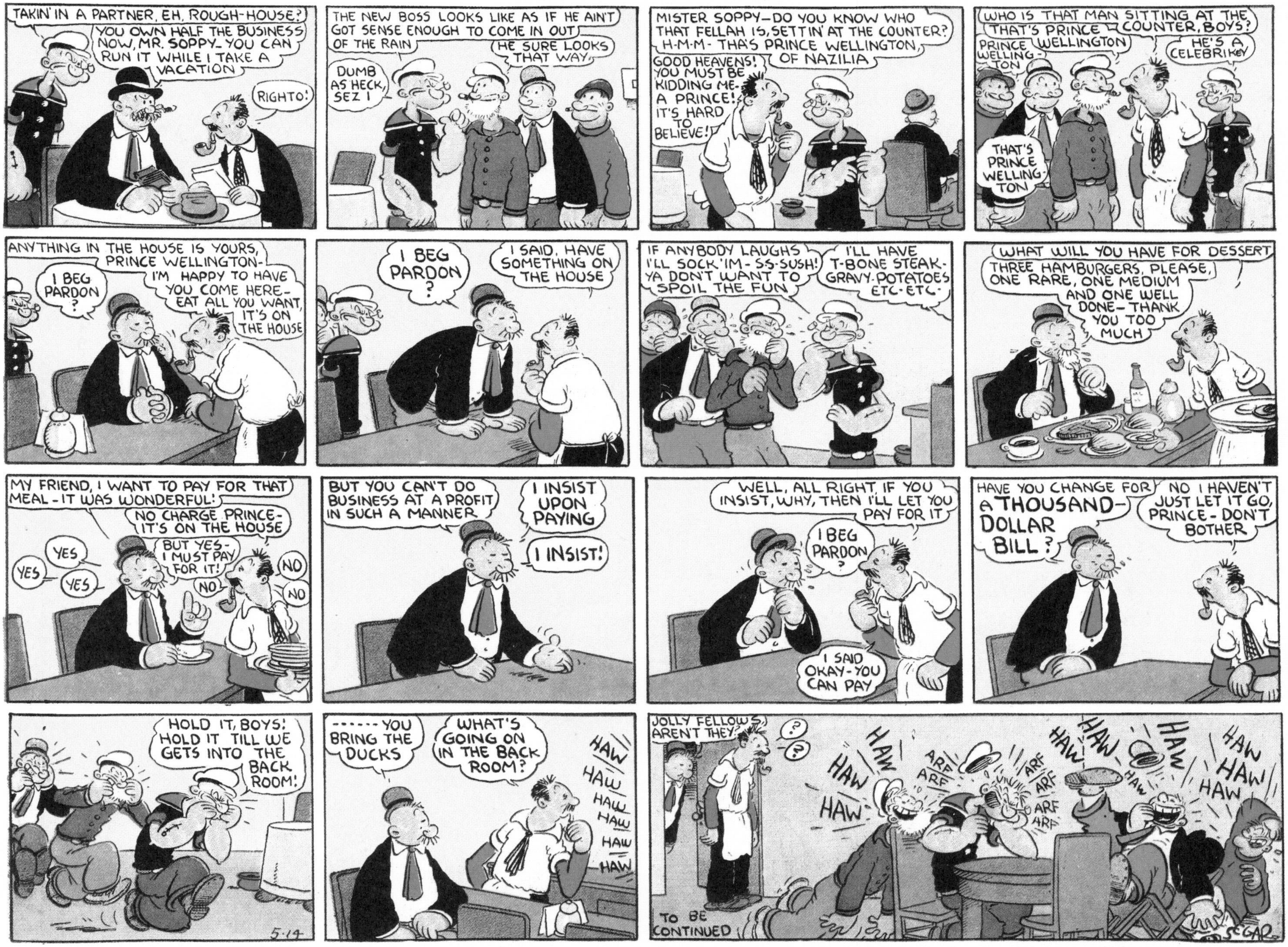
TAKIN' IN A PARTNER, EH, ROUGH-HOUSE?
YOU OWN HALF THE BUSINESS NOW, MR. SOPPY- YOU CAN RUN IT WHILE I TAKE A VACATION
RIGHTO!
THE NEW BOSS LOOKS LIKE AS IF HE AIN'T GOT SENSE ENOUGH TO COME IN OUT OF THE RAIN
HE SURE LOOKS THAT WAY
DUMB AS HECK, SEZ I
MISTER SOPPY—DO YOU KNOW WHO THAT FELLAH IS, SETTIN' AT THE COUNTER?
H-M-M- THA'S PRINCE WELLINGTON, OF NAZILIA
GOOD HEAVENS! YOU MUST BE KIDDING ME- A PRINCE! IT'S HARD TO BELIEVE!
WHO IS THAT MAN SITTING AT THE COUNTER, BOYS?
THAT'S PRINCE WELLINGTON
PRINCE WELLING-TON
HE'S A CELEBRIKEY
THAT'S PRINCE WELLING-TON
ANYTHING IN THE HOUSE IS YOURS, PRINCE WELLINGTON- I'M HAPPY TO HAVE YOU COME HERE- EAT ALL YOU WANT, IT'S ON THE HOUSE
I BEG PARDON ?
I BEG PARDON ?
I SAID, HAVE SOMETHING ON THE HOUSE
IF ANYBODY LAUGHS I'LL SOCK 'IM- SS-SUSH! YA DON'T WANT TO SPOIL THE FUN
I'LL HAVE T-BONE STEAK- GRAVY- POTATOES ETC-ETC-
WHAT WILL YOU HAVE FOR DESSERT
THREE HAMBURGERS, PLEASE, ONE RARE, ONE MEDIUM AND ONE WELL DONE- THANK YOU TOO MUCH
MY FRIEND, I WANT TO PAY FOR THAT MEAL- IT WAS WONDERFUL!
NO CHARGE PRINCE- IT'S ON THE HOUSE
BUT YES- I MUST PAY FOR IT!
YES
YES
YES
NO
NO
NO
BUT YOU CAN'T DO BUSINESS AT A PROFIT IN SUCH A MANNER
I INSIST UPON PAYING
I INSIST!
WELL, ALL RIGHT, IF YOU INSIST, WHY, THEN I'LL LET YOU PAY FOR IT
I BEG PARDON ?
I SAID OKAY- YOU CAN PAY
HAVE YOU CHANGE FOR A THOUSAND- DOLLAR BILL?
NO I HAVEN'T JUST LET IT GO, PRINCE- DON'T BOTHER
HOLD IT, BOYS! HOLD IT TILL WE GETS INTO THE BACK ROOM!
5-14
------ YOU BRING THE DUCKS
WHAT'S GOING ON IN THE BACK ROOM?
HAW HAW HAW HAW HAW HAW
JOLLY FELLOWS, AREN'T THEY?
?
?
HAW HAW HAW HAW
ARF ARF ARF ARF ARF ARF
HAW HAW HAW HAW HAW HAW HAW HAW
TO BE CONTINUED
SEGAR

71. May 14, 1933

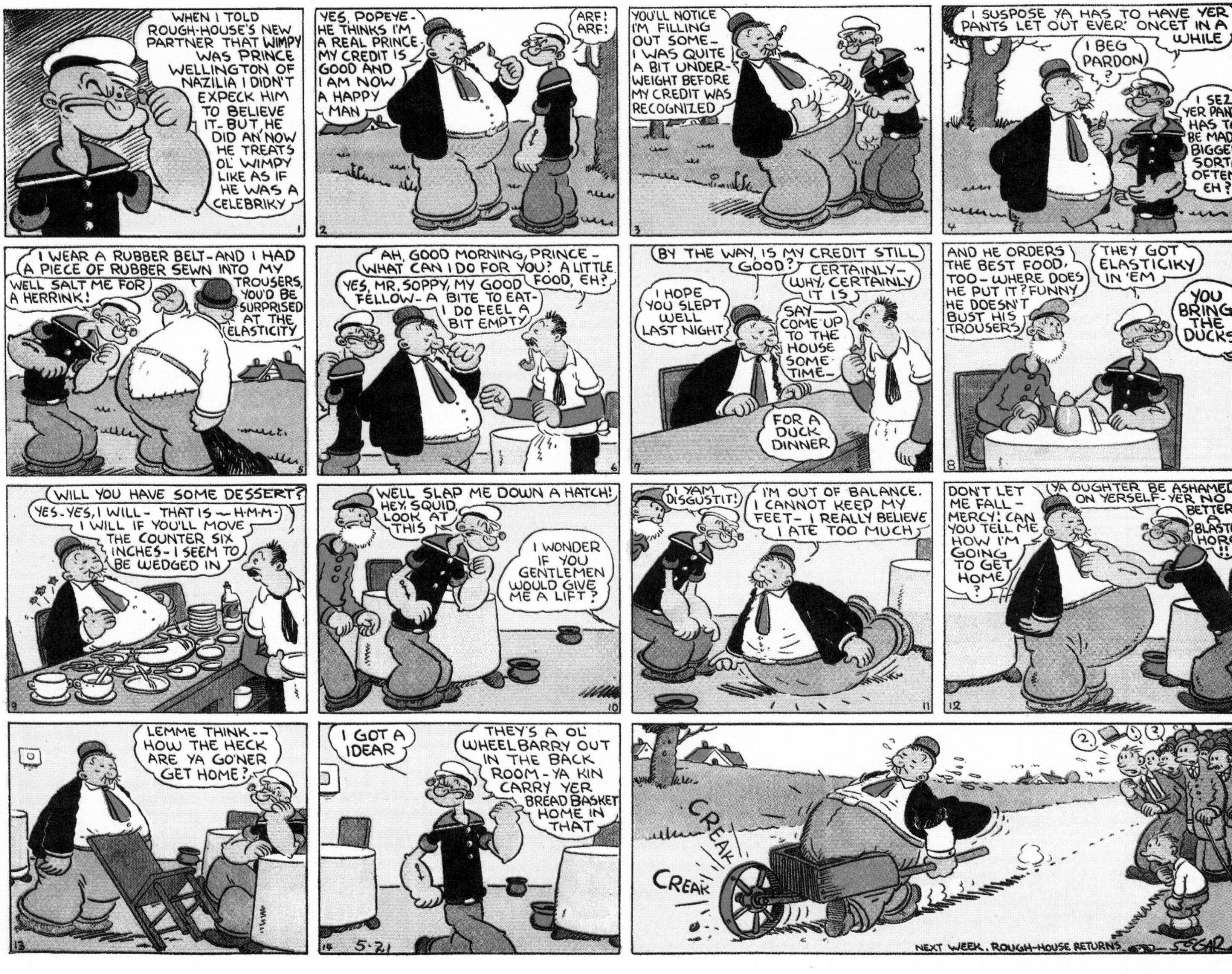
WHEN I TOLD ROUGH-HOUSE'S NEW PARTNER THAT WIMPY WAS PRINCE WELLINGTON OF NAZILIA I DIDN'T EXPECK HIM TO BELIEVE IT- BUT HE DID AN' NOW HE TREATS OL' WIMPY LIKE AS IF HE WAS A CELEBRIKY
YES, POPEYE- HE THINKS I'M A REAL PRINCE- MY CREDIT IS GOOD AND I AM NOW A HAPPY MAN
ARF! ARF!
YOU'LL NOTICE I'M FILLING OUT SOME- I WAS QUITE A BIT UNDER-WEIGHT BEFORE MY CREDIT WAS RECOGNIZED
I SUSPOSE YA HAS TO HAVE YER PANTS LET OUT EVER' ONCET IN A WHILE
I BEG PARDON ?
I SEZ YER PANTS HAS TO BE MADE BIGGER SORTA OFTEN, EH?
I WEAR A RUBBER BELT- AND I HAD A PIECE OF RUBBER SEWN INTO MY TROUSERS, YOU'D BE SURPRISED AT THE ELASTICITY
WELL SALT ME FOR A HERRINK!
AH, GOOD MORNING, PRINCE- WHAT CAN I DO FOR YOU? A LITTLE FOOD, EH?
YES, MR. SOPPY, MY GOOD FELLOW- A BITE TO EAT- I DO FEEL A BIT EMPTY
BY THE WAY, IS MY CREDIT STILL GOOD?
CERTAINLY- WHY, CERTAINLY IT IS
I HOPE YOU SLEPT WELL LAST NIGHT
SAY—— COME UP TO THE HOUSE SOME-TIME-
FOR A DUCK DINNER
AND HE ORDERS THE BEST FOOD, TOO- WHERE DOES HE PUT IT? FUNNY HE DOESN'T BUST HIS TROUSERS
THEY GOT ELASTICIKY IN 'EM
YOU BRING THE DUCKS
WILL YOU HAVE SOME DESSERT?
YES-YES, I WILL- THAT IS — H-M-M- I WILL IF YOU'LL MOVE THE COUNTER SIX INCHES- I SEEM TO BE WEDGED IN
WELL SLAP ME DOWN A HATCH! HEY, SQUID, LOOK AT THIS
I WONDER IF YOU GENTLEMEN WOULD GIVE ME A LIFT?
I YAM DISGUSTIT!
I'M OUT OF BALANCE. I CANNOT KEEP MY FEET- I REALLY BELIEVE I ATE TOO MUCH
DON'T LET ME FALL- MERCY! CAN YOU TELL ME HOW I'M GOING TO GET HOME ?
YA OUGHTER BE ASHAMED ON YERSELF- YER NO BETTERN A BLASTED HORG !!
LEMME THINK-- HOW THE HECK ARE YA GO'NER GET HOME?
I GOT A IDEAR
THEY'S A OL' WHEELBARRY OUT IN THE BACK ROOM- YA KIN CARRY YER BREAD BASKET HOME IN THAT
5-21
CREAK
CREAK
NEXT WEEK, ROUGH-HOUSE RETURNS
SEGAR

72. May 21, 1933

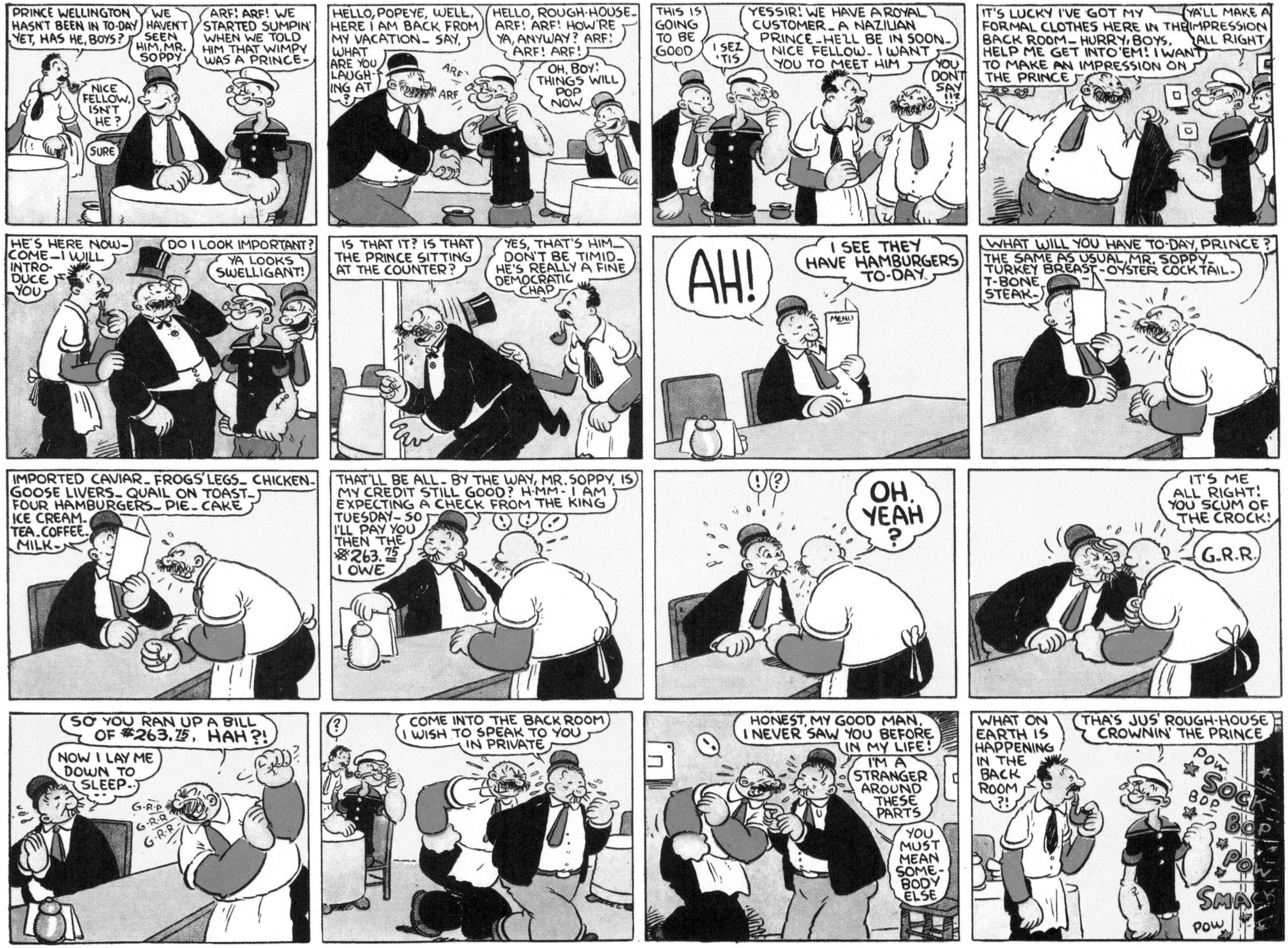
PRINCE WELLINGTON HASN'T BEEN IN TO-DAY YET, HAS HE, BOYS?
WE HAVEN'T SEEN HIM, MR. SOPPY
ARF! ARF! WE STARTED SUMPIN' WHEN WE TOLD HIM THAT WIMPY WAS A PRINCE-
NICE FELLOW, ISN'T HE?
SURE
HELLO, POPEYE, WELL, HERE I AM BACK FROM MY VACATION- SAY, WHAT ARE YOU LAUGHING AT?
HELLO, ROUGH-HOUSE- ARF! ARF! HOW'RE YA, ANYWAY? ARF! ARF! ARF!
ARF
ARF
OH, BOY! THINGS WILL POP NOW
THIS IS GOING TO BE GOOD
I SEZ 'TIS
YESSIR! WE HAVE A ROYAL CUSTOMER- A NAZILIAN PRINCE- HE'LL BE IN SOON- NICE FELLOW- I WANT YOU TO MEET HIM
YOU DON'T SAY !!?
IT'S LUCKY I'VE GOT MY FORMAL CLOTHES HERE IN THE BACK ROOM- HURRY, BOYS, HELP ME GET INTO 'EM! I WANT TO MAKE AN IMPRESSION ON THE PRINCE
YA'LL MAKE A IMPRESSION ALL RIGHT
HE'S HERE NOW- COME- I WILL INTRODUCE YOU
DO I LOOK IMPORTANT?
YA LOOKS SWELLIGANT!
IS THAT IT? IS THAT THE PRINCE SITTING AT THE COUNTER?
YES, THAT'S HIM- DON'T BE TIMID- HE'S REALLY A FINE DEMOCRATIC CHAP
AH!
I SEE THEY HAVE HAMBURGERS TO-DAY
MENU
WHAT WILL YOU HAVE TO-DAY, PRINCE?
THE SAME AS USUAL, MR. SOPPY- TURKEY BREAST- OYSTER COCKTAIL- T-BONE STEAK-
IMPORTED CAVIAR- FROGS' LEGS- CHICKEN- GOOSE LIVERS- QUAIL ON TOAST- FOUR HAMBURGERS- PIE- CAKE ICE CREAM- TEA- COFFEE- MILK-
THAT'LL BE ALL- BY THE WAY, MR. SOPPY, IS MY CREDIT STILL GOOD? H-MM- I AM EXPECTING A CHECK FROM THE KING TUESDAY- SO I'LL PAY YOU THEN THE $263.75 I OWE
! ! ?
! ?
OH, YEAH?
IT'S ME ALL RIGHT! YOU SCUM OF THE CROCK!
G-R-R.
SO YOU RAN UP A BILL OF $263.75, HAH?!
NOW I LAY ME DOWN TO SLEEP..
G-R-R
G-R-R
G-R-R
?
COME INTO THE BACK ROOM I WISH TO SPEAK TO YOU IN PRIVATE
!
HONEST, MY GOOD MAN, I NEVER SAW YOU BEFORE IN MY LIFE!
I'M A STRANGER AROUND THESE PARTS
YOU MUST MEAN SOMEBODY ELSE
WHAT ON EARTH IS HAPPENING IN THE BACK ROOM ?!
THA'S JUS' ROUGH-HOUSE CROWNIN' THE PRINCE
POW
BOP
SOCK
BOP
POW
SMACK
POW

73. May 28, 1933

74. June 4, 1933

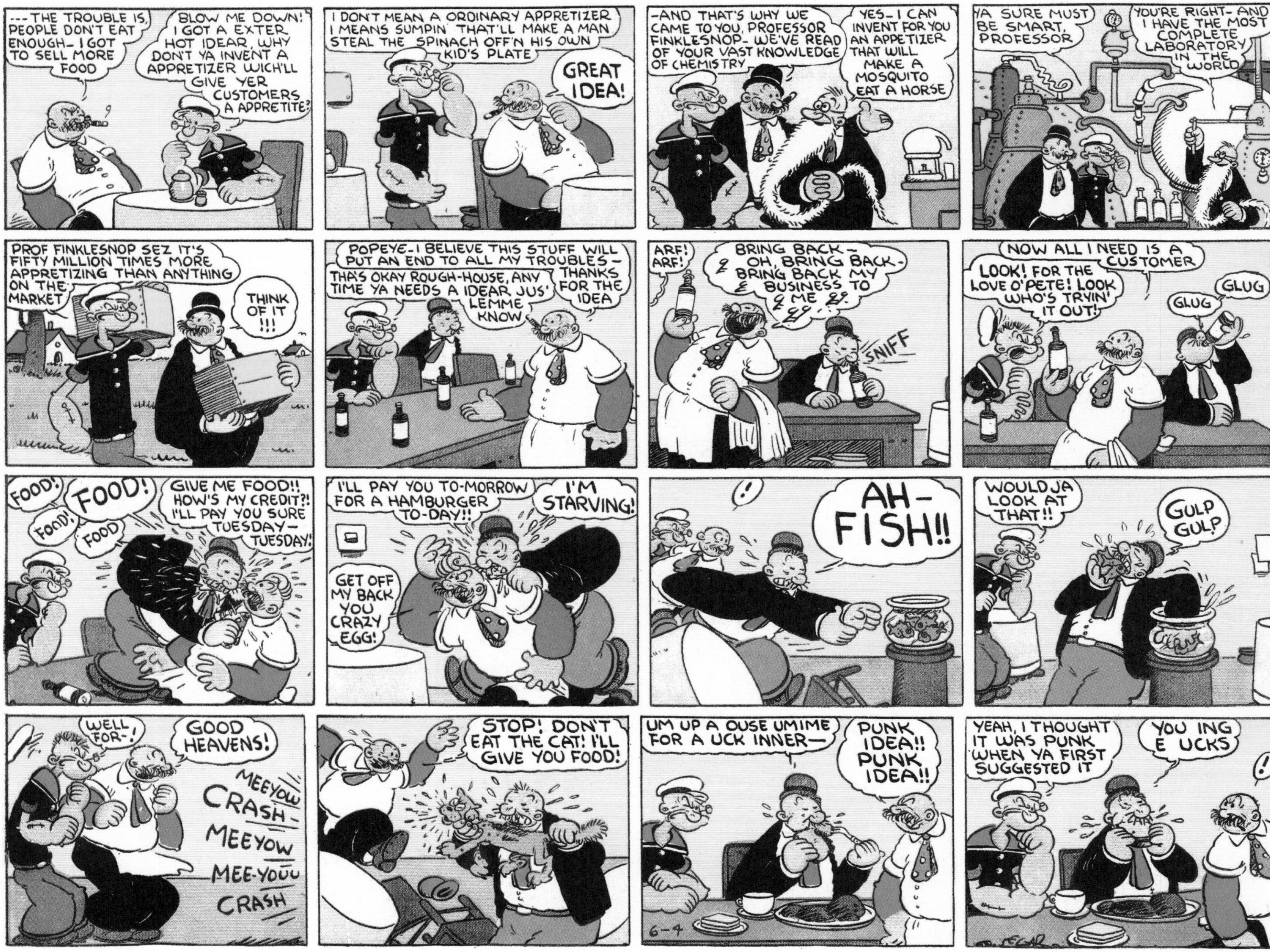
---THE TROUBLE IS, PEOPLE DON'T EAT ENOUGH- I GOT TO SELL MORE FOOD
BLOW ME DOWN! I GOT A EXTER HOT IDEAR, WHY DON'T YA INVENT A APPRETIZER WICH'LL GIVE YER CUSTOMERS A APPRETITE?
I DON'T MEAN A ORDINARY APPRETIZER I MEANS SUMPIN' THAT'LL MAKE A MAN STEAL THE SPINACH OFF'N HIS OWN KID'S PLATE
GREAT IDEA!
-AND THAT'S WHY WE CAME TO YOU, PROFESSOR FINKLESNOP- WE'VE READ OF YOUR VAST KNOWLEDGE OF CHEMISTRY
YES- I CAN INVENT FOR YOU AN APPETIZER THAT WILL MAKE A MOSQUITO EAT A HORSE
YA SURE MUST BE SMART, PROFESSOR
YOU'RE RIGHT- AND I HAVE THE MOST COMPLETE LABORATORY IN THE WORLD
PROF FINKLESNOP SEZ IT'S FIFTY MILLION TIMES MORE APPRETIZING THAN ANYTHING ON THE MARKET
THINK OF IT !!!
POPEYE- I BELIEVE THIS STUFF WILL PUT AN END TO ALL MY TROUBLES-
THA'S OKAY ROUGH-HOUSE, ANY TIME YA NEEDS A IDEAR JUS' LEMME KNOW
THANKS FOR THE IDEA
ARF! ARF!
BRING BACK- OH, BRING BACK- BRING BACK MY BUSINESS TO ME
SNIFF
NOW ALL I NEED IS A CUSTOMER
LOOK! FOR THE LOVE O'PETE! LOOK WHO'S TRYIN' IT OUT!
GLUG
GLUG
FOOD!
FOOD!
FOOD!
FOOD
GIVE ME FOOD!! HOW'S MY CREDIT?! I'LL PAY YOU SURE TUESDAY- TUESDAY!
I'LL PAY YOU TO-MORROW FOR A HAMBURGER TO-DAY!!
I'M STARVING!
GET OFF MY BACK YOU CRAZY EGG!
!
AH- FISH!!
WOULD JA LOOK AT THAT!!
GULP GULP
WELL FOR-!
GOOD HEAVENS!
MEEYOW
CRASH
MEEYOW
MEE-YOUU
CRASH
STOP! DON'T EAT THE CAT! I'LL GIVE YOU FOOD!
UM UP A OUSE UMIME FOR A UCK INNER—
PUNK IDEA!! PUNK IDEA!!
6-4
YEAH, I THOUGHT IT WAS PUNK WHEN YA FIRST SUGGESTED IT
YOU ING E UCKS
!

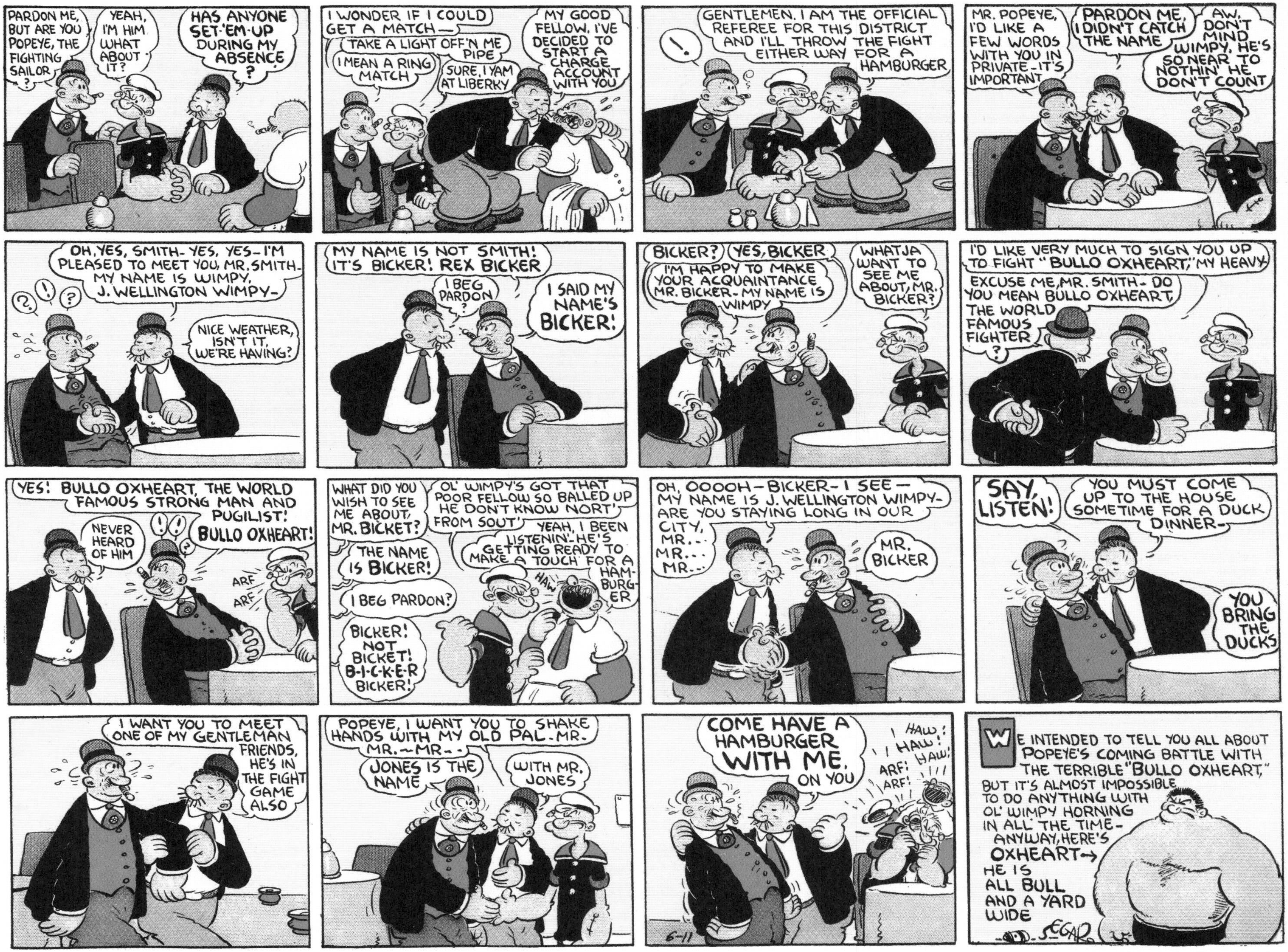
PARDON ME, BUT ARE YOU POPEYE, THE FIGHTING SAILOR ?
YEAH, I'M HIM WHAT ABOUT IT?
HAS ANYONE SET-'EM-UP DURING MY ABSENCE ?
I WONDER IF I COULD GET A MATCH—
TAKE A LIGHT OFF'N ME PIPE
I MEAN A RING MATCH
SURE, I YAM AT LIBERKY
MY GOOD FELLOW, I'VE DECIDED TO START A CHARGE ACCOUNT WITH YOU
!
GENTLEMEN, I AM THE OFFICIAL REFEREE FOR THIS DISTRICT AND I'LL THROW THE FIGHT EITHER WAY FOR A HAMBURGER
MR. POPEYE, I'D LIKE A FEW WORDS WITH YOU IN PRIVATE—IT'S IMPORTANT
PARDON ME, I DIDN'T CATCH THE NAME
AW, DON'T MIND WIMPY, HE'S SO NEAR TO NOTHIN' HE DON'T COUNT
OH, YES, SMITH—YES, YES—I'M PLEASED TO MEET YOU, MR. SMITH—MY NAME IS WIMPY, J. WELLINGTON WIMPY—
? ! ?
NICE WEATHER, ISN'T IT, WE'RE HAVING?
MY NAME IS NOT SMITH! IT'S BICKER! REX BICKER
I BEG PARDON ?
I SAID MY NAME'S BICKER!
BICKER?
YES, BICKER
I'M HAPPY TO MAKE YOUR ACQUAINTANCE MR. BICKER—MY NAME IS WIMPY
WHATJA WANT TO SEE ME ABOUT, MR. BICKER?
I'D LIKE VERY MUCH TO SIGN YOU UP TO FIGHT "BULLO OXHEART," MY HEAVY
EXCUSE ME, MR. SMITH—DO YOU MEAN BULLO OXHEART, THE WORLD FAMOUS FIGHTER ?
YES! BULLO OXHEART, THE WORLD FAMOUS STRONG MAN AND PUGILIST! BULLO OXHEART!
NEVER HEARD OF HIM
! ! ?
ARF ARF
WHAT DID YOU WISH TO SEE ME ABOUT, MR. BICKET?
OL' WIMPY'S GOT THAT POOR FELLOW SO BALLED UP HE DON'T KNOW NORT' FROM SOUT'
YEAH, I BEEN LISTENIN'—HE'S GETTING READY TO MAKE A TOUCH FOR A HAMBURGER
THE NAME IS BICKER!
HAW
I BEG PARDON?
BICKER! NOT BICKET! B-I-C-K-E-R BICKER!
OH, OOOOH—BICKER—I SEE—MY NAME IS J. WELLINGTON WIMPY—ARE YOU STAYING LONG IN OUR CITY, MR.— MR... MR...
MR. BICKER
SAY, LISTEN!
YOU MUST COME UP TO THE HOUSE SOMETIME FOR A DUCK DINNER—
YOU BRING THE DUCKS
I WANT YOU TO MEET ONE OF MY GENTLEMAN FRIENDS, HE'S IN THE FIGHT GAME ALSO
POPEYE, I WANT YOU TO SHAKE HANDS WITH MY OLD PAL—MR. MR.—MR.—
JONES IS THE NAME
WITH MR. JONES
COME HAVE A HAMBURGER WITH ME, ON YOU
HAW! HAW! HAW!
ARF! ARF!
6-11
WE INTENDED TO TELL YOU ALL ABOUT POPEYE'S COMING BATTLE WITH THE TERRIBLE "BULLO OXHEART," BUT IT'S ALMOST IMPOSSIBLE TO DO ANYTHING WITH OL' WIMPY HORNING IN ALL THE TIME—ANYWAY, HERE'S OXHEART→ HE IS ALL BULL AND A YARD WIDE
SEGAR

75. June 11, 1933

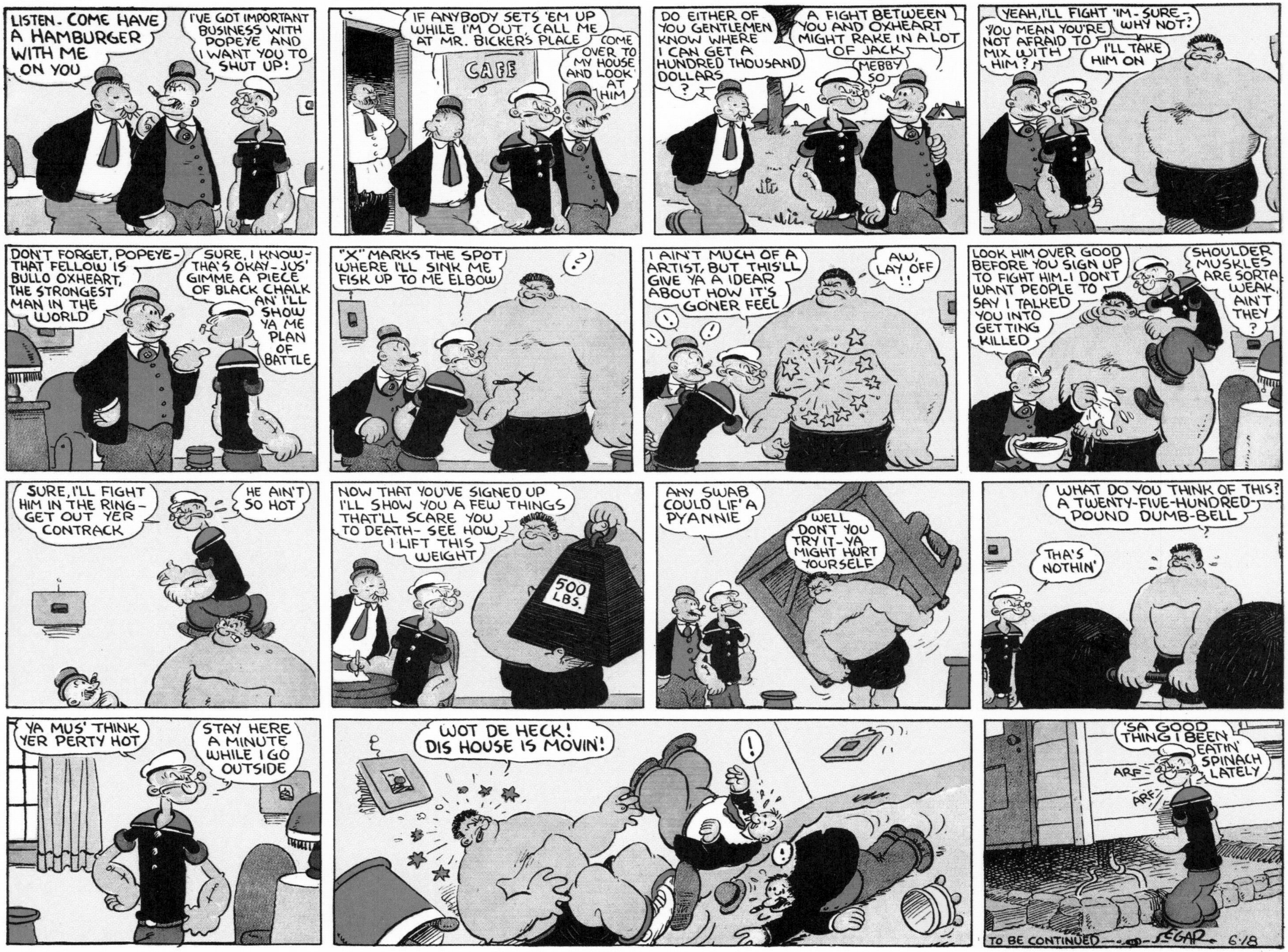

LISTEN- COME HAVE A HAMBURGER WITH ME ON YOU
I'VE GOT IMPORTANT BUSINESS WITH POPEYE AND I WANT YOU TO SHUT UP!
IF ANYBODY SETS 'EM UP WHILE I'M OUT, CALL ME AT MR. BICKER'S PLACE
CAFE
COME OVER TO MY HOUSE AND LOOK AT HIM
DO EITHER OF YOU GENTLEMEN KNOW WHERE I CAN GET A HUNDRED THOUSAND DOLLARS ?
A FIGHT BETWEEN YOU AND OXHEART MIGHT RAKE IN A LOT OF JACK
MEBBY SO
YOU MEAN YOU'RE NOT AFRAID TO MIX WITH HIM ?
YEAH, I'LL FIGHT 'IM- SURE- WHY NOT?
I'LL TAKE HIM ON
DON'T FORGET, POPEYE- THAT FELLOW IS BULLO OXHEART, THE STRONGEST MAN IN THE WORLD
SURE, I KNOW- THA'S OKAY- JUS' GIMME A PIECE OF BLACK CHALK AN' I'LL SHOW YA ME PLAN OF BATTLE
"X" MARKS THE SPOT WHERE I'LL SINK ME FISK UP TO ME ELBOW
?
I AIN'T MUCH OF A ARTIST, BUT THIS'LL GIVE YA A IDEAR ABOUT HOW IT'S GONER FEEL
AW, LAY OFF !!
LOOK HIM OVER GOOD BEFORE YOU SIGN UP TO FIGHT HIM- I DON'T WANT PEOPLE TO SAY I TALKED YOU INTO GETTING KILLED
SHOULDER MUSKLES ARE SORTA WEAK, AIN'T THEY ?
SURE, I'LL FIGHT HIM IN THE RING- GET OUT YER CONTRACK
HE AIN'T SO HOT
NOW THAT YOU'VE SIGNED UP I'LL SHOW YOU A FEW THINGS THAT'LL SCARE YOU TO DEATH- SEE HOW I LIFT THIS WEIGHT
500 LBS.
ANY SWAB COULD LIF' A PYANNIE
WELL DON'T YOU TRY IT- YA MIGHT HURT YOURSELF
WHAT DO YOU THINK OF THIS? A TWENTY-FIVE-HUNDRED-POUND DUMB-BELL
THA'S NOTHIN'
YA MUS' THINK YER PERTY HOT
STAY HERE A MINUTE WHILE I GO OUTSIDE
WOT DE HECK! DIS HOUSE IS MOVIN'!
!
'SA GOOD THING I BEEN EATIN' SPINACH LATELY
ARF
ARF
TO BE CONTINUED
SEGAR 6-18

76. June 18, 1933

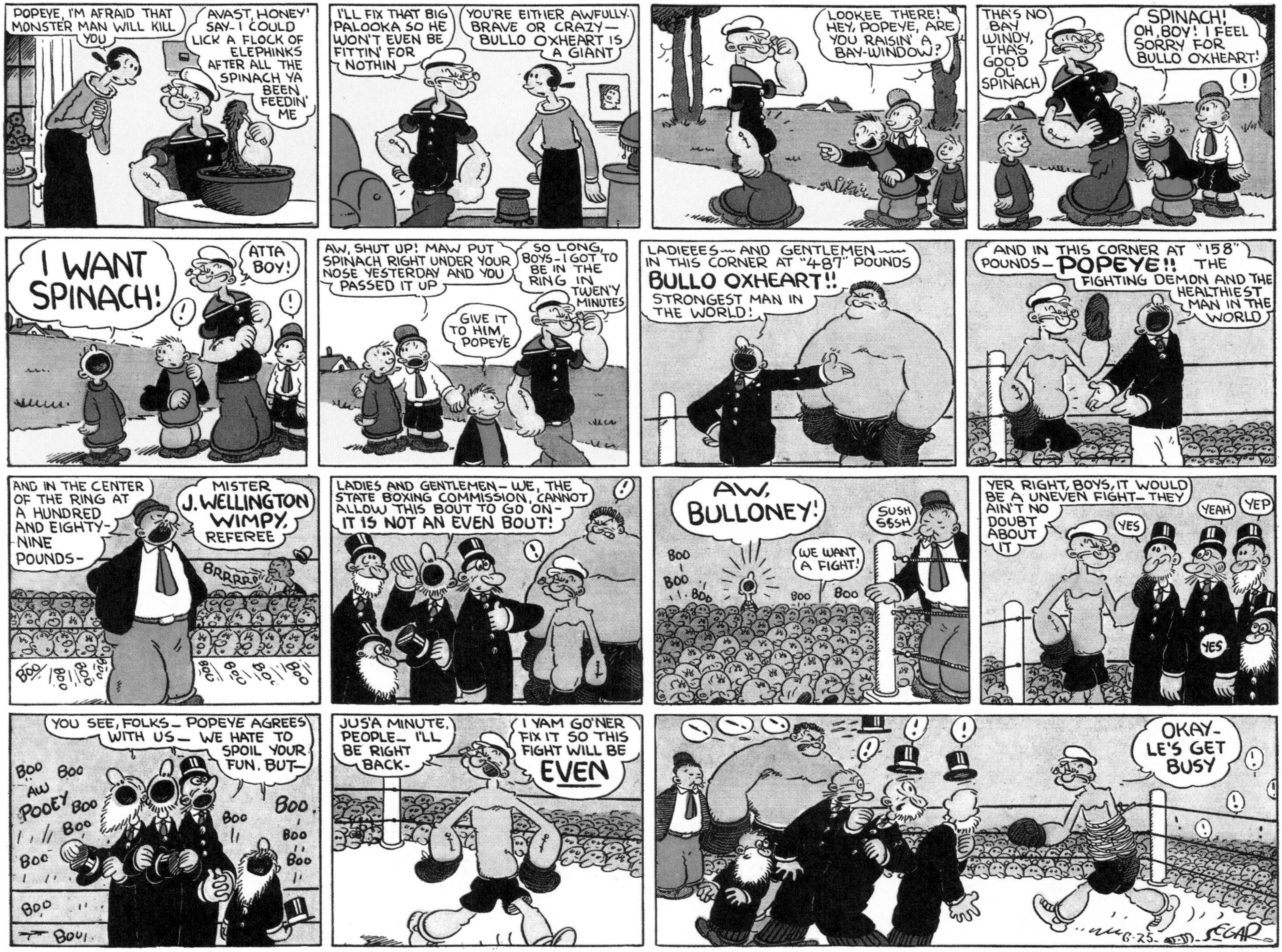
POPEYE, I'M AFRAID THAT MONSTER MAN WILL KILL YOU
AVAST, HONEY! SAY- I COULD LICK A FLOCK OF ELEPHINKS AFTER ALL THE SPINACH YA BEEN FEEDIN' ME
I'LL FIX THAT BIG PALOOKA SO HE WON'T EVEN BE FITTIN' FOR NOTHIN
YOU'RE EITHER AWFULLY BRAVE OR CRAZY— BULLO OXHEART IS A GIANT
LOOKEE THERE! HEY, POPEYE, ARE YOU RAISIN' A BAY-WINDOW?
THA'S NO BAY WINDY, THA'S GOOD OL' SPINACH
SPINACH! OH, BOY! I FEEL SORRY FOR BULLO OXHEART!
!
I WANT SPINACH!
ATTA BOY!
!
!
AW, SHUT UP! MAW PUT SPINACH RIGHT UNDER YOUR NOSE YESTERDAY AND YOU PASSED IT UP
SO LONG, BOYS- I GOT TO BE IN THE RING IN TWEN'Y MINUTES
GIVE IT TO HIM, POPEYE
LADIEEES— AND GENTLEMEN— IN THIS CORNER AT "487" POUNDS BULLO OXHEART!! STRONGEST MAN IN THE WORLD!
AND IN THIS CORNER AT "158" POUNDS- POPEYE!! THE FIGHTING DEMON AND THE HEALTHIEST MAN IN THE WORLD
AND IN THE CENTER OF THE RING AT A HUNDRED AND EIGHTY-NINE POUNDS-
MISTER J. WELLINGTON WIMPY, REFEREE
BRRRRR
BOO BOO BOO BOO BOO BOO BOO BOO
LADIES AND GENTLEMEN- WE, THE STATE BOXING COMMISSION, CANNOT ALLOW THIS BOUT TO GO ON- IT IS NOT AN EVEN BOUT!
!
!
AW, BULLONEY!
SUSH S$SH
WE WANT A FIGHT!
BOO BOO BOO BOO BOO
YER RIGHT, BOYS, IT WOULD BE A UNEVEN FIGHT- THEY AIN'T NO DOUBT ABOUT IT
YES
YEAH
YEP
YES
YOU SEE, FOLKS- POPEYE AGREES WITH US- WE HATE TO SPOIL YOUR FUN. BUT-
BOO BOO AW POOEY BOO BOO BOO BOO BOO BOO BOO BOO BOO BOO
JUS'A MINUTE, PEOPLE- I'LL BE RIGHT BACK-
I YAM GO'NER FIX IT SO THIS FIGHT WILL BE EVEN
OKAY- LE'S GET BUSY
6-25
SEGAR

77. June 25, 1933

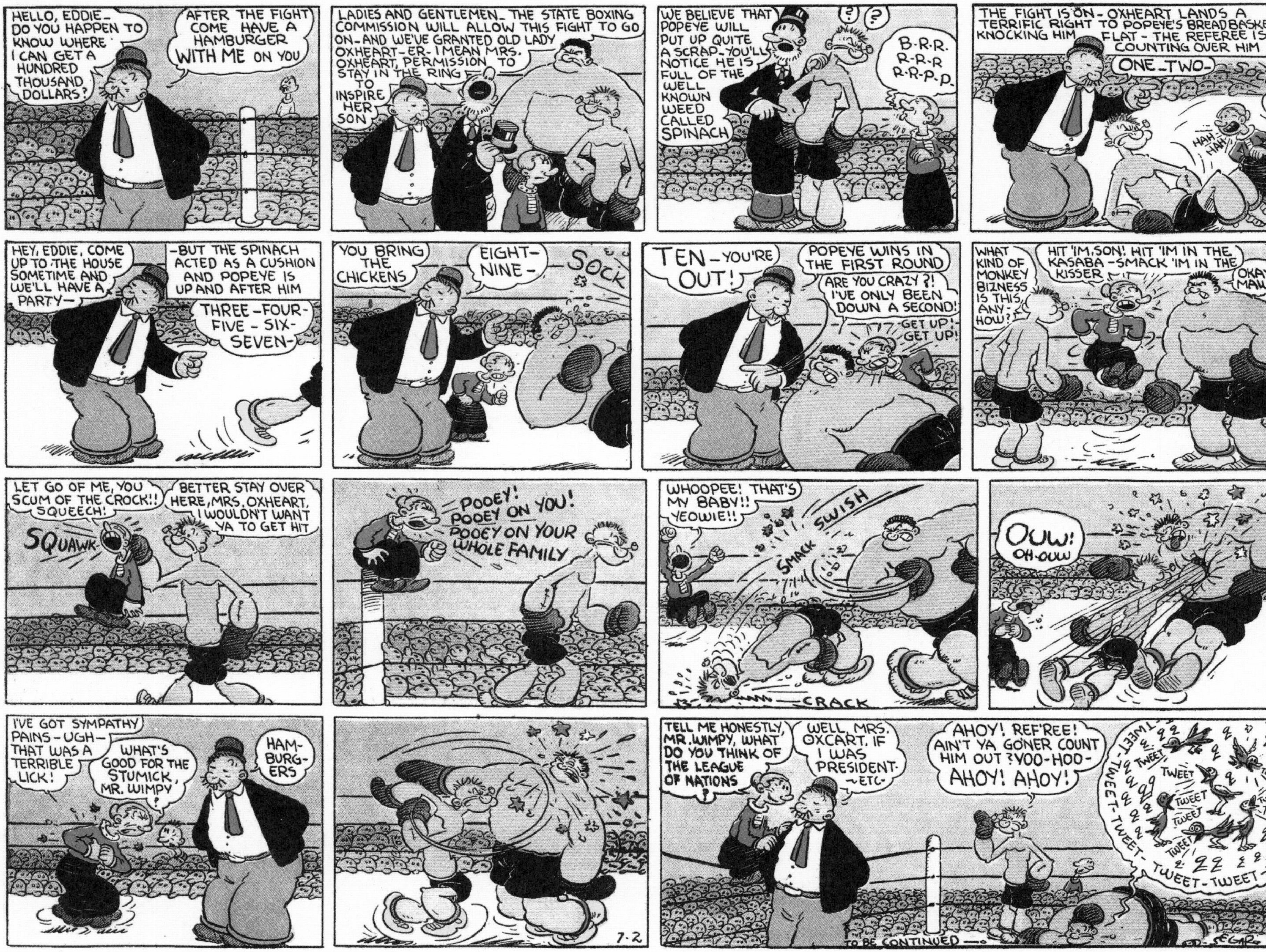

HELLO, EDDIE— DO YOU HAPPEN TO KNOW WHERE I CAN GET A HUNDRED THOUSAND DOLLARS?
AFTER THE FIGHT COME HAVE A HAMBURGER WITH ME ON YOU
LADIES AND GENTLEMEN— THE STATE BOXING COMMISSION WILL ALLOW THIS FIGHT TO GO ON—AND WE'VE GRANTED OLD LADY OXHEART—ER—I MEAN MRS. OXHEART, PERMISSION TO STAY IN THE RING TO INSPIRE HER SON
WE BELIEVE THAT POPEYE WILL PUT UP QUITE A SCRAP—YOU'LL NOTICE HE IS FULL OF THE WELL KNOWN WEED CALLED SPINACH
?
?
B-R-R. R-R-R R-R-P-P.
THE FIGHT IS ON—OXHEART LANDS A TERRIFIC RIGHT TO POPEYE'S BREADBASKET KNOCKING HIM FLAT—THE REFEREE IS COUNTING OVER HIM
ONE—TWO—
SOCK
HAH-HAH
HEY, EDDIE, COME UP TO THE HOUSE SOMETIME AND WE'LL HAVE A PARTY—
—BUT THE SPINACH ACTED AS A CUSHION AND POPEYE IS UP AND AFTER HIM
THREE—FOUR—FIVE—SIX—SEVEN—
YOU BRING THE CHICKENS
EIGHT—NINE—
SOCK
TEN—YOU'RE OUT!
POPEYE WINS IN THE FIRST ROUND
ARE YOU CRAZY?! I'VE ONLY BEEN DOWN A SECOND!
GET UP! GET UP!
WHAT KIND OF MONKEY BIZNESS IS THIS, ANY-HOW?
HIT 'IM, SON! HIT 'IM IN THE KASABA—SMACK 'IM IN THE KISSER
OKAY, MAW
LET GO OF ME, YOU SCUM OF THE CROCK!! SQUEECH!
BETTER STAY OVER HERE, MRS. OXHEART, I WOULDN'T WANT YA TO GET HIT
SQUAWK
POOEY! POOEY ON YOU! POOEY ON YOUR WHOLE FAMILY
WHOOPEE! THAT'S MY BABY!! YEOWIE!!
SWISH
SMACK
CRACK
OUW! OH-OUW
I'VE GOT SYMPATHY PAINS—UGH—THAT WAS A TERRIBLE LICK!
WHAT'S GOOD FOR THE STUMICK, MR. WIMPY?
HAM-BURG-ERS
7-2
TELL ME HONESTLY, MR. WIMPY, WHAT DO YOU THINK OF THE LEAGUE OF NATIONS?
WELL, MRS. OXCART, IF I WAS PRESIDENT— —ETC—
AHOY! REF'REE! AIN'T YA GONER COUNT HIM OUT? YOO-HOO— AHOY! AHOY!
TWEET
TO BE CONTINUED—
SEGAR

78. July 2, 1933

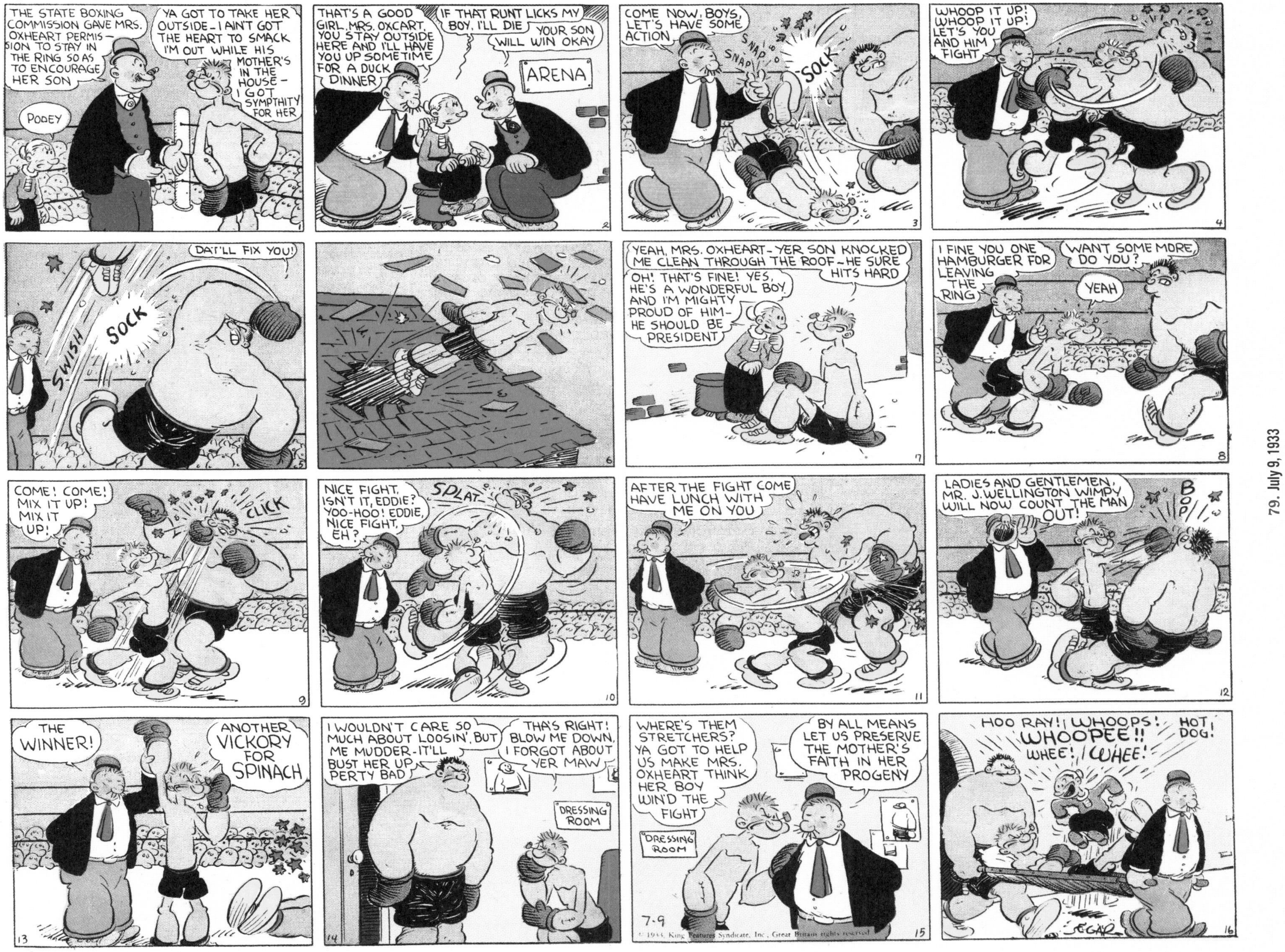
THE STATE BOXING COMMISSION GAVE MRS. OXHEART PERMISSION TO STAY IN THE RING SO AS TO ENCOURAGE HER SON
YA GOT TO TAKE HER OUTSIDE - I AIN'T GOT THE HEART TO SMACK I'M OUT WHILE HIS MOTHER'S IN THE HOUSE - I GOT SYMPTHITY FOR HER
PODEY
THAT'S A GOOD GIRL, MRS. OXCART, YOU STAY OUTSIDE HERE AND I'LL HAVE YOU UP SOMETIME FOR A DUCK DINNER
IF THAT RUNT LICKS MY BOY, I'LL DIE
YOUR SON WILL WIN OKAY
ARENA
COME NOW, BOYS, LET'S HAVE SOME ACTION
SNAP
SNAP
SOCK
WHOOP IT UP! WHOOP IT UP! LET'S YOU AND HIM FIGHT
DAT'LL FIX YOU!
SOCK
SWISH
YEAH, MRS. OXHEART - YER SON KNOCKED ME CLEAN THROUGH THE ROOF - HE SURE HITS HARD
OH! THAT'S FINE! YES, HE'S A WONDERFUL BOY, AND I'M MIGHTY PROUD OF HIM - HE SHOULD BE PRESIDENT
I FINE YOU ONE HAMBURGER FOR LEAVING THE RING
WANT SOME MORE, DO YOU?
YEAH
COME! COME! MIX IT UP! MIX IT UP!
CLICK
NICE FIGHT, ISN'T IT, EDDIE? YOO-HOO! EDDIE, NICE FIGHT, EH?
SPLAT
AFTER THE FIGHT COME HAVE LUNCH WITH ME ON YOU
LADIES AND GENTLEMEN, MR. J. WELLINGTON WIMPY WILL NOW COUNT THE MAN OUT!
BOP
THE WINNER!
ANOTHER VICKORY FOR SPINACH
I WOULDN'T CARE SO MUCH ABOUT LOOSIN', BUT ME MUDDER - IT'LL BUST HER UP PERTY BAD
THA'S RIGHT! BLOW ME DOWN, I FORGOT ABOUT YER MAW
DRESSING ROOM
WHERE'S THEM STRETCHERS? YA GOT TO HELP US MAKE MRS. OXHEART THINK HER BOY WIN'D THE FIGHT
BY ALL MEANS LET US PRESERVE THE MOTHER'S FAITH IN HER PROGENY
DRESSING ROOM
7-9
© 1933, King Features Syndicate, Inc., Great Britain rights reserved
HOO RAY!! WHOOPS! HOT DOG!
WHOOPEE!!
WHEE! WHEE!
SEGAR

79. July 9, 1933

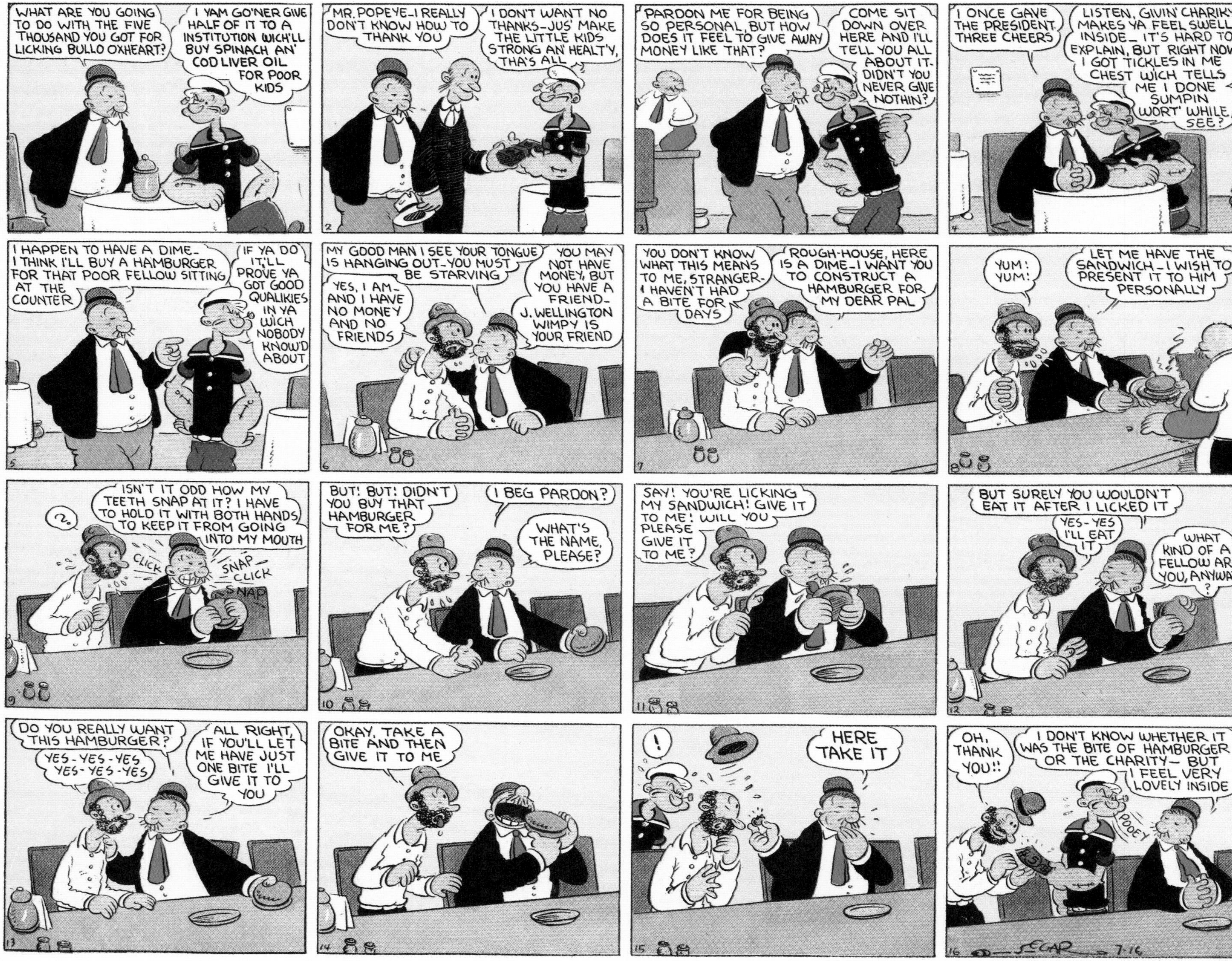
WHAT ARE YOU GOING TO DO WITH THE FIVE THOUSAND YOU GOT FOR LICKING BULLO OXHEART?
I YAM GO'NER GIVE HALF OF IT TO A INSTITUTION WICH'LL BUY SPINACH AN' COD LIVER OIL FOR POOR KIDS
MR. POPEYE-I REALLY DON'T KNOW HOW TO THANK YOU
I DON'T WANT NO THANKS-JUS' MAKE THE LITTLE KIDS STRONG AN' HEALT'Y, THA'S ALL
PARDON ME FOR BEING SO PERSONAL, BUT HOW DOES IT FEEL TO GIVE AWAY MONEY LIKE THAT?
COME SIT DOWN OVER HERE AND I'LL TELL YOU ALL ABOUT IT. DIDN'T YOU NEVER GIVE NOTHIN?
I ONCE GAVE THE PRESIDENT THREE CHEERS
LISTEN, GIVIN' CHARIKY MAKES YA FEEL SWELL INSIDE_ IT'S HARD TO EXPLAIN, BUT RIGHT NOW I GOT TICKLES IN ME CHEST WICH TELLS ME I DONE SUMPIN WORT' WHILE, SEE?
I HAPPEN TO HAVE A DIME-I THINK I'LL BUY A HAMBURGER FOR THAT POOR FELLOW SITTING AT THE COUNTER
IF YA DO IT,'LL PROVE YA GOT GOOD QUALIKIES IN YA WICH NOBODY KNOW'D ABOUT
MY GOOD MAN I SEE YOUR TONGUE IS HANGING OUT-YOU MUST BE STARVING
YES, I AM-AND I HAVE NO MONEY AND NO FRIENDS
YOU MAY NOT HAVE MONEY, BUT YOU HAVE A FRIEND-J. WELLINGTON WIMPY IS YOUR FRIEND
YOU DON'T KNOW WHAT THIS MEANS TO ME, STRANGER-I HAVEN'T HAD A BITE FOR DAYS
ROUGH-HOUSE, HERE IS A DIME-I WANT YOU TO CONSTRUCT A HAMBURGER FOR MY DEAR PAL
YUM! YUM!
LET ME HAVE THE SANDWICH-I WISH TO PRESENT IT TO HIM PERSONALLY
?
ISN'T IT ODD HOW MY TEETH SNAP AT IT? I HAVE TO HOLD IT WITH BOTH HANDS TO KEEP IT FROM GOING INTO MY MOUTH
CLICK
SNAP
CLICK
SNAP
BUT! BUT! DIDN'T YOU BUY THAT HAMBURGER FOR ME?
I BEG PARDON?
WHAT'S THE NAME, PLEASE?
SAY! YOU'RE LICKING MY SANDWICH! GIVE IT TO ME! WILL YOU PLEASE GIVE IT TO ME?
BUT SURELY YOU WOULDN'T EAT IT AFTER I LICKED IT
YES-YES I'LL EAT IT
WHAT KIND OF A FELLOW ARE YOU, ANYWAY?
DO YOU REALLY WANT THIS HAMBURGER?
YES-YES-YES YES-YES-YES
ALL RIGHT, IF YOU'LL LET ME HAVE JUST ONE BITE I'LL GIVE IT TO YOU
OKAY, TAKE A BITE AND THEN GIVE IT TO ME
!
HERE TAKE IT
OH, THANK YOU!!
I DON'T KNOW WHETHER IT WAS THE BITE OF HAMBURGER OR THE CHARITY- BUT I FEEL VERY LOVELY INSIDE
POOEY
SEGAR 7-16

80. July 16, 1933

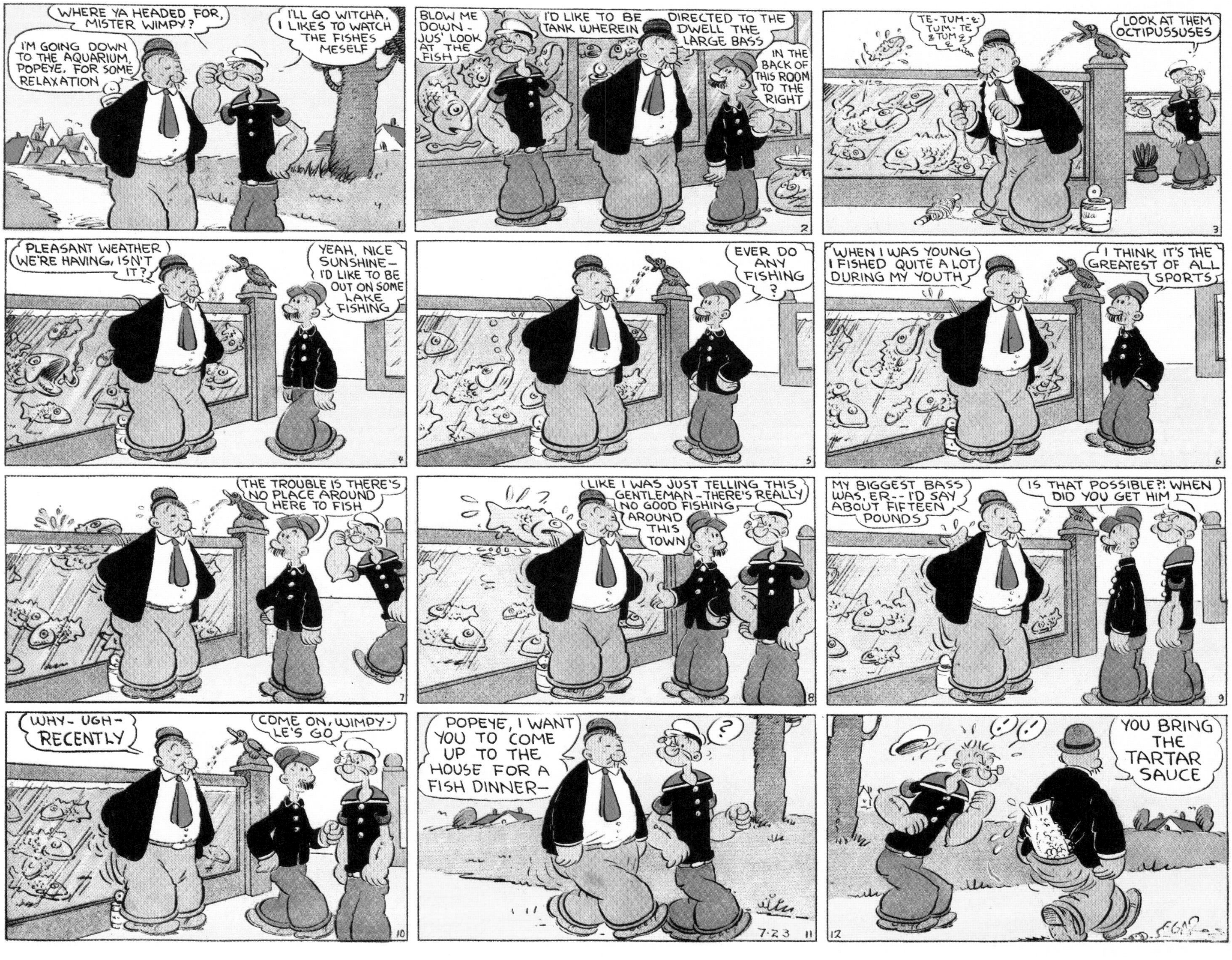
WHERE YA HEADED FOR, MISTER WIMPY?
I'M GOING DOWN TO THE AQUARIUM, POPEYE, FOR SOME RELAXATION
I'LL GO WITCHA, I LIKES TO WATCH THE FISHES MESELF
BLOW ME DOWN - JUS' LOOK AT THE FISH
I'D LIKE TO BE DIRECTED TO THE TANK WHEREIN DWELL THE LARGE BASS
IN THE BACK OF THIS ROOM TO THE RIGHT
TE-TUM-TUM-TE & TUM
LOOK AT THEM OCTIPUSSUSES
PLEASANT WEATHER WE'RE HAVING, ISN'T IT?
YEAH, NICE SUNSHINE— I'D LIKE TO BE OUT ON SOME LAKE FISHING
EVER DO ANY FISHING?
WHEN I WAS YOUNG I FISHED QUITE A LOT DURING MY YOUTH
I THINK IT'S THE GREATEST OF ALL SPORTS
THE TROUBLE IS THERE'S NO PLACE AROUND HERE TO FISH
LIKE I WAS JUST TELLING THIS GENTLEMAN - THERE'S REALLY NO GOOD FISHING AROUND THIS TOWN
MY BIGGEST BASS WAS, ER-- I'D SAY ABOUT FIFTEEN POUNDS
IS THAT POSSIBLE?! WHEN DID YOU GET HIM
WHY- UGH- RECENTLY
COME ON, WIMPY- LE'S GO
POPEYE, I WANT YOU TO COME UP TO THE HOUSE FOR A FISH DINNER—
?
7-23
! !
YOU BRING THE TARTAR SAUCE

81 . July 23, 1933

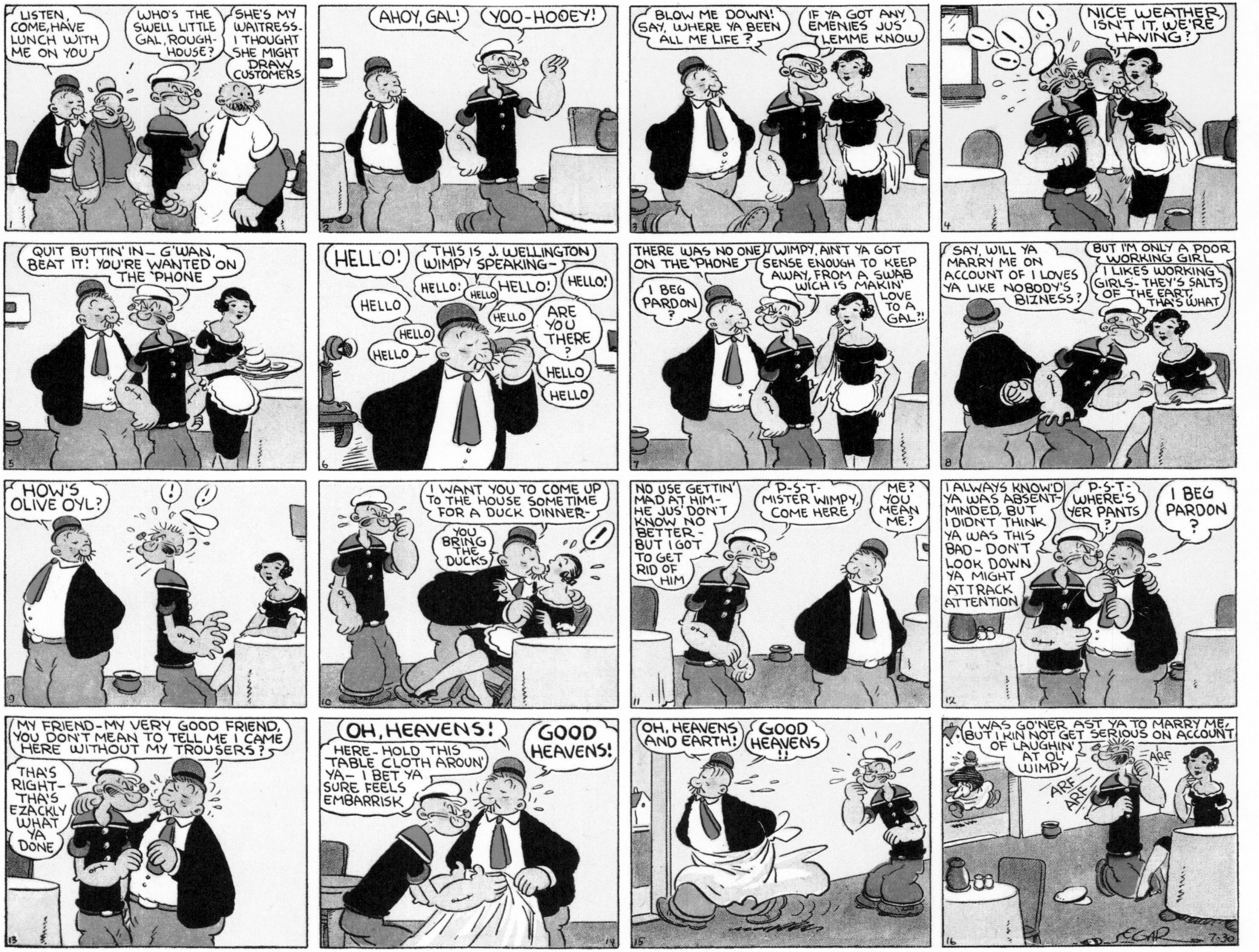
LISTEN, COME, HAVE LUNCH WITH ME ON YOU
WHO'S THE SWELL LITTLE GAL, ROUGH-HOUSE?
SHE'S MY WAITRESS- I THOUGHT SHE MIGHT DRAW CUSTOMERS
AHOY, GAL!
YOO-HOOEY!
BLOW ME DOWN! SAY, WHERE YA BEEN ALL ME LIFE?
IF YA GOT ANY EMENIES JUS' LEMME KNOW
NICE WEATHER, ISN'T IT, WE'RE HAVING?
QUIT BUTTIN' IN— G'WAN, BEAT IT! YOU'RE WANTED ON THE 'PHONE
HELLO!
THIS IS J. WELLINGTON WIMPY SPEAKING—
HELLO!
HELLO
HELLO!
HELLO!
HELLO
HELLO
HELLO
HELLO
ARE YOU THERE?
HELLO
HELLO
THERE WAS NO ONE ON THE 'PHONE
I BEG PARDON?
WIMPY, AIN'T YA GOT SENSE ENOUGH TO KEEP AWAY, FROM A SWAB WICH IS MAKIN' LOVE TO A GAL?!
SAY, WILL YA MARRY ME ON ACCOUNT OF I LOVES YA LIKE NOBODY'S BIZNESS?
BUT I'M ONLY A POOR WORKING GIRL
I LIKES WORKING GIRLS- THEY'S SALTS OF THE EART, THA'S WHAT
HOW'S OLIVE OYL?
I WANT YOU TO COME UP TO THE HOUSE SOMETIME FOR A DUCK DINNER-
YOU BRING THE DUCKS
NO USE GETTIN' MAD AT HIM- HE JUS' DON'T KNOW NO BETTER- BUT I GOT TO GET RID OF HIM
P-S-T- MISTER WIMPY, COME HERE
ME? YOU MEAN ME?
I ALWAYS KNOW'D YA WAS ABSENT-MINDED, BUT I DIDN'T THINK YA WAS THIS BAD- DON'T LOOK DOWN YA MIGHT ATTRACK ATTENTION
P-S-T- WHERE'S YER PANTS?
I BEG PARDON?
MY FRIEND- MY VERY GOOD FRIEND, YOU DON'T MEAN TO TELL ME I CAME HERE WITHOUT MY TROUSERS?
THA'S RIGHT- THA'S EZACKLY WHAT YA DONE
OH, HEAVENS!
HERE- HOLD THIS TABLE CLOTH AROUN' YA- I BET YA SURE FEELS EMBARRISK
GOOD HEAVENS!
OH, HEAVENS AND EARTH!
GOOD HEAVENS!!
I WAS GO'NER AST YA TO MARRY ME, BUT I KIN NOT GET SERIOUS ON ACCOUNT OF LAUGHIN' AT OL' WIMPY
ARF
ARF
ARF
SEGAR
7-30

82. July 30, 1933

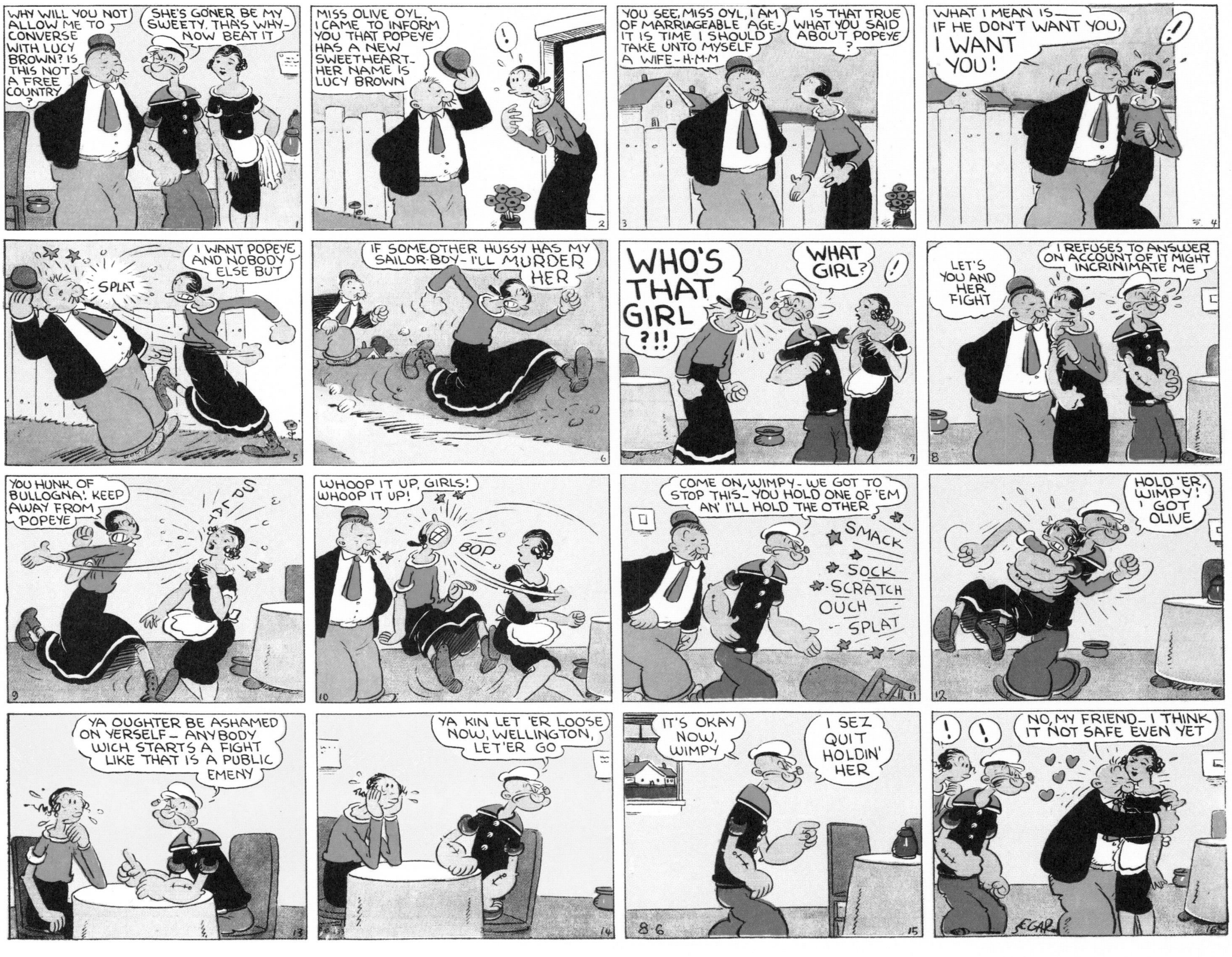
WHY WILL YOU NOT ALLOW ME TO CONVERSE WITH LUCY BROWN? IS THIS NOT A FREE COUNTRY ?
SHE'S GONER BE MY SWEETY. THA'S WHY- NOW BEAT IT
MISS OLIVE OYL, I CAME TO INFORM YOU THAT POPEYE HAS A NEW SWEETHEART- HER NAME IS LUCY BROWN
!
YOU SEE, MISS OYL, I AM OF MARRIAGEABLE AGE- IT IS TIME I SHOULD TAKE UNTO MYSELF A WIFE- H-M-M
IS THAT TRUE WHAT YOU SAID ABOUT POPEYE ?
WHAT I MEAN IS— IF HE DON'T WANT YOU, I WANT YOU!
!
SPLAT
I WANT POPEYE AND NOBODY ELSE BUT
IF SOMEOTHER HUSSY HAS MY SAILOR-BOY- I'LL MURDER HER
WHO'S THAT GIRL ?!!
WHAT GIRL?
!
LET'S YOU AND HER FIGHT
I REFUSES TO ANSWER ON ACCOUNT OF IT MIGHT INCRINIMATE ME
YOU HUNK OF BULLOGNA! KEEP AWAY FROM POPEYE
WHOOP IT UP, GIRLS! WHOOP IT UP!
BOP
COME ON, WIMPY- WE GOT TO STOP THIS- YOU HOLD ONE OF 'EM AN' I'LL HOLD THE OTHER
SMACK
SOCK
SCRATCH
OUCH
SPLAT
HOLD 'ER, WIMPY! I GOT OLIVE
YA OUGHTER BE ASHAMED ON YERSELF – ANYBODY WICH STARTS A FIGHT LIKE THAT IS A PUBLIC EMENY
YA KIN LET 'ER LOOSE NOW, WELLINGTON, LET'ER GO
IT'S OKAY NOW, WIMPY
I SEZ QUIT HOLDIN' HER
!
!
NO, MY FRIEND- I THINK IT NOT SAFE EVEN YET
8-6
E.C. SEGAR

83. August 6, 1933

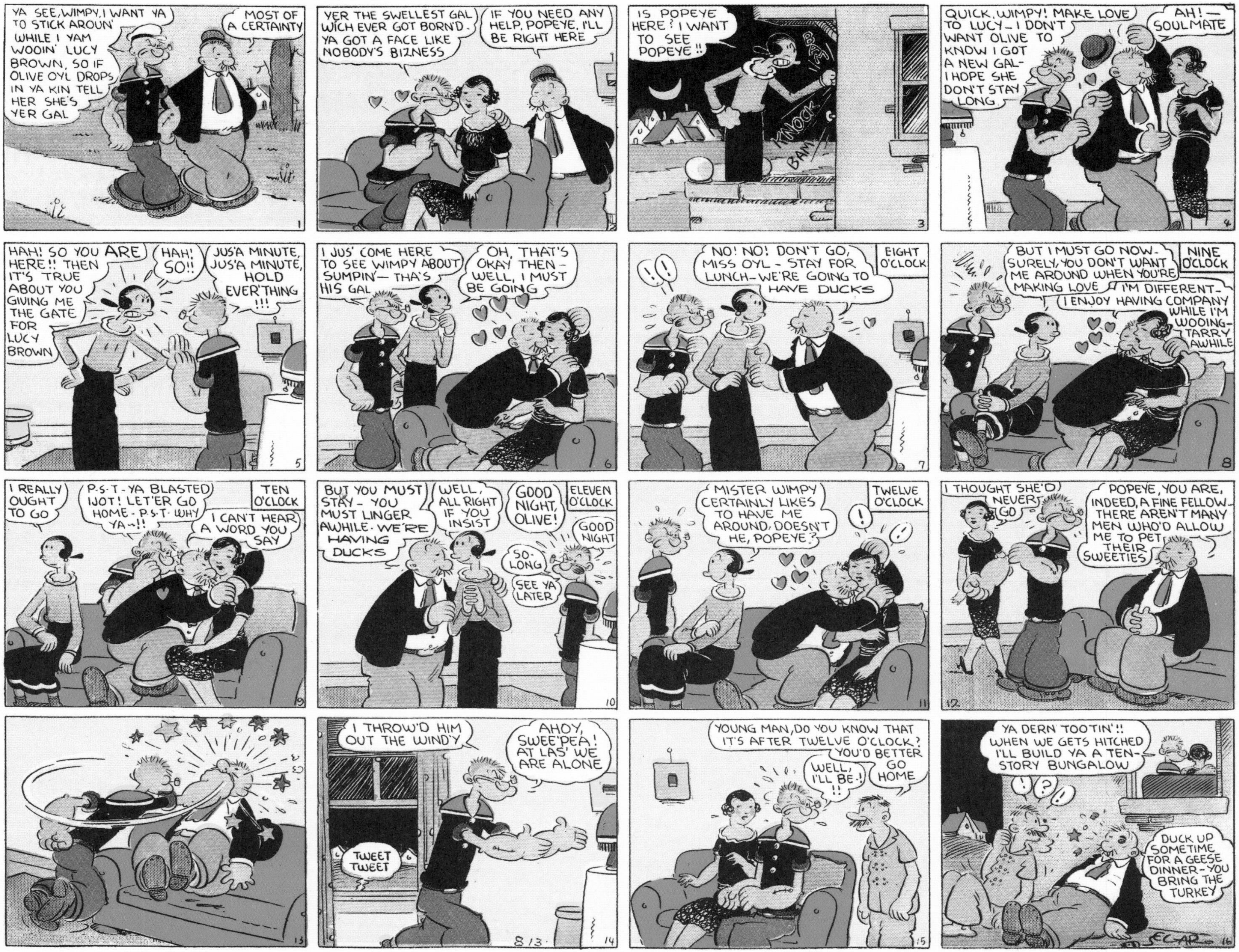
YA SEE, WIMPY, I WANT YA TO STICK AROUN' WHILE I YAM WOOIN' LUCY BROWN, SO IF OLIVE OYL DROPS IN YA KIN TELL HER SHE'S YER GAL
MOST OF A CERTAINTY
YER THE SWELLEST GAL WICH EVER GOT BORN'D - YA GOT A FACE LIKE NOBODY'S BIZNESS
IF YOU NEED ANY HELP, POPEYE, I'LL BE RIGHT HERE
IS POPEYE HERE? I WANT TO SEE POPEYE !!
BAM
KNOCK
BAM
QUICK, WIMPY! MAKE LOVE TO LUCY - I DON'T WANT OLIVE TO KNOW I GOT A NEW GAL - I HOPE SHE DON'T STAY LONG
AH! — SOULMATE
HAH! SO YOU ARE HERE!! THEN IT'S TRUE ABOUT YOU GIVING ME THE GATE FOR LUCY BROWN
HAH! SO!!
JUS'A MINUTE, JUS'A MINUTE, HOLD EVER'THING !!!
I JUS' COME HERE TO SEE WIMPY ABOUT SUMPIN' — THA'S HIS GAL
OH, THAT'S OKAY THEN - WELL, I MUST BE GOING
EIGHT O'CLOCK
!!
NO! NO! DON'T GO, MISS OYL - STAY FOR LUNCH - WE'RE GOING TO HAVE DUCKS
NINE O'CLOCK
BUT I MUST GO NOW - SURELY, YOU DON'T WANT ME AROUND WHEN YOU'RE MAKING LOVE
I'M DIFFERENT - I ENJOY HAVING COMPANY WHILE I'M WOOING - TARRY AWHILE
TEN O'CLOCK
I REALLY OUGHT TO GO
P.S.T - YA BLASTED IJOT! LET'ER GO HOME - P.S.T. WHY YA~!!
I CAN'T HEAR A WORD YOU SAY
ELEVEN O'CLOCK
BUT YOU MUST STAY - YOU MUST LINGER AWHILE. WE'RE HAVING DUCKS
WELL, ALL RIGHT IF YOU INSIST
GOOD NIGHT, OLIVE!
GOOD NIGHT
SO-LONG
SEE YA LATER
TWELVE O'CLOCK
MISTER WIMPY CERTAINLY LIKES TO HAVE ME AROUND, DOESN'T HE, POPEYE?
I THOUGHT SHE'D NEVER GO
POPEYE, YOU ARE, INDEED, A FINE FELLOW - THERE AREN'T MANY MEN WHO'D ALLOW ME TO PET THEIR SWEETIES
I THROW'D HIM OUT THE WIND'Y
AHOY, SWEE'PEA! AT LAS' WE ARE ALONE
TWEET TWEET
8.13.
YOUNG MAN, DO YOU KNOW THAT IT'S AFTER TWELVE O'CLOCK? YOU'D BETTER GO HOME
WELL, I'LL BE.! !!
YA DERN TOOTIN'!! WHEN WE GETS HITCHED I'LL BUILD YA A TEN-STORY BUNGALOW
DUCK UP SOMETIME FOR A GEESE DINNER - YOU BRING THE TURKEY
SEGAR

84. August 13, 1933

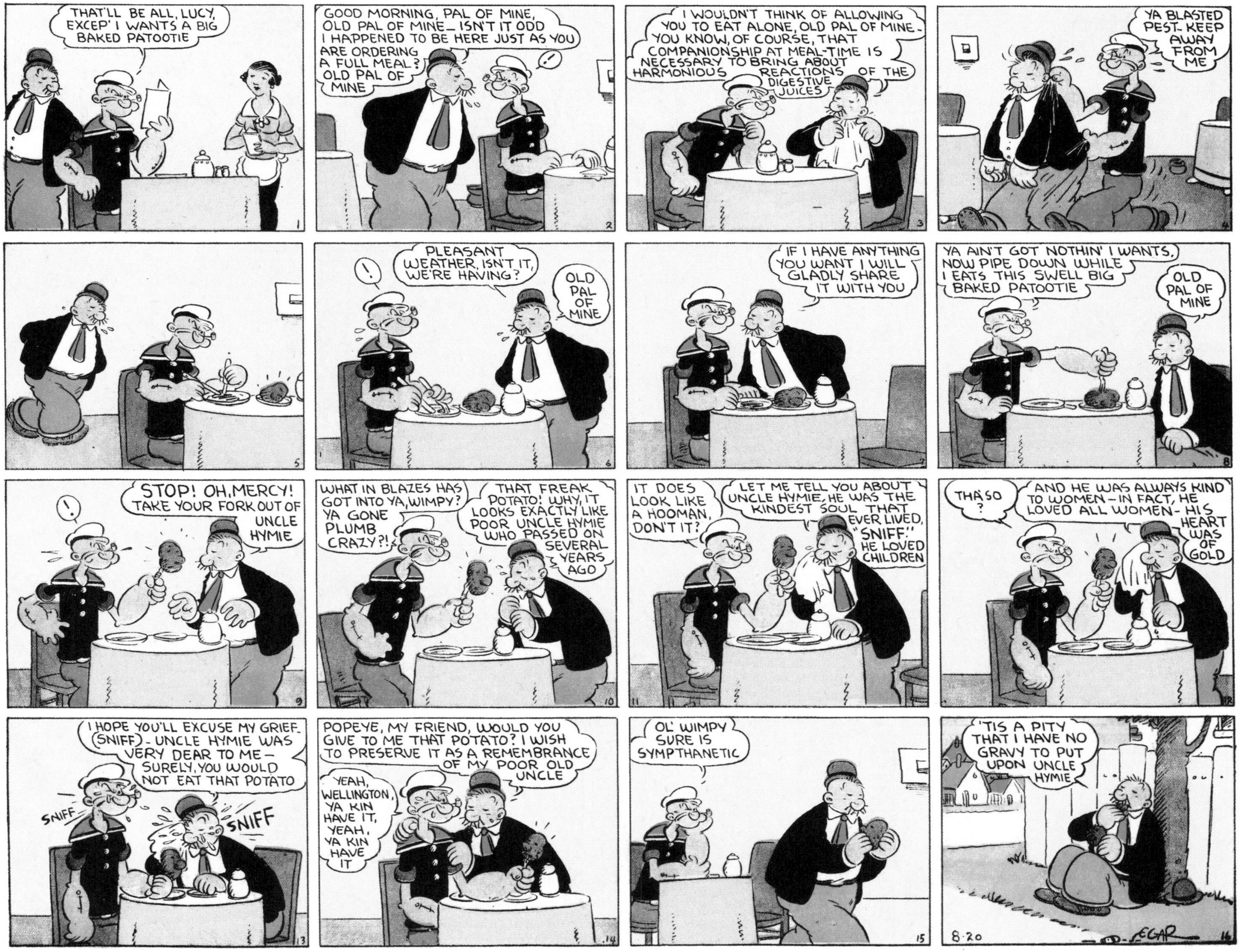

THAT'LL BE ALL, LUCY, EXCEP' I WANTS A BIG BAKED PATOOTIE
GOOD MORNING, PAL OF MINE, OLD PAL OF MINE— ISN'T IT ODD I HAPPENED TO BE HERE JUST AS YOU ARE ORDERING A FULL MEAL? OLD PAL OF MINE
!
I WOULDN'T THINK OF ALLOWING YOU TO EAT ALONE, OLD PAL OF MINE— YOU KNOW, OF COURSE, THAT COMPANIONSHIP AT MEAL-TIME IS NECESSARY TO BRING ABOUT HARMONIOUS REACTIONS OF THE DIGESTIVE JUICES
YA BLASTED PEST- KEEP AWAY FROM ME
!
PLEASANT WEATHER, ISN'T IT, WE'RE HAVING?
OLD PAL OF MINE
IF I HAVE ANYTHING YOU WANT I WILL GLADLY SHARE IT WITH YOU
YA AIN'T GOT NOTHIN' I WANTS, NOW PIPE DOWN WHILE I EATS THIS SWELL BIG BAKED PATOOTIE
OLD PAL OF MINE
!
STOP! OH, MERCY! TAKE YOUR FORK OUT OF UNCLE HYMIE
WHAT IN BLAZES HAS GOT INTO YA, WIMPY? YA GONE PLUMB CRAZY?!
THAT FREAK POTATO! WHY, IT LOOKS EXACTLY LIKE POOR UNCLE HYMIE WHO PASSED ON SEVERAL YEARS AGO
IT DOES LOOK LIKE A HOOMAN, DON'T IT?
LET ME TELL YOU ABOUT UNCLE HYMIE, HE WAS THE KINDEST SOUL THAT EVER LIVED, "SNIFF." HE LOVED CHILDREN
THA'S SO ?
AND HE WAS ALWAYS KIND TO WOMEN - IN FACT, HE LOVED ALL WOMEN - HIS HEART WAS OF GOLD
I HOPE YOU'LL EXCUSE MY GRIEF. (SNIFF) - UNCLE HYMIE WAS VERY DEAR TO ME — SURELY, YOU WOULD NOT EAT THAT POTATO
SNIFF
SNIFF
POPEYE, MY FRIEND, WOULD YOU GIVE TO ME THAT POTATO? I WISH TO PRESERVE IT AS A REMEMBRANCE OF MY POOR OLD UNCLE
YEAH, WELLINGTON, YA KIN HAVE IT, YEAH, YA KIN HAVE IT
OL' WIMPY SURE IS SYMPTHANETIC
'TIS A PITY THAT I HAVE NO GRAVY TO PUT UPON UNCLE HYMIE
8·20
SEGAR

85. August 20, 1933

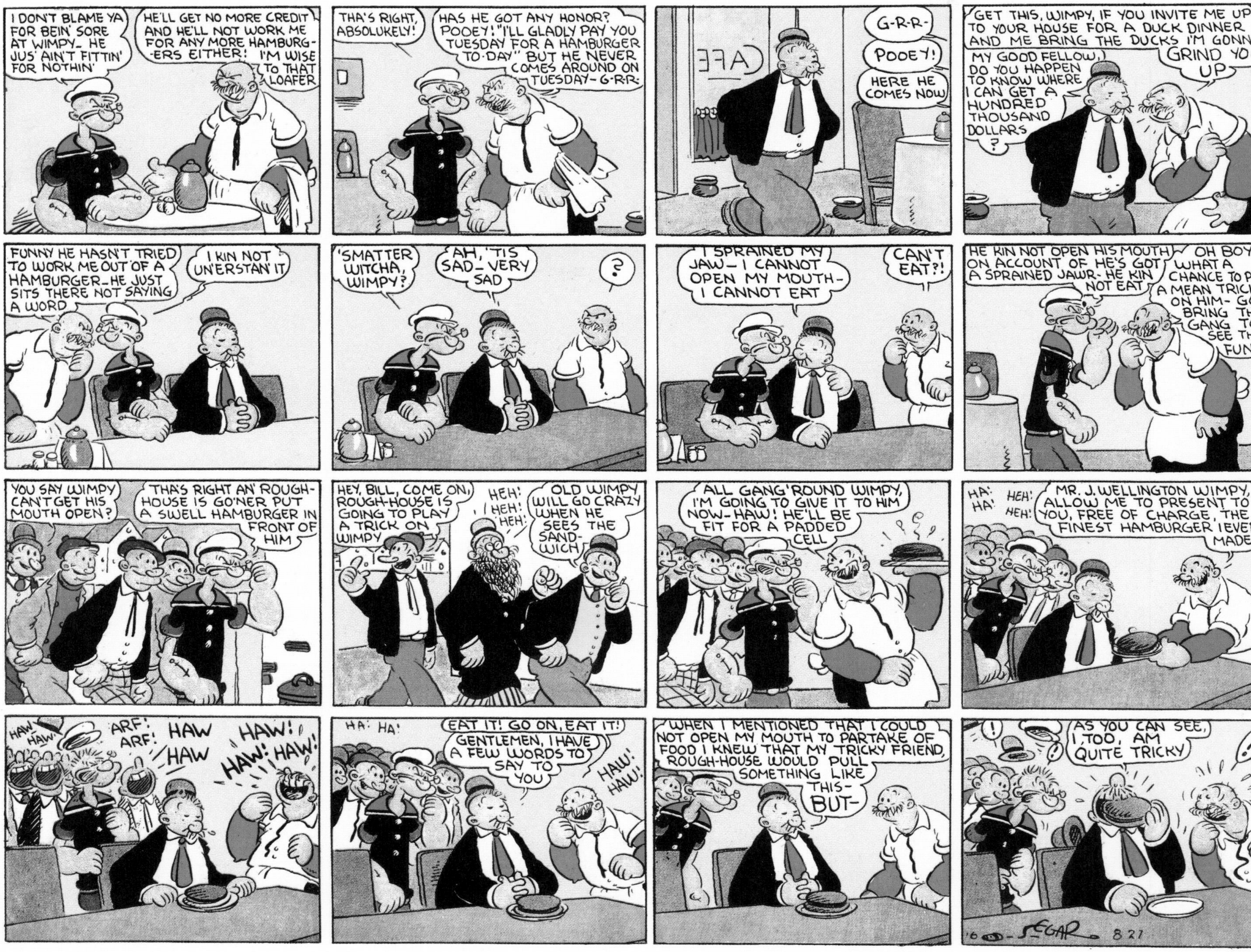
I DON'T BLAME YA FOR BEIN' SORE AT WIMPY_ HE JUS' AIN'T FITTIN' FOR NOTHIN'
HE'LL GET NO MORE CREDIT AND HE'LL NOT WORK ME FOR ANY MORE HAMBURG-ERS EITHER!
I'M WISE TO THAT LOAFER
THA'S RIGHT, ABSOLUKELY!
HAS HE GOT ANY HONOR? POOEY! "I'LL GLADLY PAY YOU TUESDAY FOR A HAMBURGER TO-DAY" BUT HE NEVER COMES AROUND ON TUESDAY-G-R-R-
G-R-R-
POOEY!
HERE HE COMES NOW
GET THIS, WIMPY, IF YOU INVITE ME UP TO YOUR HOUSE FOR A DUCK DINNER AND ME BRING THE DUCKS I'M GONNA GRIND YOU UP
MY GOOD FELLOW, DO YOU HAPPEN TO KNOW WHERE I CAN GET A HUNDRED THOUSAND DOLLARS ?
FUNNY HE HASN'T TRIED TO WORK ME OUT OF A HAMBURGER_HE JUST SITS THERE NOT SAYING A WORD
I KIN NOT UN'ERSTAN' IT
'SMATTER WITCHA, WIMPY?
AH, 'TIS SAD_ VERY SAD
?
I SPRAINED MY JAW_ I CANNOT OPEN MY MOUTH- I CANNOT EAT
CAN'T EAT?!
HE KIN NOT OPEN HIS MOUTH ON ACCOUNT OF HE'S GOT A SPRAINED JAWR- HE KIN NOT EAT
OH BOY! WHAT A CHANCE TO PLAY A MEAN TRICK ON HIM- GO BRING THE GANG TO SEE THE FUN
YOU SAY WIMPY CAN'T GET HIS MOUTH OPEN?
THA'S RIGHT AN' ROUGH-HOUSE IS GO'NER PUT A SWELL HAMBURGER IN FRONT OF HIM
HEY, BILL, COME ON, ROUGH-HOUSE IS GOING TO PLAY A TRICK ON WIMPY
HEH! HEH! HEH!
OLD WIMPY WILL GO CRAZY WHEN HE SEES THE SAND-WICH
ALL GANG 'ROUND WIMPY, I'M GOING TO GIVE IT TO HIM NOW-HAW! HE'LL BE FIT FOR A PADDED CELL
HA! HA!
HEH! HEH!
MR. J. WELLINGTON WIMPY, ALLOW ME TO PRESENT TO YOU, FREE OF CHARGE, THE FINEST HAMBURGER I EVER MADE
HAW! HAW!
ARF! ARF!
HAW HAW
HAW! HAW! HAW!
HA! HA!
EAT IT! GO ON, EAT IT!
GENTLEMEN, I HAVE A FEW WORDS TO SAY TO YOU
HAW! HAW!
WHEN I MENTIONED THAT I COULD NOT OPEN MY MOUTH TO PARTAKE OF FOOD I KNEW THAT MY TRICKY FRIEND, ROUGH-HOUSE WOULD PULL SOMETHING LIKE THIS- BUT-
!
AS YOU CAN SEE, I, TOO, AM QUITE TRICKY
!
SEGAR 8-27

86. August 27, 1933

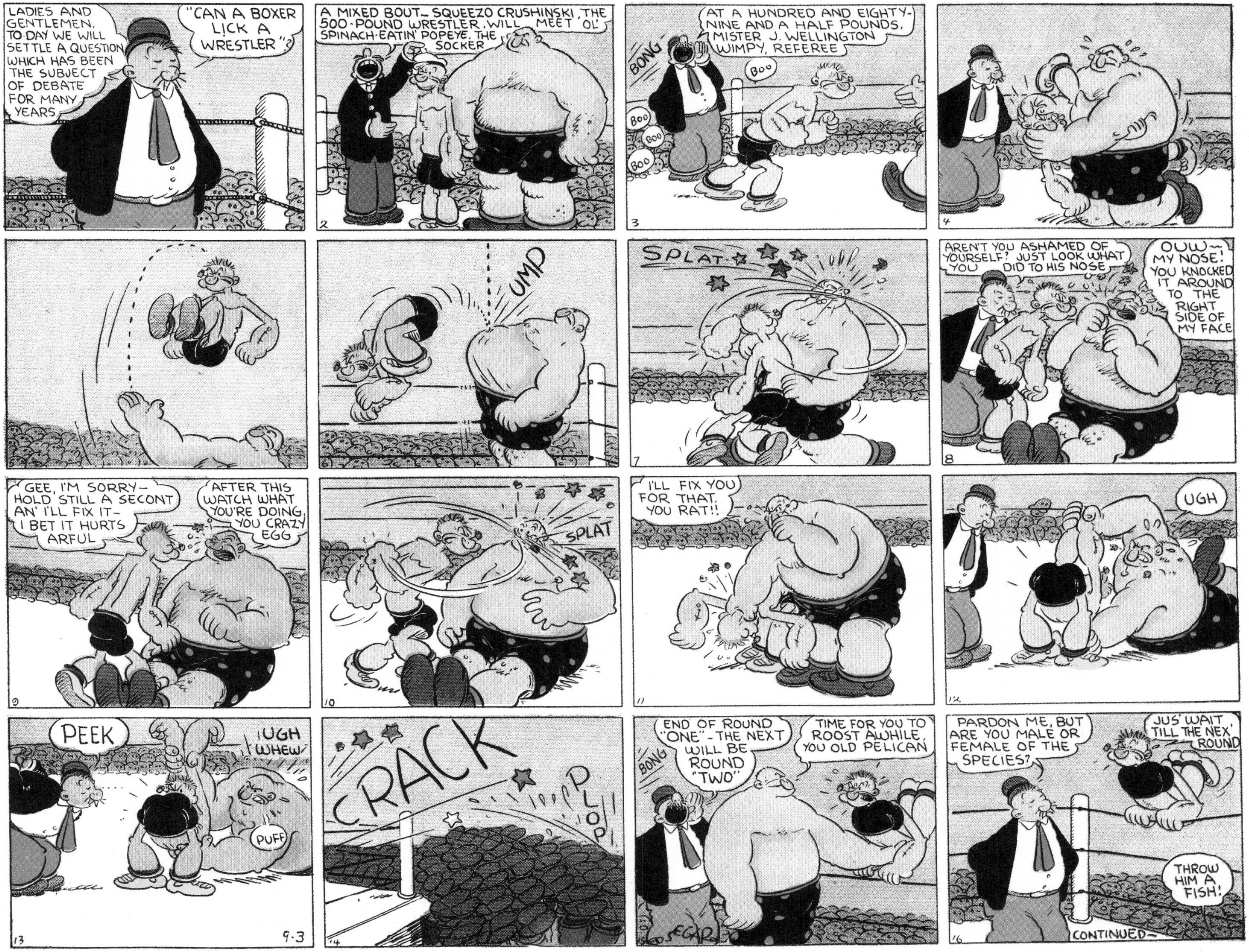
LADIES AND GENTLEMEN, TO-DAY WE WILL SETTLE A QUESTION WHICH HAS BEEN THE SUBJECT OF DEBATE FOR MANY YEARS
"CAN A BOXER LICK A WRESTLER"?
A MIXED BOUT– SQUEEZO CRUSHINSKI, THE 500-POUND WRESTLER, WILL MEET 'OL' SPINACH-EATIN' POPEYE, THE SOCKER
BONG
AT A HUNDRED AND EIGHTY-NINE AND A HALF POUNDS, MISTER J. WELLINGTON WIMPY, REFEREE
BOO
BOO
BOO
BOO
UMP
SPLAT
AREN'T YOU ASHAMED OF YOURSELF? JUST LOOK WHAT YOU DID TO HIS NOSE
OUW– MY NOSE! YOU KNOCKED IT AROUND TO THE RIGHT SIDE OF MY FACE
GEE, I'M SORRY– HOLD STILL A SECONT AN' I'LL FIX IT– I BET IT HURTS ARFUL
AFTER THIS WATCH WHAT YOU'RE DOING, YOU CRAZY EGG
SPLAT
I'LL FIX YOU FOR THAT, YOU RAT!!
UGH
PEEK
UGH WHEW
PUFF
CRACK
PLOP
BONG
END OF ROUND "ONE"– THE NEXT WILL BE ROUND "TWO"
TIME FOR YOU TO ROOST AWHILE, YOU OLD PELICAN
PARDON ME, BUT ARE YOU MALE OR FEMALE OF THE SPECIES?
JUS' WAIT TILL THE NEX' ROUND
THROW HIM A FISH!
CONTINUED–

87. September 3, 1933

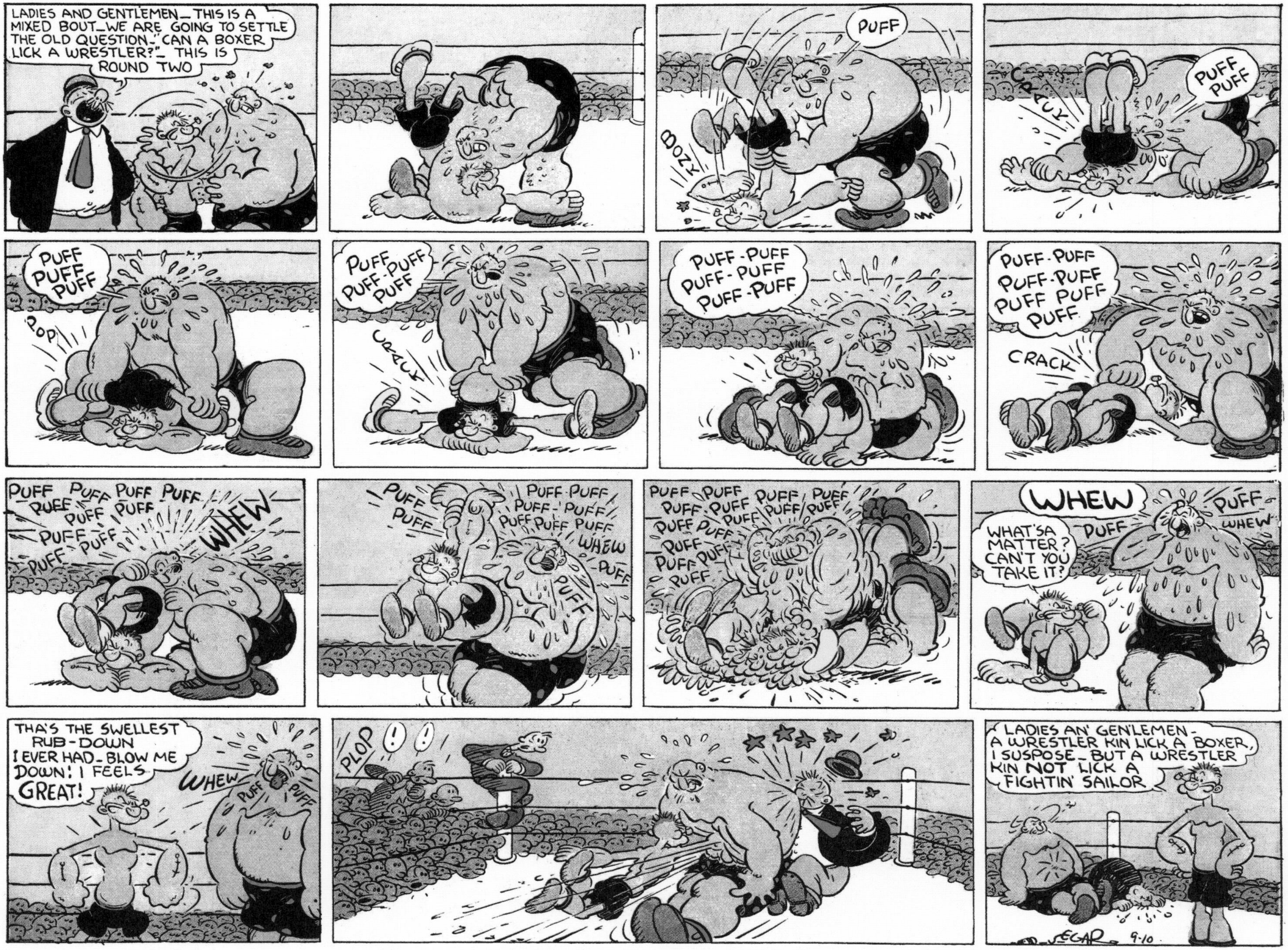
LADIES AND GENTLEMEN_ THIS IS A MIXED BOUT_ WE ARE GOING TO SETTLE THE OLD QUESTION-"CAN A BOXER LICK A WRESTLER?"_ THIS IS ROUND TWO
PUFF
BOZZ
PUFF PUFF
CRACK
PUFF PUFF PUFF
POP
PUFF PUFF-PUFF PUFF
CRACK
PUFF-PUFF PUFF-PUFF PUFF-PUFF
PUFF-PUFF PUFF-PUFF PUFF PUFF PUFF
CRACK
PUFF PUFF PUFF PUFF PUFF PUFF PUFF PUFF PUFF PUFF
WHEW
PUFF PUFF
PUFF-PUFF PUFF-PUFF PUFF PUFF PUFF
WHEW
PUFF
PUFF
WHEW
PUFF
WHAT'SA MATTER? CAN'T YOU TAKE IT?
PUFF
WHEW
THA'S THE SWELLEST RUB-DOWN I EVER HAD- BLOW ME DOWN! I FEELS GREAT!
WHEW
PUFF PUFF
PLOP
! !
LADIES AN' GEN'LEMEN- A WRESTLER KIN LICK A BOXER, I SUSPOSE_ BUT A WRESTLER KIN NOT LICK A FIGHTIN' SAILOR
SEGAR
9-10

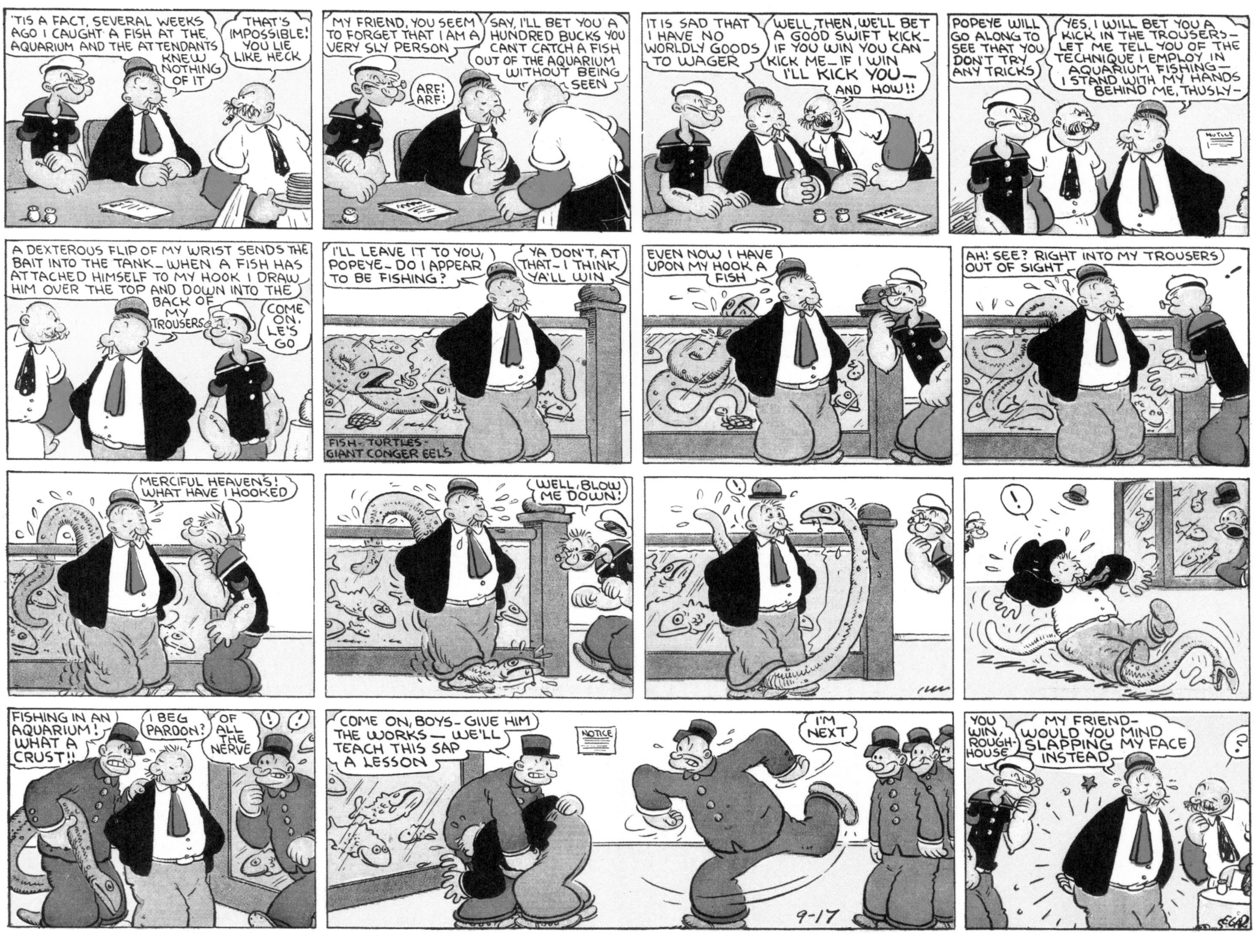
'TIS A FACT, SEVERAL WEEKS AGO I CAUGHT A FISH AT THE AQUARIUM AND THE ATTENDANTS KNEW NOTHING OF IT
THAT'S IMPOSSIBLE! YOU LIE LIKE HECK
MY FRIEND, YOU SEEM TO FORGET THAT I AM A VERY SLY PERSON
ARF! ARF!
SAY, I'LL BET YOU A HUNDRED BUCKS YOU CAN'T CATCH A FISH OUT OF THE AQUARIUM WITHOUT BEING SEEN
IT IS SAD THAT I HAVE NO WORLDLY GOODS TO WAGER
WELL, THEN, WE'LL BET A GOOD SWIFT KICK— IF YOU WIN YOU CAN KICK ME— IF I WIN I'LL KICK YOU— AND HOW!!
POPEYE WILL GO ALONG TO SEE THAT YOU DON'T TRY ANY TRICKS
YES, I WILL BET YOU A KICK IN THE TROUSERS— LET ME TELL YOU OF THE TECHNIQUE I EMPLOY IN AQUARIUM FISHING— I STAND WITH MY HANDS BEHIND ME, THUSLY—
A DEXTEROUS FLIP OF MY WRIST SENDS THE BAIT INTO THE TANK— WHEN A FISH HAS ATTACHED HIMSELF TO MY HOOK I DRAW HIM OVER THE TOP AND DOWN INTO THE BACK OF MY TROUSERS
COME ON. LE'S GO
I'LL LEAVE IT TO YOU, POPEYE— DO I APPEAR TO BE FISHING?
YA DON'T, AT THAT— I THINK YA'LL WIN
FISH - TURTLES - GIANT CONGER EELS
EVEN NOW I HAVE UPON MY HOOK A FISH
AH! SEE? RIGHT INTO MY TROUSERS OUT OF SIGHT
!
MERCIFUL HEAVENS! WHAT HAVE I HOOKED
WELL, BLOW ME DOWN!
!
!
FISHING IN AN AQUARIUM! WHAT A CRUST!!
I BEG PARDON?
OF ALL THE NERVE
! !
COME ON, BOYS— GIVE HIM THE WORKS— WE'LL TEACH THIS SAP A LESSON
NOTICE
I'M NEXT
9-17
YOU WIN, ROUGH-HOUSE
MY FRIEND— WOULD YOU MIND SLAPPING MY FACE INSTEAD
?
SEGAR

89. September 17, 1933

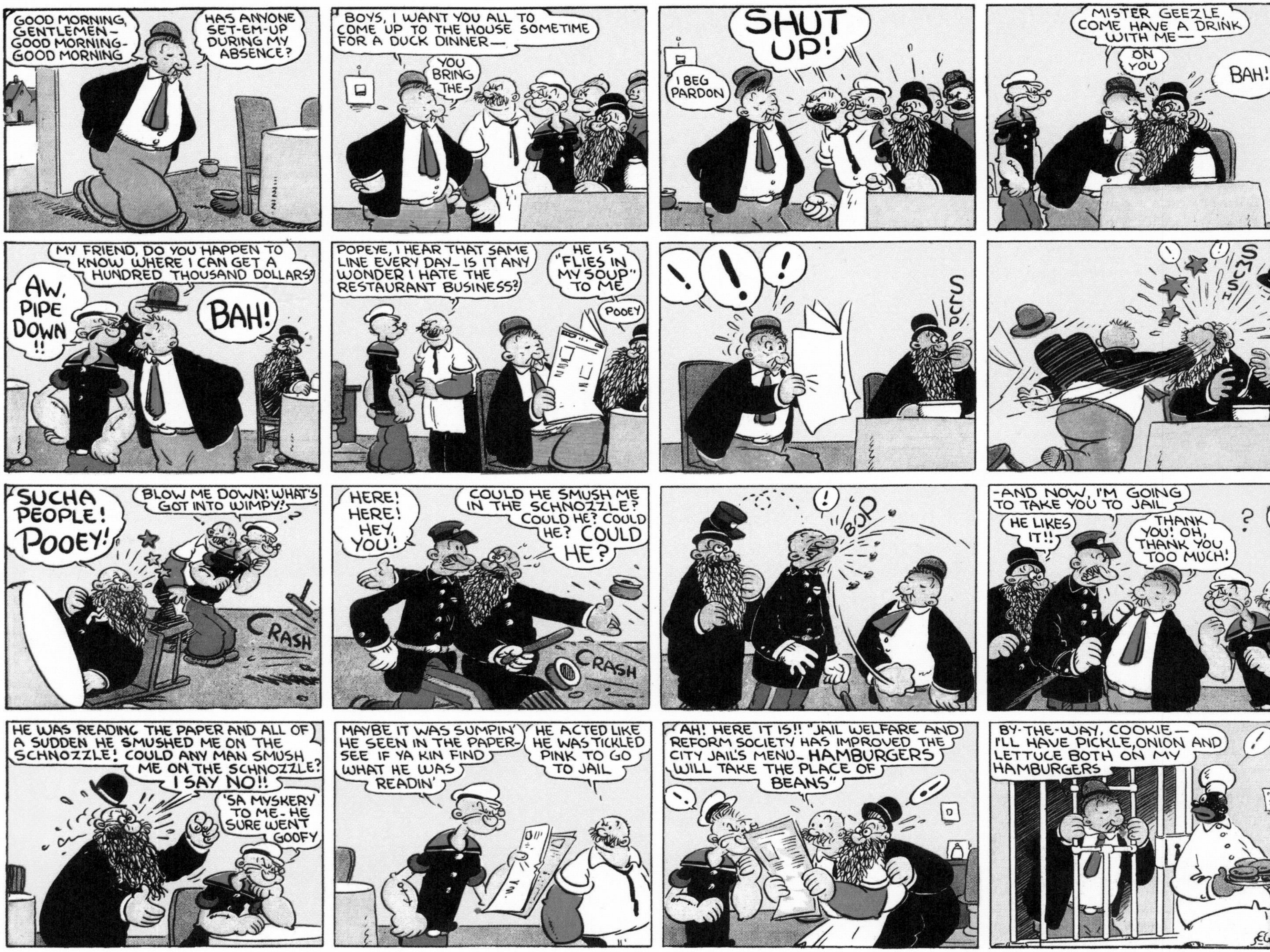
GOOD MORNING, GENTLEMEN— GOOD MORNING— GOOD MORNING
HAS ANYONE SET-EM-UP DURING MY ABSENCE?
BOYS, I WANT YOU ALL TO COME UP TO THE HOUSE SOMETIME FOR A DUCK DINNER—
YOU BRING THE-
SHUT UP!
I BEG PARDON
MISTER GEEZLE, COME HAVE A DRINK WITH ME—
ON YOU
BAH!
MY FRIEND, DO YOU HAPPEN TO KNOW WHERE I CAN GET A HUNDRED THOUSAND DOLLARS?
AW, PIPE DOWN!!
BAH!
POPEYE, I HEAR THAT SAME LINE EVERY DAY— IS IT ANY WONDER I HATE THE RESTAURANT BUSINESS?
HE IS "FLIES IN MY SOUP" TO ME
POOEY
! ! !
SLUP
!
!
SMUSH
SUCHA PEOPLE! POOEY!
BLOW ME DOWN! WHAT'S GOT INTO WIMPY?
CRASH
HERE! HERE! HEY, YOU!
COULD HE SMUSH ME IN THE SCHNOZZLE? COULD HE? COULD HE? COULD HE?
CRASH
!
BOP
—AND NOW, I'M GOING TO TAKE YOU TO JAIL
HE LIKES IT!!
THANK YOU! OH, THANK YOU TOO MUCH!
?
!
HE WAS READING THE PAPER AND ALL OF A SUDDEN HE SMUSHED ME ON THE SCHNOZZLE! COULD ANY MAN SMUSH ME ON THE SCHNOZZLE? I SAY NO!!
'SA MYSKERY TO ME— HE SURE WENT GOOFY
MAYBE IT WAS SUMPIN' HE SEEN IN THE PAPER— SEE IF YA KIN FIND WHAT HE WAS READIN'
HE ACTED LIKE HE WAS TICKLED PINK TO GO TO JAIL
AH! HERE IT IS!! "JAIL WELFARE AND REFORM SOCIETY HAS IMPROVED THE CITY JAIL'S MENU— HAMBURGERS WILL TAKE THE PLACE OF BEANS"
!
!
BY-THE-WAY, COOKIE— I'LL HAVE PICKLE, ONION AND LETTUCE BOTH ON MY HAMBURGERS
!
SEGAR

90. September 24, 1933

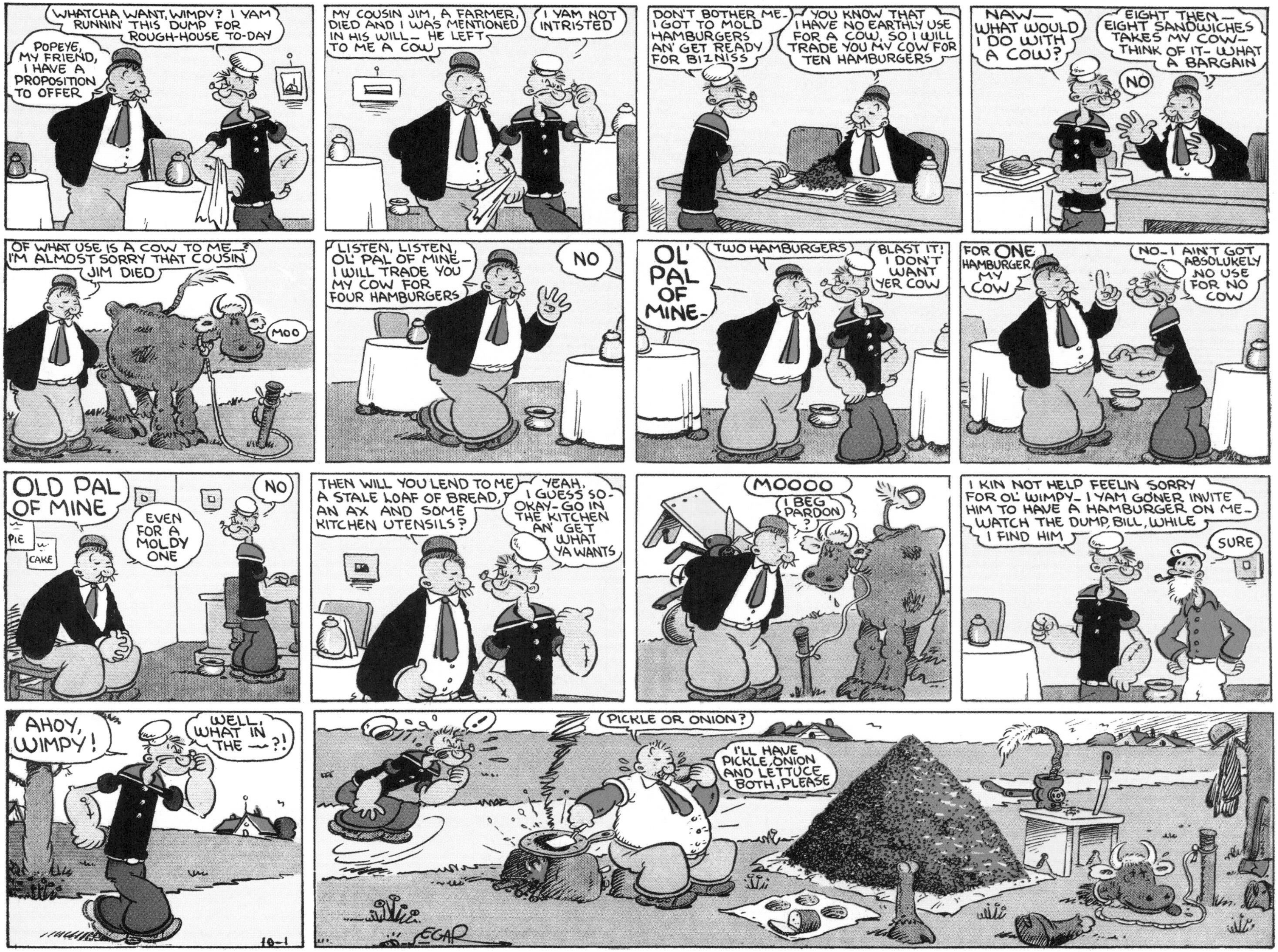
WHATCHA WANT, WIMPY? I YAM RUNNIN' THIS DUMP FOR ROUGH-HOUSE TO-DAY
POPEYE, MY FRIEND, I HAVE A PROPOSITION TO OFFER
MY COUSIN JIM, A FARMER, DIED AND I WAS MENTIONED IN HIS WILL— HE LEFT TO ME A COW
I YAM NOT INTRISTED
DON'T BOTHER ME— I GOT TO MOLD HAMBURGERS AN' GET READY FOR BIZNISS
YOU KNOW THAT I HAVE NO EARTHLY USE FOR A COW, SO I WILL TRADE YOU MY COW FOR TEN HAMBURGERS
NAW— WHAT WOULD I DO WITH A COW?
EIGHT THEN— EIGHT SANDWICHES TAKES MY COW— THINK OF IT— WHAT A BARGAIN
NO
OF WHAT USE IS A COW TO ME—? I'M ALMOST SORRY THAT COUSIN JIM DIED
MOO
LISTEN, LISTEN, OL' PAL OF MINE— I WILL TRADE YOU MY COW FOR FOUR HAMBURGERS
NO
OL' PAL OF MINE—
TWO HAMBURGERS
BLAST IT! I DON'T WANT YER COW
FOR ONE HAMBURGER, MY COW
NO— I AIN'T GOT ABSOLUKELY NO USE FOR NO COW
OLD PAL OF MINE
PIE
CAKE
EVEN FOR A MOLDY ONE
NO
THEN WILL YOU LEND TO ME A STALE LOAF OF BREAD, AN AX AND SOME KITCHEN UTENSILS?
YEAH, I GUESS SO— OKAY— GO IN THE KITCHEN AN' GET WHAT YA WANTS
MOOOO
I BEG PARDON?
I KIN NOT HELP FEELIN SORRY FOR OL' WIMPY— I YAM GONER INVITE HIM TO HAVE A HAMBURGER ON ME— WATCH THE DUMP, BILL, WHILE I FIND HIM
SURE
AHOY, WIMPY!
WELL, WHAT IN THE —?!
PICKLE OR ONION?
I'LL HAVE PICKLE, ONION AND LETTUCE BOTH, PLEASE
10-1
SEGAR

91. October 1, 1933

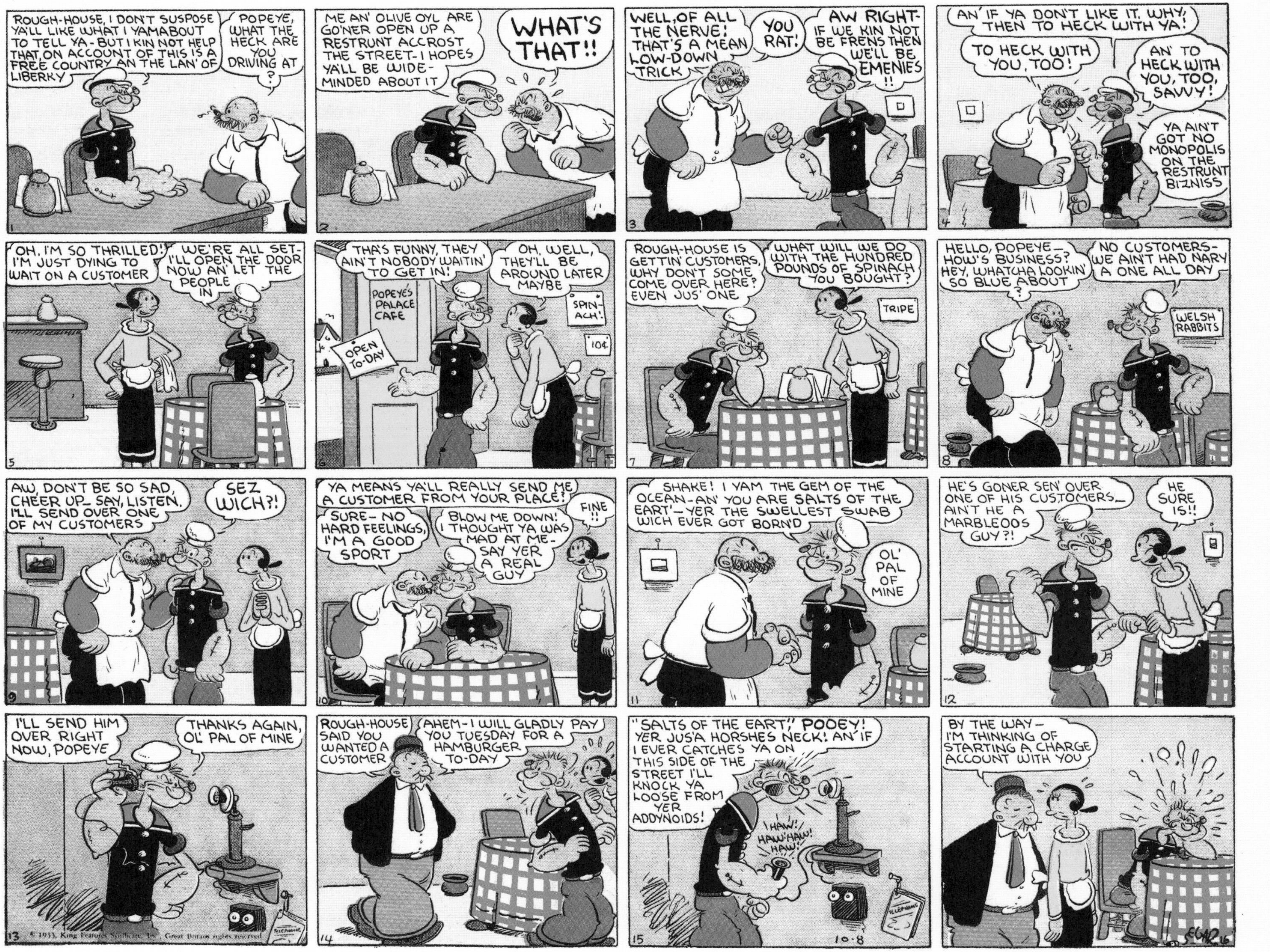
ROUGH-HOUSE, I DON'T SUSPOSE YA'LL LIKE WHAT I YAMABOUT TO TELL YA - BUT I KIN NOT HELP THAT, ON ACCOUNT OF THIS IS A FREE COUNTRY AN THE LAN' OF LIBERKY
POPEYE, WHAT THE HECK ARE YOU DRIVING AT ?
ME AN' OLIVE OYL ARE GO'NER OPEN UP A RESTRUNT ACCROST THE STREET - I HOPES YA'LL BE WIDE-MINDED ABOUT IT
WHAT'S THAT!!
WELL, OF ALL THE NERVE! THAT'S A MEAN LOW-DOWN TRICK
YOU RAT!
AW RIGHT- IF WE KIN NOT BE FRENS THEN WE'LL BE EMENIES !!
AN' IF YA DON'T LIKE IT, WHY, THEN TO HECK WITH YA!
TO HECK WITH YOU, TOO!
AN' TO HECK WITH YOU, TOO, SAVVY!
YA AIN'T GOT NO MONOPOLIS ON THE RESTRUNT BIZNISS
OH, I'M SO THRILLED! I'M JUST DYING TO WAIT ON A CUSTOMER
WE'RE ALL SET- I'LL OPEN THE DOOR NOW AN' LET THE PEOPLE IN
THA'S FUNNY, THEY AIN'T NOBODY WAITIN' TO GET IN!
OH, WELL, THEY'LL BE AROUND LATER MAYBE
POPEYE'S PALACE CAFE
OPEN TO-DAY
SPIN-ACH!
10¢
ROUGH-HOUSE IS GETTIN' CUSTOMERS, WHY DON'T SOME COME OVER HERE? EVEN JUS' ONE
WHAT WILL WE DO WITH THE HUNDRED POUNDS OF SPINACH YOU BOUGHT?
TRIPE
HELLO, POPEYE— HOW'S BUSINESS? HEY, WHATCHA LOOKIN' SO BLUE ABOUT ?
NO CUSTOMERS- WE AIN'T HAD NARY A ONE ALL DAY
WELSH RABBITS
AW, DON'T BE SO SAD, CHEER UP- SAY, LISTEN, I'LL SEND OVER ONE OF MY CUSTOMERS
SEZ WICH?!
YA MEANS YA'LL REALLY SEND ME A CUSTOMER FROM YOUR PLACE?
SURE- NO HARD FEELINGS, I'M A GOOD SPORT
BLOW ME DOWN! I THOUGHT YA WAS MAD AT ME- SAY YER A REAL GUY
FINE !!
SHAKE! I YAM THE GEM OF THE OCEAN- AN' YOU ARE SALTS OF THE EART'- YER THE SWELLEST SWAB WICH EVER GOT BORN'D
OL' PAL OF MINE
HE'S GONER SEN' OVER ONE OF HIS CUSTOMERS— AIN'T HE A MARBLEOOS GUY?!
HE SURE IS!!
I'LL SEND HIM OVER RIGHT NOW, POPEYE
THANKS AGAIN, OL' PAL OF MINE
© 1933, King Features Syndicate, Inc., Great Britain rights reserved.
ROUGH-HOUSE SAID YOU WANTED A CUSTOMER
AHEM- I WILL GLADLY PAY YOU TUESDAY FOR A HAMBURGER TO-DAY
"SALTS OF THE EART," POOEY! YER JUS'A HORSHES NECK! AN' IF I EVER CATCHES YA ON THIS SIDE OF THE STREET I'LL KNOCK YA LOOSE FROM YER ADDYNOIDS!
HAW! HAW! HAW! HAW!
10-8
BY THE WAY- I'M THINKING OF STARTING A CHARGE ACCOUNT WITH YOU

92. October 8, 1933

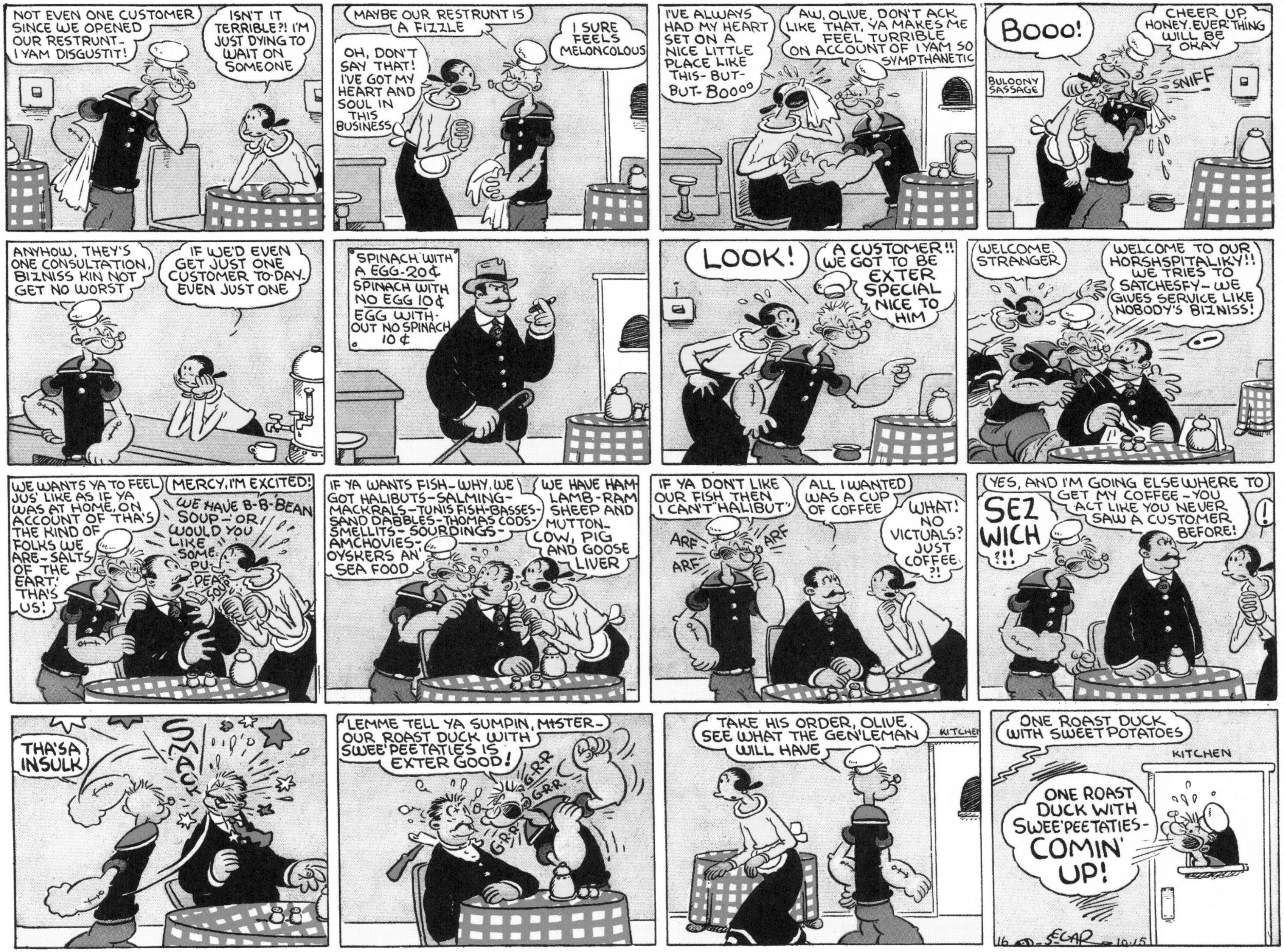
NOT EVEN ONE CUSTOMER SINCE WE OPENED OUR RESTRUNT- I YAM DISGUSTIT!
ISN'T IT TERRIBLE?! I'M JUST DYING TO WAIT ON SOMEONE
MAYBE OUR RESTRUNT IS A FIZZLE
I SURE FEELS MELONCOLOUS
OH, DON'T SAY THAT! I'VE GOT MY HEART AND SOUL IN THIS BUSINESS
I'VE ALWAYS HAD MY HEART SET ON A NICE LITTLE PLACE LIKE THIS- BUT- BUT- BOOoo
AW, OLIVE, DON'T ACK LIKE THAT, YA MAKES ME FEEL TURRIBLE ON ACCOUNT OF I YAM SO SYMPTHANETIC
BOOO!
CHEER UP, HONEY, EVER'THING WILL BE OKAY
BULOONY SASSAGE
SNIFF
ANYHOW, THEY'S ONE CONSULTATION, BIZNISS KIN NOT GET NO WORST
IF WE'D EVEN GET JUST ONE CUSTOMER TO-DAY- EVEN JUST ONE
SPINACH WITH A EGG-20¢
SPINACH WITH NO EGG 10¢
EGG WITH-OUT NO SPINACH 10¢
LOOK!
A CUSTOMER!! WE GOT TO BE EXTER SPECIAL NICE TO HIM
WELCOME, STRANGER
WELCOME TO OUR HORSHSPITALIKY!! WE TRIES TO SATCHESFY- WE GIVES SERVICE LIKE NOBODY'S BIZNISS!
WE WANTS YA TO FEEL JUS' LIKE AS IF YA WAS AT HOME, ON ACCOUNT OF THA'S THE KIND OF FOLKS WE ARE- SALTS OF THE EART! THA'S US!
MERCY, I'M EXCITED!
WE HAVE B-B-BEAN SOUP- OR WOULD YOU LIKE SOME PU- PEA SOUP
IF YA WANTS FISH- WHY, WE GOT HALIBUTS- SALMING- MACKRALS- TUNIS FISH- BASSES- SAND DABBLES- THOMAS CODS- SMELLITS- SOURDINGS- AMCHOVIES- OYSKERS AN' SEA FOOD
WE HAVE HAM- LAMB- RAM SHEEP AND MUTTON- COW, PIG AND GOOSE LIVER
IF YA DON'T LIKE OUR FISH THEN I CAN'T "HALIBUT"
ARF ARF ARF
ALL I WANTED WAS A CUP OF COFFEE
WHAT! NO VICTUALS? JUST COFFEE ?!
YES, AND I'M GOING ELSEWHERE TO GET MY COFFEE- YOU ACT LIKE YOU NEVER SAW A CUSTOMER BEFORE!
SEZ WICH ?!!
!
THA'SA INSULK
SMACK
LEMME TELL YA SUMPIN, MISTER- OUR ROAST DUCK WITH SWEE'PEETATIES IS EXTER GOOD!
G-R-R G-R-R G-R-R
TAKE HIS ORDER, OLIVE. SEE WHAT THE GEN'LEMAN WILL HAVE
KITCHEN
ONE ROAST DUCK WITH SWEET POTATOES
KITCHEN
ONE ROAST DUCK WITH SWEE'PEETATIES- COMIN' UP!
SEGAR 10-15

93. October 15, 1933

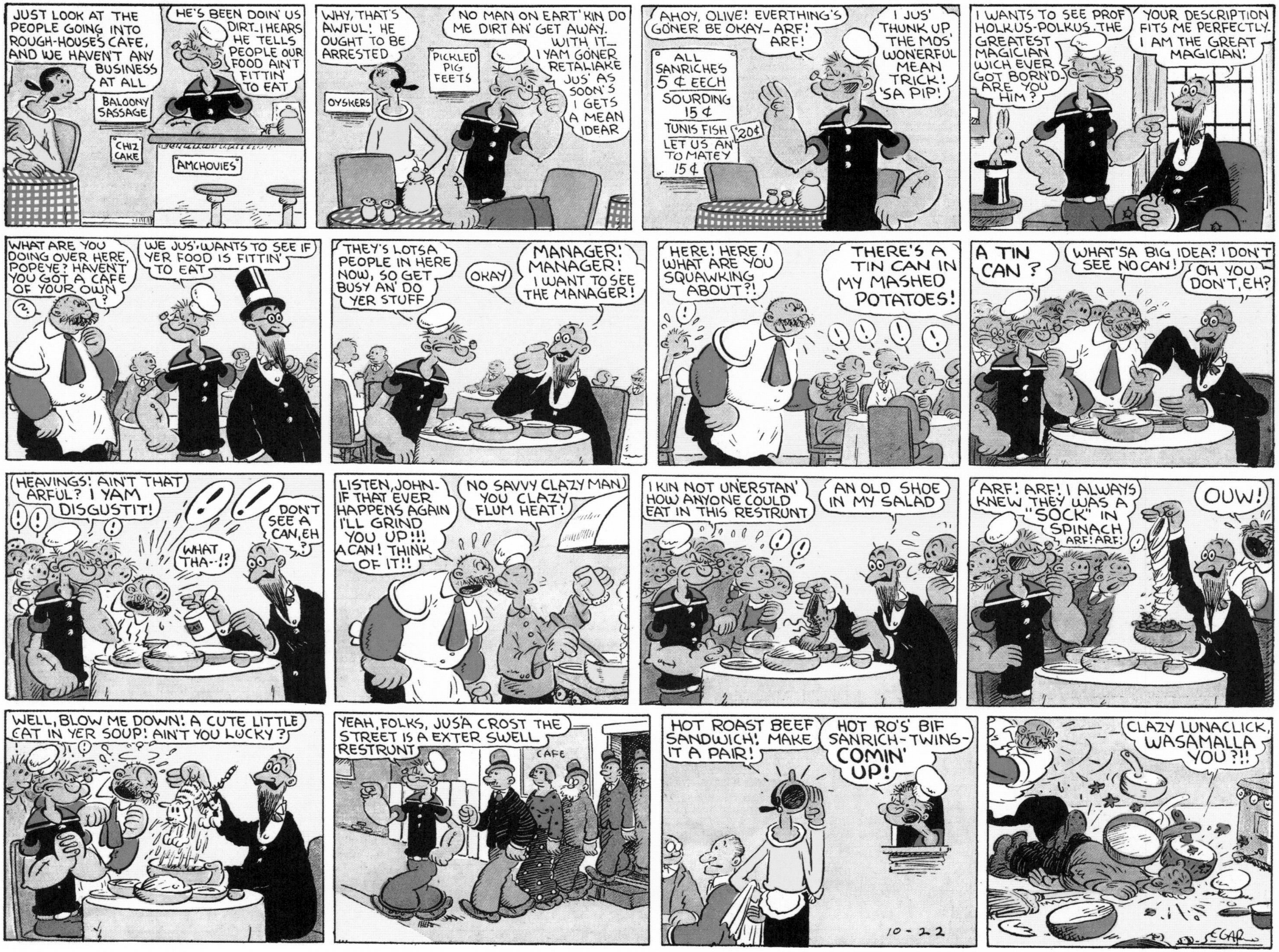
JUST LOOK AT THE PEOPLE GOING INTO ROUGH-HOUSE'S CAFE, AND WE HAVEN'T ANY BUSINESS AT ALL
HE'S BEEN DOIN' US DIRT—I HEARS HE TELLS PEOPLE OUR FOOD AIN'T FITTIN' TO EAT
BALOONY SASSAGE
CHIZ CAKE
AMCHOVIES
WHY, THAT'S AWFUL! HE OUGHT TO BE ARRESTED
NO MAN ON EART' KIN DO ME DIRT AN' GET AWAY. WITH IT— I YAM GONER RETALIAKE JUS' AS SOON'S I GETS A MEAN IDEAR
PICKLED PIG FEETS
OYSKERS
AHOY, OLIVE! EVERTHING'S GONER BE OKAY—ARF! ARF!
I JUS' THUNK UP THE MOS' WONERFUL MEAN TRICK! 'SA PIP!
ALL SANRICHES 5¢ EECH
SOURDING 15¢
TUNIS FISH 20¢
LET US AN TO MATEY 15¢
I WANTS TO SEE PROF HOLKUS-POLKUS, THE GREATEST MAGICIAN WICH EVER GOT BORN'D. ARE YOU HIM?
YOUR DESCRIPTION FITS ME PERFECTLY. I AM THE GREAT MAGICIAN!
WHAT ARE YOU DOING OVER HERE, POPEYE? HAVEN'T YOU GOT A CAFE OF YOUR OWN?
WE JUS' WANTS TO SEE IF YER FOOD IS FITTIN' TO EAT
THEY'S LOTSA PEOPLE IN HERE NOW, SO GET BUSY AN' DO YER STUFF
OKAY
MANAGER! MANAGER! I WANT TO SEE THE MANAGER!
HERE! HERE! WHAT ARE YOU SQUAWKING ABOUT?!
THERE'S A TIN CAN IN MY MASHED POTATOES!
A TIN CAN?
WHAT'SA BIG IDEA? I DON'T SEE NO CAN!
OH YOU DON'T, EH?
HEAVINGS! AIN'T THAT ARFUL? I YAM DISGUSTIT!
WHAT THA--!?
DON'T SEE A CAN, EH?
LISTEN, JOHN—IF THAT EVER HAPPENS AGAIN I'LL GRIND YOU UP!!! A CAN! THINK OF IT!!
NO SAVVY CLAZY MAN! YOU CLAZY FLUM HEAT!
I KIN NOT UNERSTAN' HOW ANYONE COULD EAT IN THIS RESTRUNT
AN OLD SHOE IN MY SALAD
ARF! ARF! I ALWAYS KNEW THEY WAS A "SOCK" IN SPINACH ARF! ARF!
OUW!
WELL, BLOW ME DOWN! A CUTE LITTLE CAT IN YER SOUP! AIN'T YOU LUCKY?
YEAH, FOLKS, JUS'A CROST THE STREET IS A EXTER SWELL RESTRUNT
CAFE
HOT ROAST BEEF SANDWICH! MAKE IT A PAIR!
HOT RO'S' BIF SANRICH—TWINS—COMIN' UP!
10-22
CLAZY LUNACLICK, WASAMALLA YOU?!!
SEGAR

94. October 22, 1933

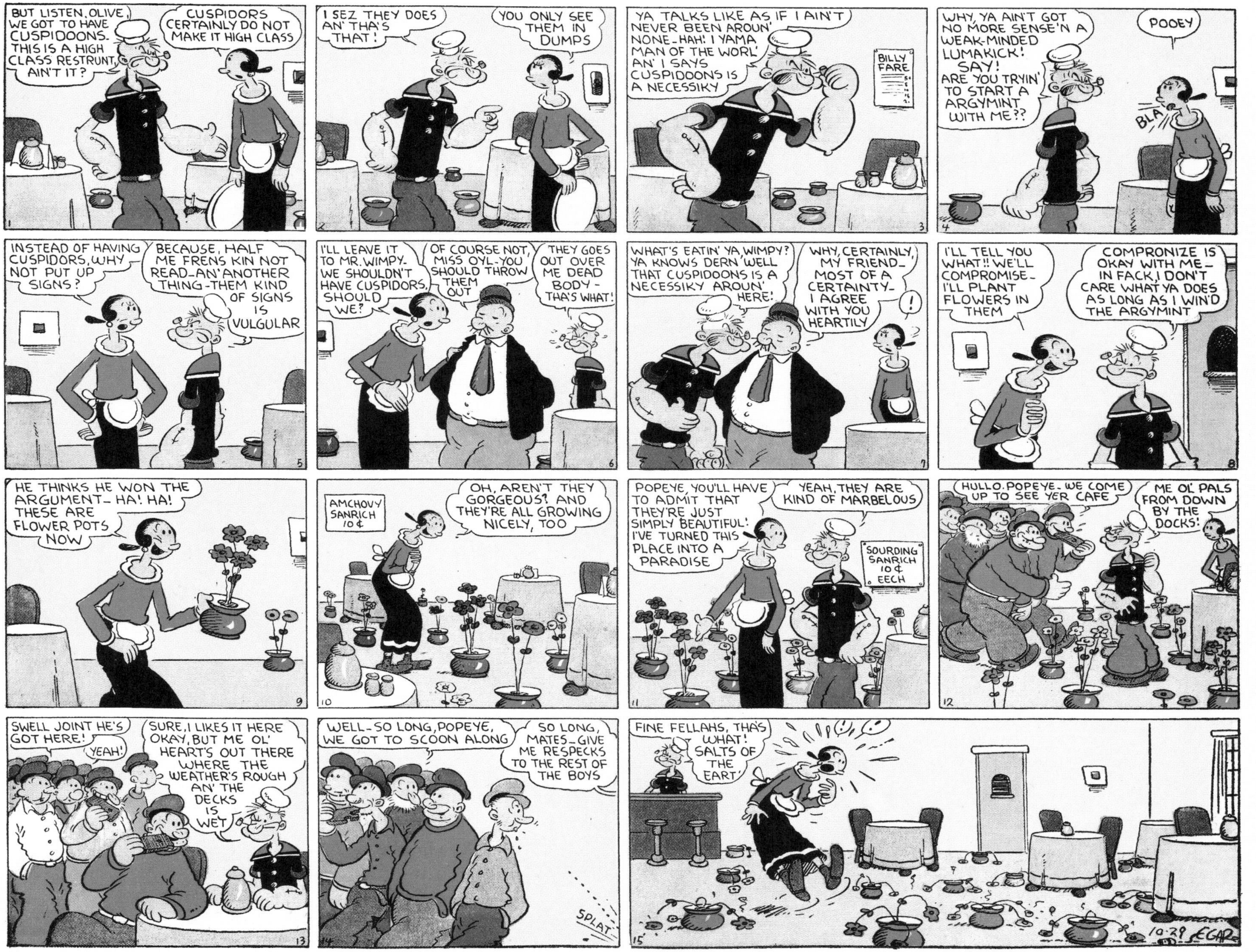
BUT LISTEN, OLIVE, WE GOT TO HAVE CUSPIDOONS. THIS IS A HIGH CLASS RESTRUNT, AIN'T IT?
CUSPIDORS CERTAINLY DO NOT MAKE IT HIGH CLASS
I SEZ THEY DOES AN' THA'S THAT!
YOU ONLY SEE THEM IN DUMPS
YA TALKS LIKE AS IF I AIN'T NEVER BEEN AROUN' NONE-HAH! I YAMA MAN OF THE WORL' AN' I SAYS CUSPIDOONS IS A NECESSIKY
BILLY FARE
WHY, YA AIN'T GOT NO MORE SENSE'N A WEAK-MINDED LUMAKICK! SAY! ARE YOU TRYIN' TO START A ARGYMINT WITH ME??
POOEY
BLA
INSTEAD OF HAVING CUSPIDORS, WHY NOT PUT UP SIGNS?
BECAUSE, HALF ME FRENS KIN NOT READ-AN' ANOTHER THING-THEM KIND OF SIGNS IS VULGULAR
I'LL LEAVE IT TO MR. WIMPY-WE SHOULDN'T HAVE CUSPIDORS, SHOULD WE?
OF COURSE NOT, MISS OYL-YOU SHOULD THROW THEM OUT
THEY GOES OUT OVER ME DEAD BODY-THA'S WHAT!
WHAT'S EATIN' YA, WIMPY? YA KNOWS DERN WELL THAT CUSPIDOONS IS A NECESSIKY AROUN' HERE!
WHY, CERTAINLY, MY FRIEND-MOST OF A CERTAINTY-I AGREE WITH YOU HEARTILY
!
I'LL TELL YOU WHAT!! WE'LL COMPROMISE-I'LL PLANT FLOWERS IN THEM
COMPRONIZE IS OKAY WITH ME-IN FACK, I DON'T CARE WHAT YA DOES AS LONG AS I WIN'D THE ARGYMINT
HE THINKS HE WON THE ARGUMENT-HA! HA! THESE ARE FLOWER POTS NOW
AMCHOVY SANRICH 10¢
OH, AREN'T THEY GORGEOUS? AND THEY'RE ALL GROWING NICELY, TOO
POPEYE, YOU'LL HAVE TO ADMIT THAT THEY'RE JUST SIMPLY BEAUTIFUL! I'VE TURNED THIS PLACE INTO A PARADISE
YEAH, THEY ARE KIND OF MARBELOUS
SOURDING SANRICH 10¢ EECH
HULLO, POPEYE-WE COME UP TO SEE YER CAFE
ME OL' PALS FROM DOWN BY THE DOCKS!
SWELL JOINT HE'S GOT HERE!
YEAH!
SURE, I LIKES IT HERE OKAY, BUT ME OL' HEART'S OUT THERE WHERE THE WEATHER'S ROUGH AN' THE DECKS IS WET
WELL-SO LONG, POPEYE, WE GOT TO SCOON ALONG
SO LONG, MATES-GIVE ME RESPECKS TO THE REST OF THE BOYS
SPLAT
FINE FELLAHS, THA'S WHAT! SALTS OF THE EART'

95. October 29, 1933

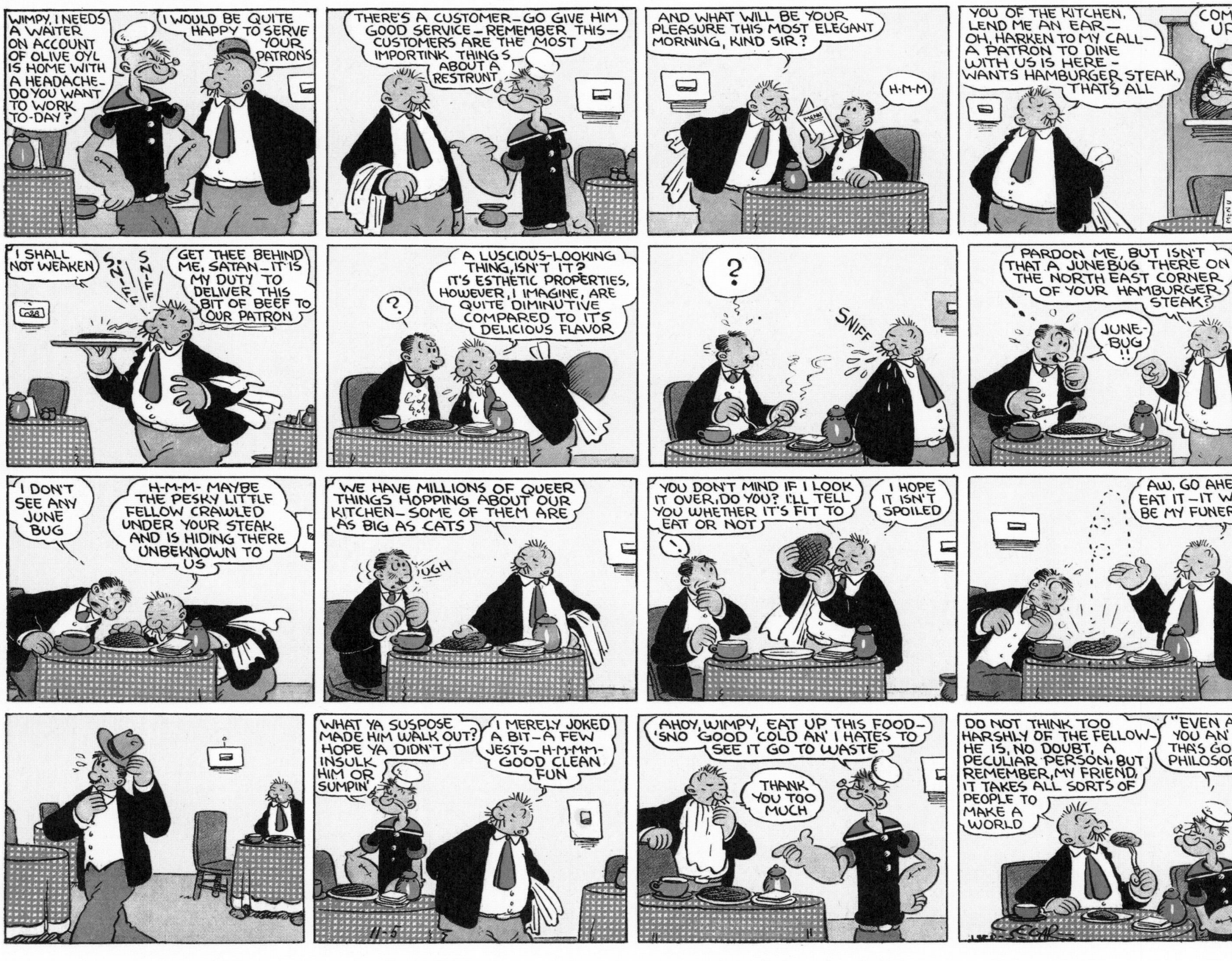
WIMPY, I NEEDS A WAITER ON ACCOUNT OF OLIVE OYL IS HOME WITH A HEADACHE-DO YOU WANT TO WORK TO-DAY?
I WOULD BE QUITE HAPPY TO SERVE YOUR PATRONS
THERE'S A CUSTOMER—GO GIVE HIM GOOD SERVICE—REMEMBER THIS—CUSTOMERS ARE THE MOST IMPORTINK THINGS ABOUT A RESTRUNT
AND WHAT WILL BE YOUR PLEASURE THIS MOST ELEGANT MORNING, KIND SIR?
MENU
H-M-M
YOU OF THE KITCHEN, LEND ME AN EAR—OH, HARKEN TO MY CALL—A PATRON TO DINE WITH US IS HERE—WANTS HAMBURGER STEAK, THAT'S ALL
COMIN' UP!
I SHALL NOT WEAKEN
SNIFF
SNIFF
GET THEE BEHIND ME, SATAN—IT IS MY DUTY TO DELIVER THIS BIT OF BEEF TO OUR PATRON
?
A LUSCIOUS-LOOKING THING, ISN'T IT? IT'S ESTHETIC PROPERTIES, HOWEVER, I IMAGINE, ARE QUITE DIMINUTIVE COMPARED TO IT'S DELICIOUS FLAVOR
?
SNIFF
PARDON ME, BUT ISN'T THAT A JUNE BUG THERE ON THE NORTH EAST CORNER OF YOUR HAMBURGER STEAK?
JUNE-BUG!!
I DON'T SEE ANY JUNE BUG
H-M-M- MAYBE THE PESKY LITTLE FELLOW CRAWLED UNDER YOUR STEAK AND IS HIDING THERE UNBEKNOWN TO US
WE HAVE MILLIONS OF QUEER THINGS HOPPING ABOUT OUR KITCHEN—SOME OF THEM ARE AS BIG AS CATS
UGH
YOU DON'T MIND IF I LOOK IT OVER, DO YOU? I'LL TELL YOU WHETHER IT'S FIT TO EAT OR NOT
I HOPE IT ISN'T SPOILED
!
AW, GO AHEAD EAT IT—IT WON'T BE MY FUNERAL
WHAT YA SUSPOSE MADE HIM WALK OUT? HOPE YA DIDN'T INSULK HIM OR SUMPIN'
I MERELY JOKED A BIT—A FEW JESTS—H-M-MM—GOOD CLEAN FUN
11-5
AHOY, WIMPY, EAT UP THIS FOOD—'SNO GOOD COLD AN' I HATES TO SEE IT GO TO WASTE
THANK YOU TOO MUCH
DO NOT THINK TOO HARSHLY OF THE FELLOW—HE IS, NO DOUBT, A PECULIAR PERSON, BUT REMEMBER, MY FRIEND, IT TAKES ALL SORTS OF PEOPLE TO MAKE A WORLD
"EVEN AS YOU AN' I"—THA'S GOOD PHILOSOPY
SEGAR

96. November 5, 1933

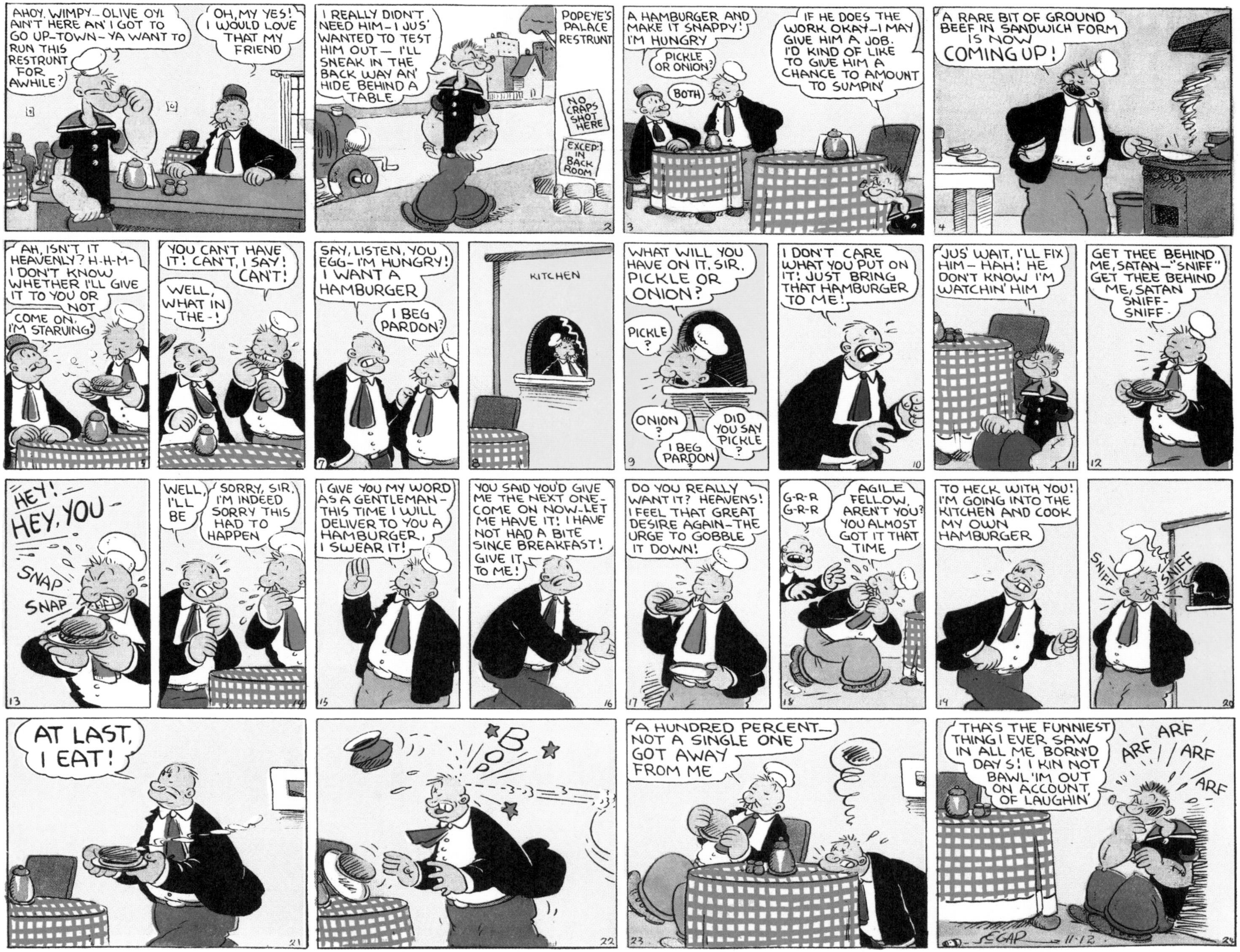
AHOY, WIMPY— OLIVE OYL AIN'T HERE AN' I GOT TO GO UP-TOWN—YA WANT TO RUN THIS RESTRUNT FOR AWHILE?
OH, MY YES! I WOULD LOVE THAT MY FRIEND
I REALLY DIDN'T NEED HIM—I JUS' WANTED TO TEST HIM OUT— I'LL SNEAK IN THE BACK WAY AN' HIDE BEHIND A TABLE
POPEYE'S PALACE RESTRUNT
NO CRAPS SHOT HERE
EXCEP' IN BACK ROOM
A HAMBURGER AND MAKE IT SNAPPY! I'M HUNGRY
PICKLE OR ONION?
BOTH
IF HE DOES THE WORK OKAY—I MAY GIVE HIM A JOB. I'D KIND OF LIKE TO GIVE HIM A CHANCE TO AMOUNT TO SUMPIN'
A RARE BIT OF GROUND BEEF IN SANDWICH FORM IS NOW COMING UP!
AH, ISN'T IT HEAVENLY? H-H-M- I DON'T KNOW WHETHER I'LL GIVE IT TO YOU OR NOT
COME ON. I'M STARVING!
YOU CAN'T HAVE IT! CAN'T, I SAY! CAN'T!
WELL, WHAT IN THE-!
SAY, LISTEN, YOU EGG—I'M HUNGRY! I WANT A HAMBURGER
I BEG PARDON?
KITCHEN
WHAT WILL YOU HAVE ON IT, SIR, PICKLE OR ONION?
PICKLE?
ONION?
I BEG PARDON?
DID YOU SAY PICKLE?
I DON'T CARE WHAT YOU PUT ON IT! JUST BRING THAT HAMBURGER TO ME!
JUS' WAIT, I'LL FIX HIM—HAH! HE DON'T KNOW I'M WATCHIN' HIM
GET THEE BEHIND ME, SATAN—"SNIFF" GET THEE BEHIND ME, SATAN SNIFF-SNIFF-
HEY! HEY, YOU—
SNAP
SNAP
WELL, I'LL BE
SORRY, SIR, I'M INDEED SORRY THIS HAD TO HAPPEN
I GIVE YOU MY WORD AS A GENTLEMAN—THIS TIME I WILL DELIVER TO YOU A HAMBURGER, I SWEAR IT!
YOU SAID YOU'D GIVE ME THE NEXT ONE—COME ON NOW—LET ME HAVE IT! I HAVE NOT HAD A BITE SINCE BREAKFAST! GIVE IT TO ME!
DO YOU REALLY WANT IT? HEAVENS! I FEEL THAT GREAT DESIRE AGAIN—THE URGE TO GOBBLE IT DOWN!
G-R-R G-R-R
AGILE FELLOW, AREN'T YOU? YOU ALMOST GOT IT THAT TIME
TO HECK WITH YOU! I'M GOING INTO THE KITCHEN AND COOK MY OWN HAMBURGER
SNIFF
SNIFF
AT LAST, I EAT!
BOP
A HUNDRED PERCENT— NOT A SINGLE ONE GOT AWAY FROM ME
THA'S THE FUNNIEST THING I EVER SAW IN ALL ME BORN'D DAYS! I KIN NOT BAWL 'IM OUT ON ACCOUNT OF LAUGHIN'
ARF
ARF
ARF
ARF
SEGAR 11-12

97. November 12, 1933

98. November 19, 1933

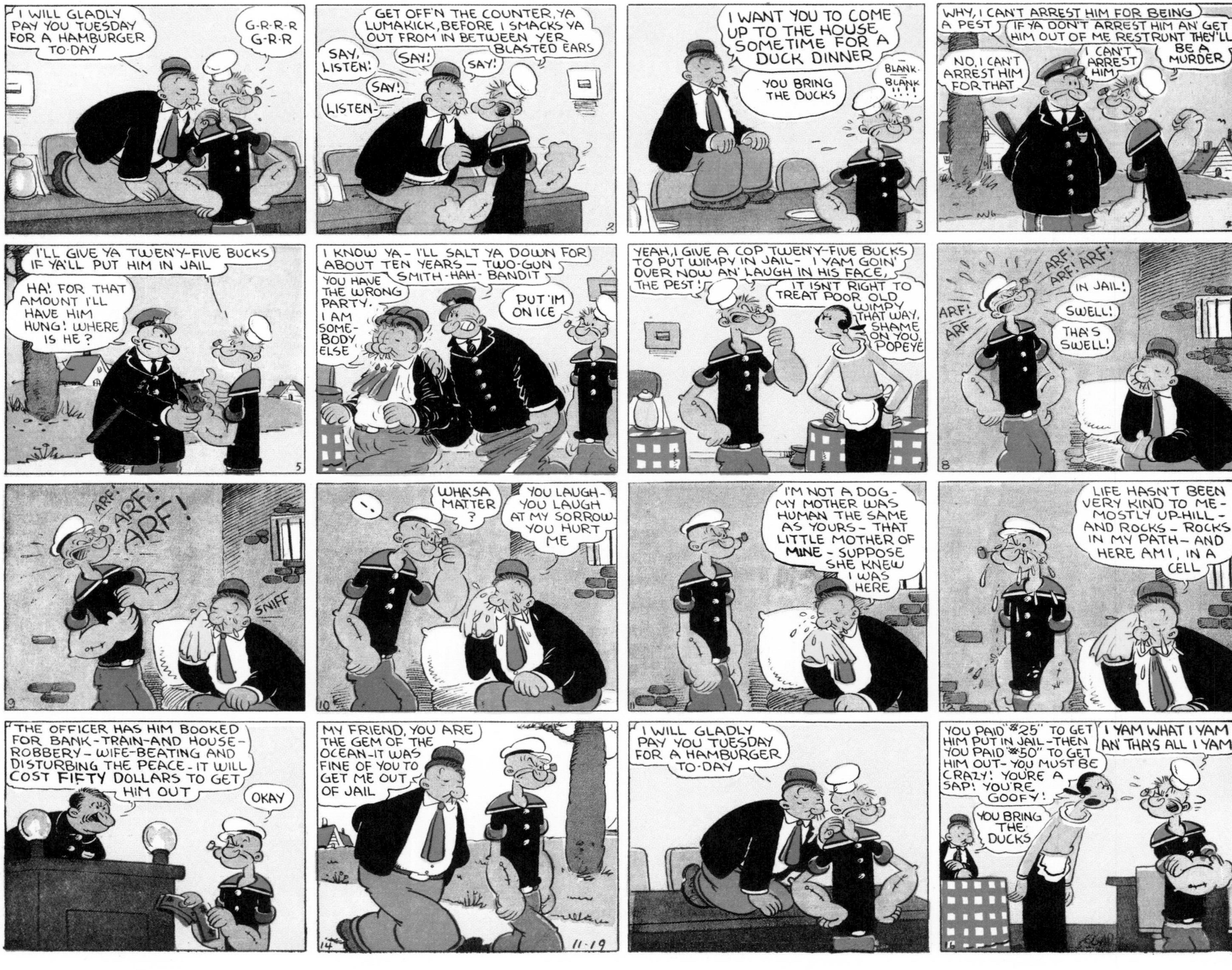
I WILL GLADLY PAY YOU TUESDAY FOR A HAMBURGER TO-DAY
G-R-R-R G-R-R
GET OFF'N THE COUNTER, YA LUMAKICK, BEFORE I SMACKS YA OUT FROM IN BETWEEN YER BLASTED EARS
SAY, LISTEN!
SAY!
SAY!
SAY!
LISTEN-
I WANT YOU TO COME UP TO THE HOUSE SOMETIME FOR A DUCK DINNER
YOU BRING THE DUCKS
BLANK- BLANK !!!!
WHY, I CAN'T ARREST HIM FOR BEING A PEST
IF YA DON'T ARREST HIM AN' GET HIM OUT OF ME RESTRUNT THEY'LL BE A MURDER
NO, I CAN'T ARREST HIM FOR THAT
I CAN'T ARREST HIM
I'LL GIVE YA TWEN'Y-FIVE BUCKS IF YA'LL PUT HIM IN JAIL
HA! FOR THAT AMOUNT I'LL HAVE HIM HUNG! WHERE IS HE?
I KNOW YA- I'LL SALT YA DOWN FOR ABOUT TEN YEARS — TWO-GUN SMITH-HAH- BANDIT
YOU HAVE THE WRONG PARTY. I AM SOMEBODY ELSE
PUT 'IM ON ICE
YEAH, I GIVE A COP TWEN'Y-FIVE BUCKS TO PUT WIMPY IN JAIL- I YAM GOIN' OVER NOW AN' LAUGH IN HIS FACE, THE PEST!
IT ISN'T RIGHT TO TREAT POOR OLD WIMPY THAT WAY, SHAME ON YOU, POPEYE
ARF! ARF! ARF!
IN JAIL!
SWELL!
THA'S SWELL!
ARF! ARF
ARF! ARF! ARF!
SNIFF
WHA'SA MATTER ?
YOU LAUGH- YOU LAUGH AT MY SORROW- YOU HURT ME
I'M NOT A DOG- MY MOTHER WAS HUMAN THE SAME AS YOURS- THAT LITTLE MOTHER OF MINE- SUPPOSE SHE KNEW I WAS HERE
LIFE HASN'T BEEN VERY KIND TO ME- MOSTLY UP-HILL- AND ROCKS- ROCKS IN MY PATH- AND HERE AM I, IN A CELL
THE OFFICER HAS HIM BOOKED FOR BANK-TRAIN-AND HOUSE-ROBBERY- WIFE-BEATING AND DISTURBING THE PEACE- IT WILL COST FIFTY DOLLARS TO GET HIM OUT
OKAY
MY FRIEND, YOU ARE THE GEM OF THE OCEAN- IT WAS FINE OF YOU TO GET ME OUT OF JAIL
11-19
I WILL GLADLY PAY YOU TUESDAY FOR A HAMBURGER TO-DAY
YOU PAID "$25" TO GET HIM PUT IN JAIL- THEN YOU PAID "$50" TO GET HIM OUT- YOU MUST BE CRAZY! YOU'RE A SAP! YOU'RE GOOFY!
I YAM WHAT I YAM AN' THA'S ALL I YAM
YOU BRING THE DUCKS

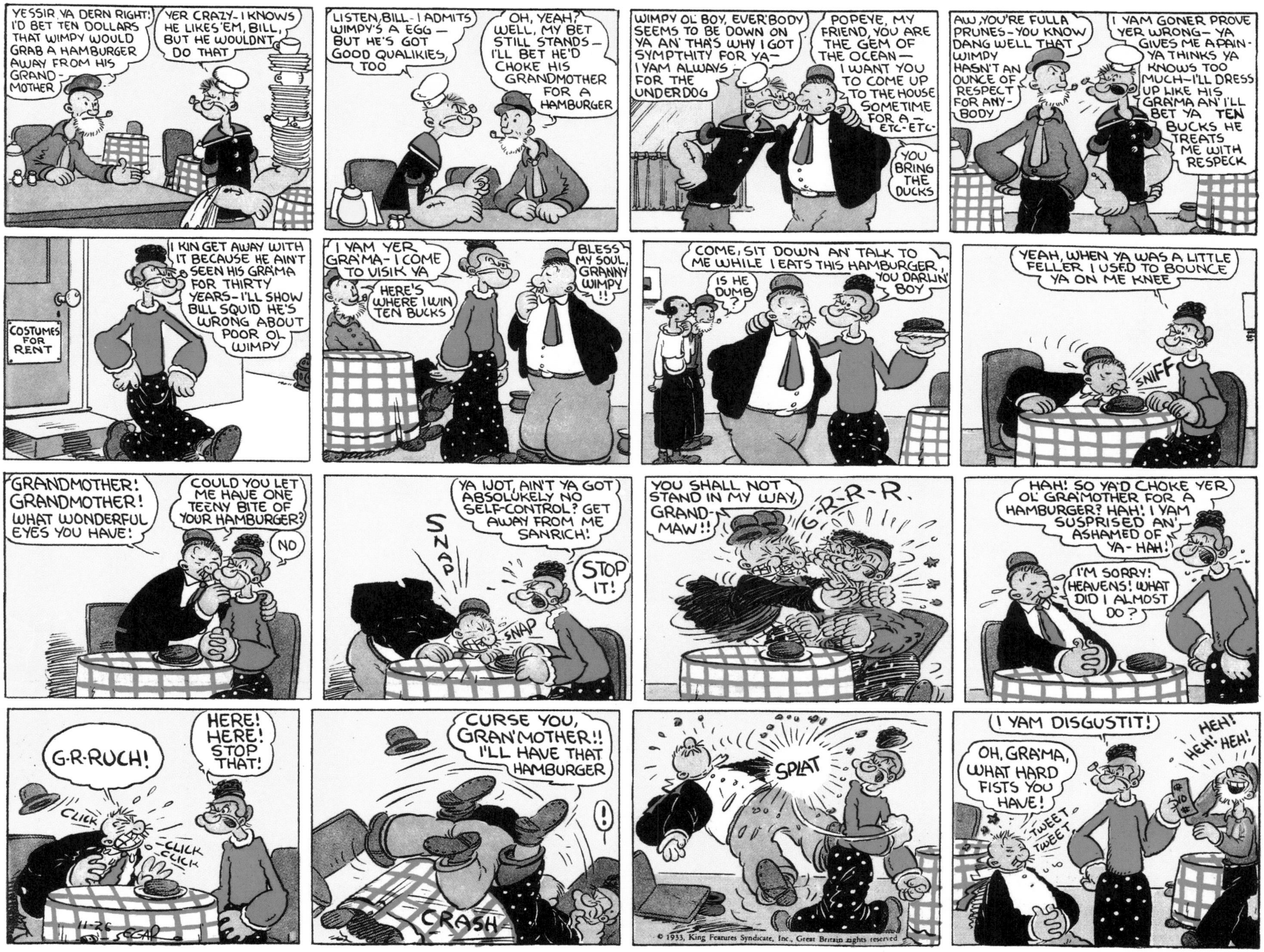
YESSIR, YA DERN RIGHT! I'D BET TEN DOLLARS THAT WIMPY WOULD GRAB A HAMBURGER AWAY FROM HIS GRAND-MOTHER
YER CRAZY - I KNOWS HE LIKES 'EM, BILL, BUT HE WOULDN'T DO THAT
LISTEN, BILL - I ADMITS WIMPY'S A EGG — BUT HE'S GOT GOOD QUALIKIES, TOO
OH, YEAH? WELL, MY BET STILL STANDS — I'LL BET HE'D CHOKE HIS GRANDMOTHER FOR A HAMBURGER
WIMPY OL' BOY, EVER'BODY SEEMS TO BE DOWN ON YA AN' THA'S WHY I GOT SYMPTHITY FOR YA - I YAM ALWAYS FOR THE UNDERDOG
POPEYE, MY FRIEND, YOU ARE THE GEM OF THE OCEAN — I WANT YOU TO COME UP TO THE HOUSE SOMETIME FOR A — ETC - ETC -
YOU BRING THE DUCKS
AW, YOU'RE FULLA PRUNES - YOU KNOW DANG WELL THAT WIMPY HASN'T AN OUNCE OF RESPECT FOR ANY-BODY
I YAM GONER PROVE YER WRONG - YA GIVES ME A PAIN - YA THINKS YA KNOWS TOO MUCH - I'LL DRESS UP LIKE HIS GRA'MA AN' I'LL BET YA TEN BUCKS HE TREATS ME WITH RESPECK
I KIN GET AWAY WITH IT BECAUSE HE AIN'T SEEN HIS GRA'MA FOR THIRTY YEARS - I'LL SHOW BILL SQUID HE'S WRONG ABOUT POOR OL' WIMPY
COSTUMES FOR RENT
I YAM YER GRA'MA - I COME TO VISIK YA
HERE'S WHERE I WIN TEN BUCKS
BLESS MY SOUL, GRANNY WIMPY!!
COME, SIT DOWN AN' TALK TO ME WHILE I EATS THIS HAMBURGER, YOU DARLIN' BOY
IS HE DUMB?
YEAH, WHEN YA WAS A LITTLE FELLER I USED TO BOUNCE YA ON ME KNEE
SNIFF
GRANDMOTHER! GRANDMOTHER! WHAT WONDERFUL EYES YOU HAVE!
COULD YOU LET ME HAVE ONE TEENY BITE OF YOUR HAMBURGER?
NO
YA WOT, AIN'T YA GOT ABSOLUKELY NO SELF-CONTROL? GET AWAY FROM ME SANRICH!
SNAP
STOP IT!
SNAP
YOU SHALL NOT STAND IN MY WAY, GRAND-MAW!!
G-R-R-R-R.
HAH! SO YA'D CHOKE YER OL' GRA'MOTHER FOR A HAMBURGER? HAH! I YAM SUSPRISED AN' ASHAMED OF YA - HAH!
I'M SORRY! HEAVENS! WHAT DID I ALMOST DO?
G-R-RUCH!
HERE! HERE! STOP THAT!
CLICK
CLICK CLICK
11-26 SEGAR
CURSE YOU, GRAN'MOTHER!! I'LL HAVE THAT HAMBURGER
!
CRASH
SPLAT
© 1933, King Features Syndicate, Inc., Great Britain rights reserved
I YAM DISGUSTIT!
OH, GRA'MA, WHAT HARD FISTS YOU HAVE!
TWEET TWEET
HEH! HEH! HEH!

99. November 26, 1933

ELZIE CRISLER SEGAR was born in Chester, IL, on December 8, 1894. At the age of 12, he got a job at the Chester Opera House, a motion-picture theater, where he drew show cards, played drums in the orchestra, and ran the projectors. This early interest in sequential storytelling led him to take a correspondence course in cartooning, which honed his drawing skills to the extent that in 1916 he was hired as a staff cartoonist at the Chicago *Herald*. There, he worked on the series *Charlie Chaplin's Comic Capers* for about a year, before he was able to create his own strip, *Barry the Boob*. In 1918, Segar joined the staff of the *Chicago Evening American*, where he created *Looping the Loop*. This strip proved popular enough that he was summoned to New York in 1919 to create a new series for the *Evening Journal* — *Thimble Theatre*, which was to become his magnum opus. Initially a parody of vaudeville shows and film serials, *Thimble Theatre* soon developed into an original story chronicling the ill-conceived schemes and romantic escapades of Olive Oyl, her brother Castor Oyl, and her boyfriend Ham Gravy. In 1920, Segar also created the long-running gag comic *Sappo*, which followed the everyday misadventures of inventor John Sappo, his wife Myrtle, and their mad scientist boarder, Professor Wotasnozzle.

Thimble Theatre's readership kept growing when, on January 17, 1929, Segar offhandedly introduced a new character to the strip — Popeye. This idiosyncratic sailor captivated readers and soon took center stage; by 1931, the series was retitled *Thimble Theatre Starring Popeye* and Segar had a hit on his hands. As the strip went on, Segar would add many memorable characters to the ensemble, including J. Wellington Wimpy, the Sea Hag and the Goon, Oscar, Bluto, Swee'pea, and Eugene the Jeep — but Popeye remained the star of the show. At the height of his cartooning career, Segar died of leukemia and liver disease on October 13, 1938, at the age of 43. However, his signature creation has lived on in print, in film, and as a fixture of pop culture today.